IN PURSUIT OF EXCELLENCE

ABOUT THE AUTHOR

Daniel D. Terry has 32 years of law enforcement experience. He began his career with the Illinois Department of Corrections where he worked at the historical Stateville Correctional Center. He joined a suburban police department outside of Chicago, Illinois, where he served for 23 years in a variety of positions. Starting out as a Patrol Officer, he worked the streets for 5 years and in 1999, became an undercover member of the Community Oriented Policing Program before earning a promotion to Detective in 2000. In 2004 he returned to Patrol as a Sergeant before being promoted to Patrol Commander in 2010. In addition to managing patrol shifts, he commanded the K-9 and Crisis Negotiations Unit and in 2012, was named Northern Illinois Critical Incident Stress Management's Team Member of the Year. He finished his career in Illinois as the Detective Commander overseeing the Criminal Investigations Division until his retirement in 2017. Two days later, he moved to North Carolina and joined a Sheriff's Office where he served as the Captain of their Criminal Investigations Division and Lieutenant of the Division of Professional Responsibility. He remained at the Sheriff's Office until accepting a position as the Chief of Police of a local agency. He holds a Master's Degree in Law Enforcement and Justice Administration from Western Illinois University. He is a graduate of the 233rd Class of the Northwestern University Center for Public Safety, School of Police Staff and Command. He also served as an adjunct professor for Kaplan University teaching criminal justice courses from 2006 to 2015. He was a board member for the Illinois Crisis Negotiators Association and the Illinois Critical Incident Stress Management Team and has published articles in multiple law enforcement publications. He is married and has five children.

IN PURSUIT OF EXCELLENCE

Leadership Lessons for Law Enforcement

By

DANIEL D. TERRY, M.A.

CHARLES C THOMAS • PUBLISHER • LTD.
Springfield • Illinois • U.S.A.

Published and Distributed Throughout the World by

CHARLES C THOMAS • PUBLISHER, LTD.
2600 South First Street
Springfield, Illinois 62704

ISBN 978-0-398-09416-4 (paper)
ISBN 978-0-398-09417-1 (ebook)

Library of Congress Catalog Card Number: 2023027703 (print)
2023027704 (ebook)

With THOMAS BOOKS *careful attention is given to all details of manufacturing and design. It is the Publisher's desire to present books that are satisfactory as to their physical qualities and artistic possibilities and appropriate for their particular use.* THOMAS BOOKS *will be true to those laws of quality that assure a good name and good will.*

Printed in the United States of America
MX-C-1

Library of Congress Cataloging-in-Publication Data

Names: Terry, Daniel D., author.
Title: In pursuit of excellence : leadership lessons for law enforcement / by Daniel D. Terry, M.A.
Description: Springfield, Illinois, USA : Charles c.. Thomas, Publisher, Ltd., [2023] I Includes bibliographical references and index.
Identifiers: LCCN 2023027703 (print) | LCCN 2023027704 (ebook) | ISBN 9780398094164 (paperback) | ISBN 9780398094171 (ebook)
Subjects: LCSH: Law enforcement. | Leadership.
Classification: LCC HV7921 .T466 2023 (print) | LCC HV7921 (ebook) | DDC 363.2--dc23/eng/20230801
LC record available at https://lccn.loc.gov/2023027703
LC ebook record available at https://lccn.loc.gov/2023027704

This book is dedicated to the memory of Officer Kyle Dieling and Deputy Ryan Hendrix. Two heroes that left us all too soon.

INTRODUCTION

Why another book on leadership? A quick search on the shelves of a local bookstore or the web will find you volumes of texts on the topic of leadership or sound management techniques. What can one more book on these topics provide the reader that the others don't? Has leadership changed to the point that a new text on leadership and management is required?

The truth is many, if not most, of these books contain sound leadership principles that any reader can learn and use to improve their leadership capabilities and the capabilities of the work groups they lead. I have referred to many of them and still do in my drive to be the best leader possible. Some of these writings and the leadership principles they recommend will be referred to in the present text as they are sound. A list of references and suggested readings will also be included at the end of the book so you can explore more fully the discussion topics within this text.

The ability to lead and motivate people, create strong teams and work groups, and create a shared vision has not changed. It still comes down to understanding and successfully interacting with people for the benefit of the organization or group. It is still all about people. True leadership implies that someone, and hopefully a group of people, consents to follow you willingly. A forced following or a cadre of subordinates who follow out of fear or intimidation has nothing to do with true leadership.

So, why another book on leadership and management? With so many texts already written on the topic, what do we hope to accomplish with this book?

First, we hope to provide a book specific to the leadership and management needs of the law enforcement professional. Frequently, we find the shelves filled with leadership books from the perspective of running a business or a division of a company. We can also find numerous leadership books from the perspective of the military or one perceived to be a great leader in military history. Again, the principles found in these documents can be sound advice. However, there are few specific texts on leadership principles related to law enforcement organizations. Most examples in this book are real-life examples and will relate directly to law enforcement, and therefore should be practical to the law enforcement professional.

The law enforcement professional, be it a police officer, a sheriff deputy, or civilian personnel working within the law enforcement environment, is unique. It typically takes a particular type of person to perform such a job. Not everyone can or is willing to do this type of work. For example, shortly before I began to write this book, Sergeant Ron Helus of the Ventura California Sheriff's Office died a hero on November 7th, 2018, because he chose to enter a bar alone to stop an active shooter from harming others.

A little closer to home for me, Deputy Ryan Hendrix made the ultimate sacrifice on September 10th, 2020, when he responded to a call that started as someone breaking into a vehicle but quickly escalated into a shootout between the vehicle owner and the offender. Despite the extreme danger present in this call, Ryan and his shift mates responded, as they had done so many times before. Unfortunately, on this occasion, Deputy Ryan Hendrix was hit by a bullet that would take his life. His co-workers, friends, brothers, and sisters of the badge would mourn and grieve for the loss of Ryan. They would gather around a week after his death to see him buried. And then what did they do? They went back to work protecting the community and responding to those same types of calls that took Ryan's life and so many other law enforcement professionals: burglaries, domestic violence calls, shootings, people drugged out, or having a mental health crisis.

The tragedy of seeing their good friend killed didn't stop them. I ask, is this normal? Who does this? Do normal people do this? Maybe normal is a relative term. Who gets to decide what is normal? How about the average person? Would they do this? Would most of America's population respond this way? I have seen people quit jobs over a lot less discomfort or frustration.

I think one of the best examples to emphasize the point is 9/11. What did we see immediately after the attacks on the Twin Towers in New York City on September 11th, 2001? Our first responders, our real heroes, including both law enforcement and firefighters, were observed running towards the towers, towards the danger, towards the unknown. In contrast, everyone else ran away in panic, a natural response for most people. It is an example that demonstrates that there is something different about those who choose law enforcement as their career and calling in life.

Our law enforcement professionals ran into harm's way to save the lives of strangers, people they neither knew nor previously met. And many of these heroes died doing their duty. Why would they do this? They certainly didn't do it for the money. You do not get rich being in law enforcement. They did it because that is who they were! They continue to do this every day in communities around the nation. They put their well-being aside and confront danger over and over as they serve their communities. We can find examples of this starting before 9/11 and up to the present day. The responsibilities of law enforcement require a unique personality and character.

The personalities you frequently find in those that choose the law enforcement profession, including the civilians, and non-sworn personnel who join law enforcement agencies to provide vital support to law enforcement activities, are often your "Type A" personalities. The police are typically individuals who come to the job with personal characteristics consistent with those required to carry out the police function in society. They are strong-willed, passionate, and action and control oriented. We seek out these people for the job, putting them through a testing process and psychological examination to ensure they have this passion and aversion for action and control; this is a good thing. When a man has just killed his family and is loose in the community, we do not want a group of police officers standing on the street breaking down emotionally, paralyzed by the gruesome scene observed moments before. We want our law enforcement heroes to take control of the situation, take the necessary action, and find and get the homicide suspect off the street, so the rest of the community can be safe.

We hire these personalities to be "action junkies and control freaks" to go towards the fight and not away. We reinforce this with the training we put them through so they can control and handle whatever bizarre, dysfunctional, or violent behavior they are confronted with, all to keep our communities safe. This reinforcement is necessary, and our communities are better because of it.

Let's restate that more accurately. It is good and necessary when law enforcement officers are responding to potentially dangerous and urgent matters in the community that require immediate attention. We need ready and prepared officers to take needed action and control to get the job done. However, it does not work well when our officers take this same need for action and control and bring it back from the field into the office or station house. Now you have a group of control-oriented people jockeying for position or power within the office, which can lead to counterproductive behavior and performance contrary to the organization's mission. Rather than improving relationships and teamwork that will enhance police performance, this strong ego can quickly weaken much-needed relationships if not recognized and kept in check.

Worse yet, they bring their ego and need for control home with them and present it to their families. That can have devastating effects on marriage and family. Many times in my career, my wife, Wendy, had to lay down the law with a proclamation to remind me that I am not "The Commander" or "Sergeant" in the house. I am grateful for those reminders, as they are certainly needed. Nonetheless, even with those reminders, the law enforcement career I chose has influenced my marriage and family, and many of those effects have been negative.

I believe there are unique challenges to leading and managing the unique personalities of most people who choose law enforcement as their career. I don't know that these same challenges are as prevalent in most other chosen professions. What works efficiently in a business environment might not fit the police culture. Where the bottom line in business is profit, the bottom line in law enforcement is much harder to identify and measure. It involves adding value to the community. But what does that look like, and how do we measure it to ensure we are successful? The resources available to law enforcement are also limited, as the taxpayers provide the needed resources. Not many taxpayers get excited about paying more taxes, hence the often-heard phrase the police need to "do more with less." In this book, I hope to provide sound advice to leading and managing law enforcement professionals while keeping the police personality and these unique challenges in mind.

With all the resources available on leadership, shouldn't our so-called "leaders" have already mastered these skills? Look around your organization. How are those in management and supervisory positions doing? Would you call them true leaders? Have they mastered the principles of leadership found throughout the literature and in the many training courses and seminars?

The truth is there is no mastering the ability to lead. Leadership is an ongoing process that you can never wholly master. Leadership is a constant balancing act. Think of a three-legged stool with the organization being one leg, the people you supervise being the second leg, and you the third. You are trying to balance the organization's interests, the people you lead within the organization, and your interests. The scales are constantly moving. In one instance, a course of action may benefit all three groups. Then the next moment, what is in the organization's best interest might not serve the best interest of the organization's employees. Consider a business' need to downsize and lay off hundreds of employees. It may be best for the organization, but not for those poor employees who may end up unemployed. Or there may be a recommendation from your subordinates that would improve their work environment and morale but come at a tremendous financial cost to the organization. Perhaps better morale and motivation will eventually increase the organization's success, but maybe not. The leader must balance these varying interests and decide what the best course of action is at that very moment.

A leadership position requires this balancing act daily. And what of your interests? Well, those must frequently be sacrificed for the benefit of the organization and the people you lead. But sacrifice your interests all the time, never consider your needs or those of your family, and grave consequences await you that ultimately harm your ability to lead. Divorce, alcoholism and suicide rates are high for those in the field of law enforcement because some often make decisions that are not in their best interests. Finding the right balance is a constant for law enforcement leaders if they are to be successful and last an entire career.

In his book Eisenhower on Leadership, author Alan Axelrod puts it this way: "As a leader, you must balance your own perceptions with the demands of those above you, the realities of overall strategy and the big picture, and the concerns of those immediately surrounding you. The success of the entire enterprise depends on the skill and consistency with which you achieve and maintain this balance."[1]

Again, you do not get to graduate from leadership. It is a constant process where learning should never stop for the person who truly desires to be a "true leader" and improve his ability to make a difference in their organization. So yes, we constantly need to think, talk, and consider what a good leader looks like.

Look around your organization. Is it full of leaders or just people filling supervisory positions? When asking law enforcement personnel what percentage of their supervisors practice true leadership behaviors, Jack E. Enter, Ph.D. author of Challenging the Law Enforcement Organization: Proactive Leadership Strategies, reports that most estimate between 5-10%.[2] Sometimes it might be downright challenging to spot a great leader.

Much easier, however, is to spot a poor leader. It doesn't take long, and everyone knows what they look like. They are leaders who seem to have the opposite effect of good leaders. Instead of motivating employees, they de-motivate them. They are not well-liked or respected, tend to frustrate employees, and when not standing over and directing them in their efforts, performance or production may suffer. Working for this person might be outright miserable. Employees do not feel valued or appreciated. Ironically, bad leaders, who may put their subordinates through this negative experience, also recognize poor leadership when they are the victims. They are quick to recognize and complain about it without realizing they do the same to their people and organizations.

This difference between these two types of leaders and the practical consequences, one being positive and one negative, caught my attention early in my life and instilled my interest in the topic of leadership. I observed the same dynamics over and over from those who supervised me, whether: as a teenager working in the kitchen of a nursing home; on the docks of United Parcel Service as a young adult; or within in confines of the Illinois Department of Corrections as a correctional officer, or as a police officer on the streets of suburban Chicago. There were those supervisors who made me feel good and motivated me; I bent over backward to please them. And then there were those supervisors I tried desperately to avoid, who seemed to bring down the entire work group, and maybe the group's performance along with it. I would watch

---

[1] Used with permission of John Wiley & Sons Books, from *Eisenhower on Leadership: Ike's Enduring Lessons in Total Victory Management* by Alan Axelrod, copyright © 2006, p. 182. Permission conveyed through Copyright Clearance Center, Inc.

[2] Enter, Jack E. (2006). *Challenging the Law Enforcement Organization: Proactive Leadership Strategies.* Narrow Road Press, Dacula, GA, p. 27.

as my co-workers would complain about these supervisors and do just enough to get by, not wanting to do anything that might make this supervisor look good. I observed this repeatedly. I saw it but never really understood it. I saw the effects it had on the work group. I saw the fluctuation in morale between the two groups or the change in the work group after a preceding change in leadership. Even as I write this, supervisors - great, good, and poor - come to mind. If you are reading this, I know you have seen them too. You have worked for these same people. They have different names and different faces, but the dynamics and what they do to the organization and people within is the same. Unfortunately, I had no real experience in a leadership position to understand what I saw until I had my chance.

It was in the first part of the year 2000. I had just been promoted to detective. I had worked as a correctional officer, a patrolman, a member of an undercover tactical team, and now a detective. Up to this point, I never held a supervisory position. Being a detective allowed me weekends off in most cases, which allowed me to return to school to pursue a Master's degree in Law Enforcement and Justice Administration.

Western Illinois University had a satellite weekend program where you could attend courses on Saturday and Sunday to obtain your degree. I was required to complete a thirty-page term paper in one of my first courses. The instructor had a list of topics you could choose from on the board, but only one student could write on each topic. As the list of topics was posted, and I saw the subject of leadership among them, I quickly spoke out to secure the topic before anyone else could. Here was my chance to study leadership, to understand and comprehend the observations I had been making for years. The desire to learn and understand leadership was instilled in me through a series of events, including being fortunate to have had the opportunity to write that leadership term paper, as well as the process of growth in obtaining my master's degree and being promoted to sergeant a few years later. I had come to possess the desire to be the best I could, to be one of the good leaders and not one of the poor ones.

Did I make it? Was I successful in being one of the good leaders? I can confidently state that I was nowhere near perfection and learned as much from the mistakes that I have made then from my successes. I will share some of those mistakes with you. Whether I was a good leader rests with those who worked with me. Being a good or great leader is not determined by what you think of yourself but by the perspective of the led. It is their opinion and assessment that matters. I can tell you I have worked with some great police officers who, again and again, made me look polished. They are true heroes and true leaders themselves. They are the ones who decided to get up in the morning and make a difference. They sacrificed and gave, and I benefited from them. I will be ever grateful to them. You will hear about some of them in the pages of this book.

There are good, even great leaders, and then there are poor leaders. A person's true leadership potential and ability will be made known by their fruits. The Bible tells us in Matthew 7:16-18, "You will know them by their fruits...every good tree bears good fruit, but the bad tree bears bad fruit. A good tree cannot produce bad fruit, nor can a bad tree produce good fruit." Indeed, no one is perfect, and every leader will make mistakes. Still, eventually, a good leader will be known by their character, how they treat people, their priorities, what they can accomplish, and how they achieve it. Do their accomplishments come with honesty and integrity?

Good leaders seem to instill a sense of pride in the work group, a sense that what is being done is of value and appreciated. They can motivate people to give more of their best. Working for a good leader is more enjoyable, less of a hardship, and more satisfying, and the desire to strive for optimal performance under this leader may be the norm.

But, be warned, even the poor or average police leader can probably recite much of what the research on leadership has to say. And many, if not most, police leaders have probably attended leadership training where these topics were emphasized. Police leaders may be able to talk about the characteristics of a good versus poor leader. Still, the question is, do they demonstrate the right characteristics in their personal leadership behaviors? Do they 'walk the talk'? and are their actions as a leader consistent with their words, or do they say one thing and do another? Knowledge and know-how are not enough if the characteristics and behaviors of a great leader aren't followed. So, where do you stand? Great leader? Poor leader?

Many of us will fall somewhere in between these two points. That is good news, as it leaves room for improvement. Hence the title of this book, In Pursuit of Excellence. This pursuit and drive for improvement are ongoing for the successful leader. I stole the title for this book from the motto of the sheriff's office I was fortunate enough to get to work for, but I think it fits the direction and purpose of this book perfectly.

Though perfection and excellence for ourselves and our organizations may be the goal, achieving it is impossible. However, the process of pursuing excellence should be what drives us to keep improving and moving forward. We can never stand still. There is no such thing as the status quo. You are either moving forward or falling behind. If you find yourself in a tremendous and outstanding agency, you can't say, "Stop, we have reached our pinnacle; things are running great, so let's just sit here and stay as we are." No, it does not work that way because change is inevitable. There may be a change in leadership within your organization. That can easily send an organization in a different direction. Eventually, there will be a change in personnel and hence personalities. There will be changes in technology, changes in law, changes in the attitudes and expectations of the community, and changes in best practices for law enforcement. If you are not actively monitoring the environment, looking for these changes, and adjusting accordingly, you are falling behind. I hope this book will help you to do better and pursue excellence.

This book will discuss many principles of leadership. It will provide stories, examples, and experiences that offer lessons and takeaways linked directly to leadership principles. It will also dive into management and law enforcement-specific topics as to how you might drive performance, maintain accountability, or just do a more effective job as a supervisor. But the ideas and suggestions made in this book will do you no good if not founded on sound leadership behaviors. Everything rises and falls on your ability to lead. All the supervisors in your organization may be carrying out the same tasks as expected of your organization's management. However, whether they are successful or whether their work group is effective will depend on the type of leaders they are.

Remember the great, good, and poor leader (or leaders) you were picturing just moments ago? You were thinking of some of those poor leaders you have had the unfortunate experience of working for or observed others suffering through. There are many out there, certainly in law enforcement, with our "Type A" control-minded personalities. Why with all the resources on leadership we have today, is poor leadership still so prevalent? I believe we have a significant void in leadership. It is, to this leadership void, that we will now turn.

ACKNOWLEDGMENTS

First and foremost, thanks to the Lord Jesus. For taking a misguided youth on a fast track to a life of pain and disappointment and allowing him to accomplish more than he ever imagined or deserved. Thank you for the humbling lessons learned along the way and for keeping me safe all these years.

A special thanks to my parents, David and Jetta Terry. For their love and support, and especially their patience and the many prayers I know went up on my behalf. I'm so very grateful I wasn't stuck with the curse of having children as problematic as I was. I don't think I would have been as good as you two.

To my sunshine, Wendy. I would not have accomplished what I have without your love and support. I know it wasn't easy. You often sacrificed, so I didn't have to. While I went missing or didn't come home because of the job, you were the rock that ensured the family had what they needed, so I could do what I needed.

To my children, Brandon, Matthew (Laura), Alex (Travis), Jack, a.k.a. "Buddy," and Super Sam. This book is part of your story too. You were part of this journey, which wasn't always a smooth ride. I love you all, and I am proud of you for who you are and will continue to be.

To my friend and mentor, Pac-Man, a.k.a. Don Pasquarella. I don't know why we clicked the way we did. What did you see in this "wet behind the ears" rookie? I am grateful for your friendship, constant support, and the wisdom you imparted as I grew into the profession. I miss the pizza dinners and cups of coffee as we shared our many laughs together.

To my red penned friend, Mike Althoff. Thanks for your willingness to read and edit this book. I know it had to be frustrating and test your patience. However, your mark on this book has no doubt made it better. You're a good man, a good friend, and a good partner in CID.

A special thanks to Chief John Millner, Chief Steve Neubauer, Chief Dominic Panico, and Chief James Doherty. You gave me the opportunities and paved the path that allowed me to be the best I could be. To my friend, Sheriff Charles McDonald. If not for you, I would not have found my way to the great State of North Carolina. And, what a treasure I would have missed. To Sheriff Lowell Griffin, thank you for your trust, confidence, and continued support as we continue to serve our communities.

Finally, to all the men and women of the badge, who worked with me, stood beside me, and made me look good. You are the real heroes who sacrificed daily to make a difference in the world. You will always have my utmost respect and admiration.

P.S. Go White Sox and Roll Tide!

CONTENTS

SECTION THREE: YOU WILL NEVER BE GREAT UNTIL YOU REALIZE YOU AREN'T GREAT

IN PURSUIT OF EXCELLENCE

Section One

THE LEADERSHIP VOID

The following section, titled; The Leadership Void, highlights several leadership areas I believe are lacking among many law enforcement agencies today. These voids, as I have chosen to call them, keep our agencies and leaders from performing at the highest level possible. The failure of leaders to recognize and make appropriate adjustments as required will prevent a leader from developing into the best leader they can be. Indeed, if forfeited or ignored, other leadership characteristics may also inhibit the "would-be" leader from obtaining the "true leader" status, which ultimately has adverse effects on the leader's work group and, subsequently, the organization as a whole. The topics (voids) chosen for discussion in this section are based upon the author's experience, observed behaviors of both good and bad leaders, as well as his very own decisions made, including the good, the bad, and the ugly, and the subsequent consequences that went along with those decisions and behaviors.

Many of the dynamics present among these leadership voids come naturally. The behaviors are a means of survival; avoiding discomfort and caring for one's interests are basic instincts learned and developed over a lifetime. Therefore, failing to recognize these voids doesn't mean a person is bad. Instead, they are not performing as leaders to their full potential. With some self-reflection, honesty, and genuine effort, a person can take action to eliminate or minimize these voids to enhance their ability to lead and develop high-performing, successful work groups. The leadership voids discussed in this section include:

- The failure to recognize that leadership is about serving others and not yourself.
- Compromising your values and integrity and doing what is right to avoid discomfort and the feeling of loneliness that sometimes comes with leadership.

- Adhering to the skills and the role of a previous position instead of accepting, learning, and mastering the skills of your present leadership level.
- Promoting people into leadership positions for any reason other than competence and ability to perform successfully.
- The failure to recognize the importance of small things that might not be so small after all to your people.
- Utilizing a leadership style inconsistent with the demands and expectations of today's community policing.

Chapter 1

THE NUMBER ONE RULE OF LEADERSHIP: IT'S NOT ABOUT YOU

It's not about you! This is what I call the number one rule of leadership. A failure to appreciate and grasp this concept will undoubtedly leave a leadership void within your organization. If you are a leader, your priority, at least as it pertains to the organization you work for, should be the success of the organization and the group of people you lead. As soon as your decision-making comes down to what is in the best interest of you personally and not the group or organization, you have lost your leadership. It takes a unique person to do this. Indeed, many rise to this challenge and call for true leadership who sacrifice for the organization's benefit and do so successfully. This type of behavior is not natural, however. It requires effort, and constant self-reflection, to continually put the interests of others above yourself.

Human nature, left to itself, is selfish. It looks out for its own interests. The Bible tells us in Mark 14:38 that "the spirit is willing, but the flesh is weak." We may genuinely desire and tell ourselves we want to be good leaders. We want to be successful and care for and support those we lead, to help the police department meet its goals, to help make the community safer, and improve the quality of life for the members of the community. In other words, "the spirit is willing." We agree these are positive things and want them to happen, but this is where the "rubber meets the road." It takes daily effort, self-reflection, and self-sacrifice to do the things necessary to make them happen. Without the constant effort required, we will fall back on human nature and what is in our best interest because "the flesh is weak."

Where do we, as law enforcement officers, get in the most trouble in police work? Indeed, everyone makes mistakes. We will have lousy judgment calls as we try to make the best decisions under complex and stressful situations. I have made many. But typically, it isn't these "good faith" decisions that go wrong that get us in our most significant trouble. When are we, the police, getting suspended, demoted, fired, and even indicted and prosecuted? When we let our self-interests and selfish desires dictate the decisions we make instead of the code of ethics and the oath of office, which we swore to uphold.

Greed, booze, and inappropriate sexual relationships certainly rank high in ruining many law enforcement careers. But, in my opinion, the number one thing that gets the police in trouble is lies! When we lie, lie, lie. We lie to cover up our mistakes, and sometimes the poor decisions we make that aren't mistakes but decisions intentionally made, though clearly wrong.

There was a police officer who worked on my patrol shift. I'll call him "Officer Smith." I liked Officer Smith and thought highly of him. In many ways, he was an asset to the shift and organization. During urgent calls for service, such as crimes in progress, I was thankful to hear him answer the radio and call out "en route." Smith did not hesitate to get involved in high-risk situations. He would not be intimidated by potential danger or conflict. He took control of those situations, and I would breathe a sigh of relief when I heard on the radio that he had arrived on the scene of particularly nasty calls with the potential for violence. However, Smith had a problem. It was his ego. He wanted to be a cowboy. He thought he could do what he wanted, and considering policy and procedure wasn't his priority. He was going to do what he thought was right or at least right for him, and any other opinion as to the matter was "stupid," which he often publicly verbalized.

Smith's attitude began to have the expected adverse effects on other members of his shift, as well as with others elsewhere in the organization. I saw his strengths and the benefit he brought to the police department, but his "I know it all" ego overshadowed that, so others could not, or refused to, see his strengths. I met with Smith on more than one occasion, commending him for the strengths he brought to the team, but I made it just as clear that he would not last long enough to retire from the police department if he didn't change his attitude. Unfortunately, my words came true, as it wasn't long after those conversations when Smith lost his job.

Smith responded with others to an incident where a man had exposed himself to a woman and her young child. Smith was the primary assigned unit, nearing the end of the shift. I heard the call on the radio and heard Smith responding to it. As I was preparing to leave the office, Smith entered the station house with his duty bag in hand as my shift concluded. He appeared to be going toward the locker room to prepare for going home. Knowing enough time had not elapsed for him to complete a thorough investigation and report, I asked him for details of the incident and who was completing the report. He briefly summarized the incident, which was clearly a sexually motivated crime requiring a report and investigation. He assured me he was completing the report. We concluded the conversation, and I went home for the night.

The next day came, and I sought out the report looking for more details of the crime. After not finding the report, I asked Smith about it. He said he had completed the report and turned it in to the front desk, which was the appropriate procedure (this was before computerized Records Management Systems when we were still handwriting reports). I checked with the front desk personnel responsible for taking reports and entering data from the reports into the computer. They had neither seen nor were familiar with the report in question. I had a second conversation with Smith, and it ended with him adamantly saying he completed and turned in the report, suggesting the front desk personnel lost it. I instructed Smith to complete the report again while I continued to investigate what happened to the first report.

During this investigation, I came to suspect Smith had been less than truthful in his story about completing and turning in the report. Because of this suspicion, the second report was reviewed with some scrutiny. I later learned that Smith had not completed a first report and had no intention of doing so. In addition, he hadn't obtained the information from the victim necessary to complete a report.

Smith's first lie was telling me he would complete the report knowing he had no intention of doing so. The second lie was telling me he had finished it and turned it into the front desk to avoid getting in trouble for the first lie. Then, being held accountable for completing a report for which he had no information, Smith committed his third lie by falsifying his report rather than being forthcoming. He searched for information in the computer system on the victim and a witness, but unfortunately for him, the information was outdated. So, his report contained false information that he wanted his supervisors to believe he obtained directly, in person, from the victim upon responding to the incident on the night in question. This incident was the final "nail in the coffin," leading to Smith's departure from the police department.

Can lying by a police officer be anything other than them promoting their personal interests above all else? Smith lost a great career with a professional police agency. Why did Smith lose his job? Because Smith lied! Why did Smith lie? To cover up the decisions he made when he put his interests above that which was right and required by his commitment to the law enforcement profession. Maybe Smith wanted to go home on time. Perhaps he didn't want to be stuck at the office on overtime. Or, maybe Smith was just being lazy at the moment. Whatever his thought process was at that moment, Smith's self-centered decision came at a price. Fortunately, he was not in a leadership position, as it is much more destructive to an agency when a person in a leadership position puts their interests above that of the organization and its good people.

How about these additional examples of things that cause the police significant troubles?

- A manager uses their position to obtain sexual favors from a subordinate of the opposite sex.
- An officer shares confidential law enforcement information to obtain a benefit or alert a friend or relative to an ongoing investigation.
- An officer becomes involved in an intimate relationship with an informant.
- An officer lies during court testimony to obtain a conviction.
- An officer puts false information on their time sheet.
- An officer decides to drive intoxicated.
- An officer shakes down a drug dealer, keeping some of the drug money for themselves.

These are just a few scenarios that bring about significant consequences for those supposed to be role models and leaders in the community. Some of these examples seem pretty serious, yet if you have been on the job in law enforcement for any time, you have personally seen or heard of these behaviors occurring within law enforcement agencies. It wouldn't take long to search for media reports of this behavior. Just yesterday, a day before writing these words, another police officer in our community ruined his career by being involved in a motor vehicle accident while driving intoxicated.

What do these examples all have in common? First, the person guilty of these offenses lets their self-interests and selfish desires dictate their decisions. They were not thinking of the community they serve, the organization's benefit, or its good members. When we put ourselves first above others, we are not leaders.

Does this often happen among police leaders? You bet! We hope we do not routinely see serious offenses like the examples above among our law enforcement leaders. Still, even small decisions and actions taken out of selfishness and not for the organization's benefit will diminish our leadership abilities.

I believe a small percentage of people seek a law enforcement career out of an unhealthy desire for power and the authority that comes with the badge. They abuse their authority from the very beginning of their career, and it usually does not take too long until we identify these personalities. Thankfully, many of their jobs will end quickly and limit the damage they cause. It is devastating for one of these personalities to hide under the radar and rise to a leadership position. More common, however, is the individual who truly desires to do right. They enter law enforcement for the right reasons. They are genuinely concerned for the community and the organization and perform admirably, moving up the ranks to a leadership position. They proudly take this leadership position intending to make a difference, be successful, and lead an influential work group. Many will desire the most productive work group and believe they can do it. So, what happens?

When tough times come, when the supervisor faces resistance from their subordinates, when progress is slow and grueling, when you don't necessarily share the same vision and opinions of the Chief or Sheriff, or when it seems you are alone and no one else cares, it is easy to fall back and take the path of least resistance. As previously said, this is human nature and a fairly natural thing to do. It happens all the time, even to some of our best leaders, at least temporarily. It doesn't necessarily mean you are a terrible employee and can't be successful. It does mean you are not living up to your true leadership potential. Our best leaders won't stay down long. They will not take this path of least resistance. There will undoubtedly be frustration and disappointment, but they will get "back in the saddle." They will keep moving forward. They have to.

I use the analogy of "banging your head against the wall." If you keep banging your head against the wall, you eventually realize it hurts and quit doing it. Likewise, when a mediocre leader realizes authentic leadership takes hard work and effort, and success does not come easy, it is an easy alternative to settle into the path of least resistance. Settling into the path of least resistance can also quickly happen to a newly appointed leader with tremendous leadership potential if the proper support and means for personal growth are unavailable.

Maybe as a leader, you are striving to have the best trained and motivated patrol shift in the organization. You prepare roll call training for your shift so they can be the best. You research applicable case law to ensure your personnel can respond quickly and legally to whatever confronts them in the field. You debrief any incidents of significance responded to by your shift to identify "lessons learned" to improve future responses to similar incidents. You hold your personnel accountable for results. You review their work to ensure it is of the best quality and correct those needing improvement. Unfortunately, none of the other patrol supervisors seem to put forth this same effort. And the results show. You have the highest-performing patrol shift. Unfortunately, however, your boss is not a good leader. After all the extra effort you put forth to be the best, you receive no recognition. Your boss never commends you or even recognizes the contributions you make. And, the supervisors of the other patrol shifts, those doing much less, are receiving the same recognition you are, allowed to get by providing mediocre results. Some people with good leadership potential will step back or settle in and join their peers in a world of mediocrity and never rise to the level of excellence they could. Before too long, this attitude becomes the norm, with no further thought to what you could have been and what you could have done for your organization, community, and work group. Law enforcement agencies around the nation are full of these "just getting by" supervisors.

Great leaders, on the other hand, will continue to excel in performance because that is who they are. They know that is best for the organization, the community, their personnel, and, yes, for themselves. They are driven by values, doing what is right and making a difference regardless of what others are doing around them. Too many so-called leaders, however, will give in. They will say, "Why bother? No one cares, so why am I doing all this extra work? It would be easier for me if I just did what I needed to do to get by." And hence, a void in leadership is born.

TO LEAD IS TO WORK

To lead is to work. Leadership is not for the faint-hearted, the lazy, or those willing to settle for mediocrity. If you want to have subordinates and a work group that excels, then you, the leader, must set the example that hard work is necessary in pursuing excellence. So, what does this leader look like? One who works and serves. To serve implies putting others above yourself. John C. Maxwell, in his book titled, *The 17 Indisputable Laws of Teamwork*, says about becoming a better leader, "No matter what kind of situation you face, remember that your responsibilities to people come in the following order: to the organization, to the team, and then to the individual. Your own interests and comfort come last."[1]

Forsaking your interests and comfort might require you to miss your lunch break to ensure your people get theirs. You may need to work overtime to finish a task, complete an important proposal or project, or just be there for your people. Are you the first to go home at the end of the workday or the last?

Every department has a front desk, where calls from citizens are received and walk-ins greeted; questions about everything and anything, including a lot of non-police related topics, are answered; and where a significant number of reports are completed and data entered. In one instance, an officer assigned to the police department front desk had an opportunity to attend a personal event that was important to her. However, she could not get off to attend the event due to minimal staffing requirements and no one else available to cover her assignment. Understanding the importance of the event, as the shift supervisor, I volunteered to cover for this officer. Working the front desk required me to complete tasks I was neither familiar with nor comfortable with, and I downright dreaded the day as it approached. I did not have to do it; under some circumstances, I wouldn't have done it. But, in this case, I was able to do it, chose to do it, and I know this officer was grateful to be able to attend an important personal event because I did it. I know my willingness to do this meant a lot to this officer.

During a crisis, when bad things happen, the leader may have to fill in and sacrifice for the benefit of others. For example, after breaking the news

---

[1] From *The 17 Indisputable Laws of Teamwork* by John C. Maxwell, copyright © 2001, p. 72. Used by permission of Thomas Nelson Publishing, a division of HarperCollins Focus LLC. https://www.harpercollinsfocus.com/

to an entire patrol shift that had just arrived at work that a shift mate had been killed in a traffic crash the night prior, I knew it was time "to lead and work." A couple leaders, who were also hurting and in pain, ran back and forth from opposite sides of town, trying to handle as many calls for service as possible. They did this to relieve officers of the responsibility and burden of responding to calls, giving them time together to remember and grieve their lost friend (see Figure 1). And then, spending time cleaning the deceased officer's blood from his equipment, which the family later received unblemished. These actions involved putting others first.

Figure 1. Shift mates erected this cross at the site of the fatal vehicle crash that took the life of their friend, Officer Kyle Dieling.

After an attempted robbery of a drug dealer, a gunfight ensued, hospitalizing two people with gunshots. A long day of investigating lay ahead, as evidence needed identification and collection, witnesses interviewed, and suspects identified, tracked down, interviewed, and hopefully arrested and charged. Two of three offenders were identified, located, and placed in custody. The police spent most of the day searching for the third offender, the gun, and the vehicle used in the shooting. About ten detectives spent their Saturday off working this case most the day. As day turned to night, leads regarding the whereabouts of the third offender waned. Detectives were relieved to head home for the remaining few hours of their day off.

I was the last one still in the office and had my bag in hand, preparing to head out the door for home when I got a call. Police units had just located the vehicle from the shooting, parked at an apartment complex where the offender's ex-girlfriend was thought to live, out of our jurisdiction, in another town. It would be critical that this vehicle be taken into custody, adequately secured, and processed for evidence. An interview with the ex-girlfriend may also prove fruitful in locating the offender. I was not happy, though. I was tired and just wanted to go home. As crucial as this vehicle may be to the case, inside, I wished they hadn't found it.

I had the authority to call other detectives, including the primary investigator, and order them to come in to deal with the recovery of this vehicle so I could go home. However, these other detectives had been working all day, starting early in the morning and working much harder than myself. So, as a leader, it was my turn to serve them and allow them what little remained of their Saturday.

I did need a second person to go with me to take custody of this vehicle and attempt to locate and speak with the ex-girlfriend. Although he too had been working this case much of the day, I called a detective supervisor at his home and requested a detective accompany me. When the supervisor answered the phone, he explained that he was just leaving home with his wife for a restaurant. This supervisor, a leader in his own right, chose to serve and join me rather than call out one of the detectives who had worked all day.

Unbeknownst to me, one of this supervisor's subordinates had not left the office yet but was in the workout room exercising. Had I known this, I would have recruited him and not bothered the detective supervisor. This supervisor, however, did know that his detective was still in the building, but he chose not to bother him. Furthermore, so his personnel could enjoy some needed downtime, this supervisor demonstrated his servant's heart by canceling his dinner plans with his wife and assisting me. This detective supervisor understood, "to lead is to work, and it's never about you!"

Work is good, and you make a difference regardless of your position. Therefore, the question that needs to be asked is, "What kind of difference are you making?" Is it a positive difference or a negative? "It is nearly impossible to remain neutral as you travel through each day... The key is to pay attention to the kinds of differences you are making...You shouldn't be asking, 'Did I make a difference today?' Of course, you did! You undoubtedly affected somebody, maybe slightly, maybe significantly. The most important question to ask yourself is, 'What *kind* of difference did I make?'"[2]

The true leader desires to make a positive difference for others. They will make mistakes. They occasionally make poor judgment calls but won't settle for "just getting by." They want the organization and its people to be successful, which only comes with hard work and making a positive difference within your organization.

When I started considering writing this book, I was about 30 days from being demoted and removed as a captain within the sheriff's office. The newly elected sheriff chose to replace me and several others with command team members of his choosing. Replacing us wasn't due to any noted performance deficiency but rather a common practice as the agency head. The sheriff has the prerogative, rightly so, to fill his administration with command-level personnel he knows, who share his vision, and whom he trusts, etc. He decided to reassign me before he ever took office, met me, or had an in-depth conversation with me. A made decision to fit his plan and vision moving forward. However, this unwanted change in assignment allowed me the extra time to start writing this book, which proved a blessing. It also proved to be a means of exercising my mind and hopefully expanding my influence on others, specifically regarding leadership and police management (see Figure 2).

Reassigned as a deputy in the courthouse, I assisted in providing security and law enforcement functions for all the courtrooms, offices, and activities on the premises. So, what did I do? After 15 years of being in a leadership, supervisory, and command position, I now found myself with no one to lead. Or did I?

---

[2] From *The Fred Factor* by Mark Sanborn, copyright © 2004, pp. 35-36. Used by permission of Waterbrook Press, a division of Random House Inc.

Figure 2. Lead from wherever you are! About a week after being demoted, I learned that part of my responsibilities was mopping inmate cells. Once I recognized this wasn't a joke, I grabbed a mop and got busy, smiling all the way.

TO LEAD IS TO SERVE

In Ecclesiastes 9:10, The Bible says, "Whatever your hand finds to do, do it with all your might." So, lead from wherever you are. My performance and efforts made a difference daily, whether positive or negative. True leaders will continue to make those positive differences regardless of their situation. If I'm a deputy assigned to the courthouse, my job is to be the best deputy

I can be, to help create the most effective courthouse team possible. I found it gratifying to support and encourage my supervisors, some of whom used to be my subordinates. Because of my experience, others sought my advice, and I reveled in the opportunity to provide some wisdom and perspective to help others excel.

My job was to set an example by informally leading others whenever and wherever. For example, what did we do when my supervisor asked my peers and me to change procedures, and they neither appeared effective nor made sense to any of us? Did we nod our head in approval and understanding of the request and then leave the discussion grumbling as to what a stupid decision that was, only to continue to do things the way we used to? Is this what a leader does? No! If a request made by the supervisor was neither illegal nor unethical, I did what was asked of me because it was not about me. If I needed to have a conversation to express my concern over the requested change in procedure, I could have done that one-on-one with the supervisor and done so respectfully. When others start talking poorly about a supervisor or coworker, I don't have to participate in that, and if possible, I can redirect the conversation in a more positive direction. In other words, I could support my work group and improve it regardless of my position. I've been on both sides, and what a difference it makes to a leader to have other leaders on the team. Lead from wherever you are!

Do true leaders automatically become leaders at the moment of their promotion? Or do they get chosen for promotion because they are already leaders? Lead from wherever you are.

About three months after being reassigned to the courthouse, as I routinely did at the end of the day, I walked the courthouse hallways checking doors to ensure they were locked. I came across a judge in one of the back hallways. It was the first time I had seen this judge inside the courthouse. However, I had met this judge on previous occasions. After greeting the judge, he exclaimed, "You are the guy they are talking about. I was wondering who it was; it's good to finally know it was you." He explained how various people working in the courthouse told him about a deputy with a lot of experience who was now assigned to work in the courthouse. The judge told me that these people had been saying how lucky they were to have me working inside the courthouse and how I was making a positive difference. Those kind words shared with me by the judge came at the perfect time. It was an encouragement and boost I needed – a reminder that we can all make a positive difference from wherever we are.

About a month later, I received some more encouragement. I had the opportunity to speak with a local social service agency leader with whom I used to frequently interact as the captain of investigations. She explained how excited some of her social workers were to see me, "Captain Dan," as a deputy at the courthouse. The social workers provide liaison services to victims of domestic violence and, therefore, spend frequent time at the courthouse with victims. They felt safer with "Captain Dan" in the building.

Were they safer because "Captain Dan" was now assigned to the courthouse? No, probably not! The perception was there, however; perception can affect people and their quality of life. We can affect the quality of life of people in our communities regardless of our position if we choose to lead. And, to lead is to serve. This was another lesson learned and a perspective I needed to hear during a time many people might perceive as a low point in life. Most of us hopefully began our careers in law enforcement with the desire to make a positive difference. Wouldn't it be great when we retire from a long career in law enforcement if we leave with that same attitude, still making a positive difference? It's up to you.

Eventually, the new sheriff and I would get to know each other better. Finally, and gratefully, I would again be promoted twice at the sheriff's office and eventually have the opportunity to lead my own police department as its police chief.

Looking back on my demotion, I could have chosen to grumble and take advantage of every opportunity to covertly attack and sabotage the new sheriff, who removed me from my position as a captain and reassigned me as a courthouse deputy. That might be the easy and instinctual response. But instead, I decided my job was to make my supervisor's job easier by providing support and exceptional service where I could. And maybe, with the combination of experience, working hard, and a positive attitude, I could make a positive difference among my peers and coworkers and perhaps even help them become successful leaders, obtaining some of the opportunities I was blessed to have. However, positively impacting my coworkers in this manner doesn't happen if I put myself first, above all others, because the number one rule of leadership is, "It's not about you!"

Chapter 2

IT'S LONELY AT THE TOP

Nobody prepares and strives with excitement for a leadership position, thinking they will be lonely. On the contrary! Looking at those leading organizations and work groups, they appear anything but lonely. Leaders are often surrounded by people. Leaders frequently interact with their subordinates, a requirement to ensure organizational functions and tasks get accomplished. They have easy access to their supervisors, those higher up the chain of command. They attend and hold meetings, meet with stakeholders that have an investment within the law enforcement agency, and are often out in front receiving significant attention during serious, complex, and critical events associated with the agency. These roles are what aspiring leaders see and are drawn towards. Unfortunately, the loneliness I'm referring to often hides below the surface, unnoticed by those outside the leadership circle. Rest assured, a true leader recognizes this loneliness. It may not present itself daily, but a true leader who pursues excellence and puts the organization's needs first will experience it. I believe the failure of some in leadership positions to not only recognize, but to willingly accept this idea that leadership is lonely is another void we have in the leadership of our law enforcement agencies. So, what is this loneliness?

In the book titled, *The Leadership Secrets of Colin Powell*, the author provides an entire chapter called "Prepare for Loneliness."[1] At the onset, the chapter confirms that "leaders are rarely alone..., however are often lonely." When leaders must make tough decisions, they may collect data and information from various sources. For example, he may have an open-door policy, encourage candid discussion, and provide everyone in the work group an opportunity to be heard. However, once a decision is made, it belongs to the leader; he owns it. Often there won't be enough information to come up with the perfect solution.

---

[1] Harari, Oren. (2002). *The Leadership Secrets of Colin Powell.* Used with permission of McGraw-Hill, New York, NY, pp. 243-253. Permission conveyed through Copyright Clearance Center.

Nonetheless, leaders must make decisions even with limited information. In policing, this often involves complex incidents involving the threat to life. Yet a decision must be made. And then, the loneliness starts as the leader questions himself in silence. "Did I make the right decision?" "Was there a better decision?" "Was there more information I should have obtained before making the decision?" "Did I base my decision on accurate and reliable information?" "What are others thinking or saying about the decision I made?" Hence the loneliness. There will be second-guessing, possibly by the leader, but certainly by others. Sometimes a person in a leadership position will stall or outright refuse to decide for fear of being second-guessed. A true leader recognizes these dynamics and accepts them, understanding that this loneliness comes with the leadership position.

I believe the dynamics involved with these feelings of loneliness and how a void in leadership originates is similar to the dynamics affecting the number one rule of leadership I discussed previously – it's not about you! In the last chapter, we explored what happens to aspiring leaders, those who have shown an indication of great potential, when confronted with resistance, when things don't go their way, or they aren't recognized for their effort. Unfortunately, when this occurs, they often settle into mediocrity, limiting their true leadership potential. In the present case, a void in leadership is created when a supervisor, a person in a leadership position, either refuses to accept responsibility for their decisions or does not do the right thing, that which is appropriate, to avoid this feeling of loneliness. Let's face it – human beings are social beings who want to belong and be liked by others. The mental health field is full of professionals who counsel people suffering from poor self-esteem, issues with their feelings of self-worth, or poor social skills. People want to be liked and feel good about themselves.

Those who choose law enforcement as a career are no different. I might argue due to the personality traits often found among our law enforcement professionals, such as a strong ego, a need to belong, and a need for control, the need for acceptance and validation may be even more vital. The leadership void is created when a leader compromises on doing what is right in hopes of being liked, avoiding being talked about negatively, or avoiding questions about their decisions. In other words, they give up authentic leadership to prevent or minimize the feeling of loneliness that comes with it.

Throughout my career, there have been numerous times when I did not take appropriate action, most frequently involving the discipline or correction of performance on behalf of those working for me. I procrastinated in allowing misbehavior to continue because I liked the person or considered them a friend whom I didn't want to offend. I feared losing their commitment or allegiance or worried about what others might say. Therefore, I provided too many chances before appropriately addressing inappropriate performance or behavior. I made excuses in my head. Rather than addressing the deficiency immediately, I told myself, "Let's just watch them for a while and see if the behavior continues." Or I met with them and discussed the inappropriate behavior, but only to find myself repeatedly having the same discussion, month after month. Instead of using progressive discipline with a reoffending officer, I might give them numerous chances, because I liked them, wanted to be a positive motivator, and was concerned about what this officer and others would think of me if I responded more harshly. In reality, I was doing nobody any favors.

The officer who refuses to follow appropriate procedures, even after being talked to, and willingly continues with their inappropriate behavior is doing the organization no good. Their deficiencies in performance often must be made up for by other officers who have to carry their weight. Had I addressed the problems more promptly and appropriately, officers may have corrected their behavior more expeditiously rather than continuing with behavior that required more drastic disciplinary measures to address their deficiencies. My reputation as a sound leader might also come into question when others saw me shun my responsibilities and not perform as a leader should. My failure to practice authentic leadership because of my fear of loneliness did more harm than good to the organization.

I am not suggesting we immediately jump to harsh disciplinary action when someone makes a mistake or shouldn't give our personnel chances to recover, grow, and do the right thing. On the contrary, as I believe most of this book will affirm, we want to create a positive environment and leadership style where our personnel can be successful. However, in my experience, the behavior rarely gets better when we choose not to address lack of performance or inappropriate behavior because we fear what others might think about us. And as a result, the good people of the organization suffer. They will have to pick up the person's slack and, all the while, look at you, the supervisor, wondering why you are not doing something about it. Why aren't you doing your job?

The need for affiliation, liking people, or being liked by people can go a long way in creating and maintaining positive relationships that will help you accomplish tasks and fulfill the mission. The necessity for such positive relationships should not be understated, and I will cover them in more depth in a future chapter. However, when a leader's affiliation needs become their priority over fulfilling the organization's mission, those needs can have a negative and distracting effect on goal attainment when the need to be liked is no longer a means to an end but become the end itself.

Besides my own experience and failures in this area, I have seen other supervisors ignore poor performance, including potentially unethical behavior, because they feared the ramifications and consequences of taking action.

They wanted to be liked by their personnel, and this desire took priority, overshadowing their commitment to putting the organization first. They looked the other way, hoping things would get better on their own, that someone else would deal with the problem, or maybe the problem would go unnoticed. I have seen my peers, commanders of other divisions alerted to problems and deficiencies among their ranks, problems that would have a long-term adverse effect on the organization if not addressed. These commanders recognized and acknowledged these problems but then refused to follow up and manage the deficiencies out of what I believe to be a fear of what others, their personnel, might think. These leaders cannot accept the idea and reality that it can be lonely at the top. So, their leadership capabilities and the organization's ability to accomplish its mission are limited.

After monitoring the work performance of a detective for about three months, it was apparent that this detective's performance in specific areas was lacking. The detective had excellent skills and potential and did a great job in those areas in which he held interest. However, his efforts and the services he provided were lacking when he didn't deem a case essential or interesting. When I received calls from victims complaining about not receiving feedback, getting status updates on their case, or getting returned phone calls after leaving messages, nine out of ten times, it was regarding this detective. There were issues of poor report writing and a lack of investigative follow-up on numerous cases. In one instance, the documentation of drug evidence was mishandled, giving the appearance that evidence had gone missing from the evidence room. In reality, it was a reporting and documentation error. With the error detected, the evidence was located. These types of mistakes, however, certainly are serious and can potentially embarrass and affect an agency's credibility.

After several months of monitoring this detective's work product and learning of his lack of service to the community, I met with this detective's sergeant. I asked this sergeant for his recommendation on how he thought these deficiencies should be addressed. The response I received somewhat surprised me. The investigation into this detective's performance came shortly after an election in which a new sheriff had been elected but had not yet taken office. The sergeant was aware the detective and the newly elected sheriff were friends, and, therefore, the sergeant's position was more about self-interest than doing what was in the organization's best interest. In addition, the sergeant believed the new sheriff would move the detective from the current unit after taking office, after which the detective would become someone else's problem in the organization. Therefore, the sergeant thought it best to ignore the issues and let the detective's work performance deficiencies go unchallenged.

The sergeant wasn't a bad sergeant, but someone I thought was committed to the organization. Someone I appreciated. We recapped the various issues with this detective's performance. I asked the sergeant what his concerns were that led him to recommend no action be taken to correct this detective's performance. It came down to concern for himself and how taking corrective action against this detective might negatively affect him and his career. I understood his position. He wasn't alone in this way of thinking, as this was prevalent within the agency's culture. The concerns I had, however, which I shared with the sergeant, were these:

1. As everyone in the division knows the detective's attitude and performance, what message is sent if no corrective action is taken?
2. How does our action or inaction impact those who already received corrective action for performance deficiencies, similar or otherwise?
3. How will our reputation and credibility as leaders be impacted if we treat people differently because of who they know or support?

In the end, I completed the investigation and handed out the discipline myself, relieving the sergeant of that burden.

Ultimately the sergeant was right. When the new sheriff took office, he transferred the poor-performing detective. And I was removed from my position, demoted, and reassigned elsewhere. Of course, my reassignment had nothing to do with this incident, as it was made long before I meted out the discipline. But it doesn't matter. True leaders do the right thing regardless, even when it leaves them alone. Quoting former Chicago Police Superintendent Phil Cline, ". . . if you wanted everyone to like you, you should have become a circus clown, not a police supervisor."[2]

LEADERS SET THE EXAMPLE

True leaders set the example. True leaders do the right thing, even when it is not the popular thing. True leaders stand up for what they believe to be right even when others may criticize them for it. But, as a leader, you are being watched. Your every move is watched and scrutinized, including the decisions you make and those you don't. As well as how you spend your time, what you focus on, the parts of the job you emphasize, the type of performance and behavior you reward and ignore, and whether you genuinely support the organization's mission or only give it simple lip service. And,

[2] Police Executive Research Forum. (2009). *Leadership Matters: Police Chiefs Talk About Their Careers.* Washington, D.C.: Police Executive Research Forum, p. 35.

let's not forget, do you mean what you say and hold people accountable for their performance, or do you procrastinate or outright ignore inappropriate behavior from subordinates?

Others will criticize the leader. Leaders will be criticized when they make mistakes and make wrong decisions; some criticism may be warranted. But they will also be unjustly criticized when they make the right decision. There will always be someone who will not agree with the decisions made. Or, even if they agree, attacking the leader may be the popular thing to do or serve their interests or agenda. This type of behind-your-back, or in some cases, not so behind-your-back, behavior is frequently observed in the world of politics, but make no mistake, these same tactics are being used in law enforcement agencies every day. The leader cannot always please everyone, and there are some people you know in your organization that the leader will never satisfy. Yet, they seem to "know it all" and always have the correct answers until they are responsible for making the decision.

Abraham Lincoln is arguably one of the best presidents the United States has ever had; however, he endured significant criticism. Lincoln was publicly called ". . . a grotesque baboon, a third-rate country lawyer who once splits rails and now splits the Union, a coarse vulgar joker, a dictator, an ape, a buffoon, and . . . even the most dishonest politician that ever disgraced an office in America."[3] This was public criticism he received. I am sure there was much more said privately behind his back. Lincoln recognized and accepted that he would be unable to please everyone. A true leader must accept this because people will be talking about the leader, the supervisor, the chief, or the sheriff behind their backs. It comes with the territory of a supervisor and a leader. If you can't live with this, leadership is not for you. If you are going to fret and balk at every decision-making opportunity in fear of what others may think, then again, leadership is not for you.

Regardless of the pleasant environment you may foster and the teamwork you encourage, they know you are the supervisor and have been watching, listening, and scrutinizing your every move. So don't forget it, because your subordinates won't.

It has always amazed me how people I considered friends, people I viewed as committed employees, who I supported, encouraged, and tried to develop and help succeed at every opportunity, turned on me as the supervisor at moment's notice when the going got tough. I have seen officers make mistakes, not perform a task or handle a call as expected by organization standards. When confronted by their supervisor, self-preservation kicked in; officers made excuses and began finger-pointing, sometimes directed at me. I considered these good officers. But remember, even good officers will

---

[3] From *Lincoln on Leadership* by Donald T. Phillips, copyright © 1991, p. 66. Reprinted by permission of Grand Central Publishing, an imprint of Hachette Book Group, Inc.

watch the leader's every move, and some will use what they observe to save themselves. All too often, when confronted, officers start making excuses, looking for a way out from taking responsibility for their decisions and actions. I have heard officers tell me, "Sergeant Smith never makes me do that"; "Sergeant Smith let officer so-and-so do it; he didn't say anything to him"; "That's how Sergeant Smith's shift does it"; "Sergeant Smith says. . . ." "I can't be at fault if the boss allows the same behavior or does the same thing himself" is the mindset. Sometimes the statements have been factual, but other times either exaggerated or taken out of context, all so this officer could save their skin. Again, I consider many of these to be good officers, but under stress, it is human nature for self-preservation to rise to the top of a person's priority list.

There was an occasion when multiple officers approached me separately to complain about the poor performance of another officer. The officer was not handling his assignments appropriately, which required other officers to "pick up his slack" and do some of his work. Some described the officer as simply lazy. I appreciated that these officers chose to pick up their deficient peer's slack instead of just ignoring the poor performance and allowing the service to victims or the community to suffer. These officers thought it important enough to provide the right level of service that they carried the load for this officer whose performance was deficient. However, they finally decided they were fed up with doing his job on top of their own. I was aware of the officer in question. He was not one of our star performers. There had been prior complaints in the past, and as previously mentioned, this was one of those cases where poor performance was probably allowed to continue much longer than it should have been.

So, after receiving these multiple complaints, I began paying closer attention, and it didn't take long to make personal observations confirming the complaints I had received. Then, I took decisive action to hold this officer accountable for not delivering the appropriate and expected level of performance. However, to this day, I remain amazed at how the officers who brought this all to my attention reacted. They turned on me while rallying around the deficient officer, supporting him as if the agency was unjustly out to get him.

I'm sure some employees weren't surprised this officer was getting disciplined for poor work performance. And others were probably thinking, "It's about time." But what about the officers who initiated the complaint against this deficient officer and then turned on me, making me out to be the bad guy? I do not know if this was an act to somehow protect themselves against allegations by the officer or fear of being held accountable themselves, sometime in the future. Exactly why, I do not know. But I have learned through experience that the reason doesn't matter. It did not matter if those complaining officers changed their minds. They were right to be fed up with having to do their peer's work because he was too lazy to do it. In addition, it would have been the right thing for any supervisor to address this officer's poor behavior and how it negatively impacted his peers, regardless of how his peers responded.

When events like these occur, and the supervisor feels they are receiving unfair or unjust criticism, it can become lonely. It is easy to give up. It's easy to say, "Why bother?" It's easy to fall back into a world of mediocrity. It's easy to want to lash back at those you feel have wronged you with an "I'm the boss, and I'll show you" attitude. Indeed, there will be times when the right thing to do for the agency's good is to stand up, set the record straight, and let the truth be known. But do not take it personally and act from the standpoint of an over-inflated ego. True leaders don't do that. Instead, they accept the loneliness that comes with being a leader.

LEADERS TAKE RESPONSIBILITY

A position of leadership is a position of responsibility. Leaders are responsible for themselves, their decisions, and their personnel's performance. A true leader craves this responsibility, as it isn't something they can delegate. The buck stops with them. They stand by their decisions and recognize that if it brings success, it is not because of them, the leader, but the workers – their personnel – who brought about the success and deserve the recognition. In his book *Good to Great,* author Jim Collins describes the best leaders, Level 5 leaders, as those who look outside of themselves when things go well and when the company achieves and is successful. They give credit for success to others, and sometimes when there is no prominent person or persons to credit success to, they credit their good fortune to good luck.

On the other hand, when things aren't going well, and decisions don't lead to the expected results, they don't blame others or bad luck; they personally take the blame and responsibility. Collins explains that other leaders, not considered Level 5 leaders, do the opposite. They enjoy taking credit for good results and blaming others for the mishaps and poor performance.[4] I suggest this is the case for poor leaders because they do not want to face the loneliness of taking responsibility for poor results and unsatisfactory performance.

In 2013, three police officers assigned as drug investigators from a suburb of Chicago were arrested for drug trafficking. They were "shaking down"

---

[4] Collins, Jim. (2001). *Good to Great* by Jim Collins copyright © 2001 by James Collins. Reprinted by permission of Curtis Brown, Ltd. All rights reserved.

drug dealers, stealing their drugs, and selling them for profit. In addition to the scandal caused by these highly publicized arrests, the police chief of the same police agency was being investigated for an unrelated crime. As a result, the village leaders hired an outside consulting firm to assess the police department to help determine or understand how the village, and specifically the police department, may have failed to identify the illegal activities conducted by members of the department. The consultants identified numerous deficiencies within the department, making innumerable recommendations for improvement. One finding was that "individuals in the Police Chief's position in the past have been reluctant to accept responsibility for difficult decisions, accepted credit for the Department's positive outcomes and blamed others when incidents went awry"[5]–the opposite of what Jim Collins' Level 5 great leaders do.

Another finding was that the officers assigned to the drug unit, from which the three arrested worked, were working with minimal supervision and oversight. According to the assessment, the proactive work group participated in high-risk activities without sufficient supervisor oversight. In addition, the supervisor of the drug unit, and the supervisor's supervisor, were not setting an example or taking responsibility, as good leaders do.

"When a subordinate did a good job, Lincoln praised, complimented, and rewarded the individual. On the other hand, he shouldered responsibility when mistakes were made . . . this included taking responsibility for the battles lost during the Civil War."[6] Imagine the loneliness in accepting such responsibility involving significant loss of life and the country's future. The leader of a law enforcement agency will also have to make decisions that affect the lives of others in significant ways. And accepting this responsibility is accepting the state of loneliness. Many people, if not most, cannot or will not. Thus, authentic leaders must.

"Being responsible sometimes means pissing people off. . . . A leader simply cannot please everyone all the time . . . leadership can't be a popularity contest. Trying not to offend anyone, or trying to get everyone to like you, will set you on the road to mediocrity . . . leaders who are afraid to make people angry are likely to waver and procrastinate when it comes time to make tough choices. Leaders who care more about being liked than about being *effective* are unlikely to confront the people who need confronting. They are unlikely to offer differential rewards based upon performance. They won't challenge the status quo. And inevitably, by not challenging tradition, they hurt both their own credibility and their organization's performance."[7]

---

[5] Hillard Heintze LLC. (2013). *The Schaumburg Police Department: An Agency in Transition, An independent assessment and strategic roadmap.* Chicago, IL, pp. 56, 24.

[6] From Donald T. Phillips, *Lincoln on Leadership,* p. 103.

[7] Oren Harari, *Leadership Secrets of Colin Powell,* pp. 17-18.

During World War 2, the day before he was to authorize the launching of Operation Overload on D-Day, General Eisenhower took time to write a note in case the operation failed. Fortunately, the operation was successful; therefore, the note was unnecessary. However, imagine his loneliness when he wrote these words, not knowing what the next day would bring. "Our landings in the Cherbourg-Havre area have failed to gain a satisfactory foothold and I have withdrawn the troops. My decision to attack at this time and place was based upon the best information available. The troops, the air and the Navy did all that bravery and devotion to duty could do. If any blame or fault attaches to the attempt it is mine alone."[8] Indeed, it would have been a lonely place to be had the operation failed. But, as history has shown, it ended as a tremendous success, and the glory went to the brave men and women of the military who took part in the D-Day invasion.

It was my first day as the new Police Commander of the Detective Division. About two hours into the day, my phone rang. It was an investigator from another jurisdiction reporting a three-year-old homicide that until now had gone unreported. The investigator informed me the homicide had occurred in my jurisdiction. I immediately thought, "This is a joke, a prank, and a very good one." What's the likelihood of this happening two hours after having taken over the reins of the detective division? I stretched the phone cord from my office phone as far as I could, trying to see into the open area of cubicles where the division's detectives sat. I expected to see the culprit smiling at the other end of this call as they tried to pull off this "Welcome to the detective division" prank. Unfortunately, it was not a prank. That may have been how my first day started, but it did not stop there.

My first week in this new and exciting position worsened. Later in the week, a detective entered my office, shutting the door behind them. Usually, this is not a good sign. He went on to tell me there were allegations against our chief, who allegedly had committed a felony. The detective told me our chief was an associate of an offender under investigation and had alerted the offender about the criminal investigation. The city recently hired the chief from outside the department. I asked the detective who within the department was aware of the allegations. He told me only two members of the detective division and the previous division commander, who had since retired. I asked the detective not to share this information with anyone else until I had the opportunity to review all case-related information.

I suspected these allegations probably started from someone unhappy with the chief. As an objective observer, I thought once I reviewed the available information, I would probably find the allegation unfounded. However, this

---

[8] Used with permission of John Wiley & Sons Books, from *Eisenhower on Leadership: Ike's Enduring Lessons in Total Victory Management* by Alan Axelrod, copyright © 2006, p. 29. Permission conveyed through Copyright Clearance Center, Inc.

was not the case. As I reviewed the information and evidence collected, it was all circumstantial evidence regarding the chief's involvement, but the evidence appeared strong.

I pondered how to handle this. If the allegations were true, then many people were in harm's way. Not necessarily physically, but their well-being, careers, and quality of life. If the chief was of the character to participate in this behavior, what else might he do? What harm might come to the good men and women of the department and the community we serve? In speaking with the two employees aware of the allegations, we agreed a separate investigation was warranted. But how should we do this, and who should conduct the investigation?

I could follow my chain of command and report the situation to my supervisor, the deputy chief. Indeed, this would be an acceptable course of action, as matters of this nature and sensitivity are routinely forwarded through the chain of command. I could have taken the "This is above my pay grade" stance, and rightly forwarded it up the chain of command, washing my hands of it altogether. However, that option didn't seem ideal. First, the deputy chief was ultimately responsible for the department's day-to-day operations and had to interact with the chief frequently. This kind of information might distract him from handling his daily responsibilities, let alone screening this knowledge from the chief during their interactions. In addition, if the allegations proved false, this could have long-term effects on their relationship, which I wanted to avoid.

Secondly, I was not only concerned for the well-being of the subordinates working for me, but I didn't want the deputy chief to experience the stress and loneliness that would undoubtedly come from this news.

Finally, the deputy chief may have decided we would have no involvement in the investigation and ordered me to drop it entirely. To do anything else at that point would be disobeying a direct order and insubordination, which I certainly wanted to avoid.

I recognized this was a significant conflict of interest, and I should not personally have any part in this investigation. Even if we found enough evidence to prove the chief's involvement, the chief's defense and his supporter's argument would be we fabricated it because we just didn't like him or his policies. We needed an outside agency to investigate the claims so we could remove ourselves from any involvement.

I decided to reach out to the District Attorney's Office, which had an investigation unit. If they took this investigation, it would remove all of us from the police department from involvement. Instead, they could conduct an objective, independent investigation and let the chips fall where they may. During my communication with an investigation unit supervisor, I learned the District Attorney's Office was already aware of the allegations. In addition, members of the city government had already received anonymous letters about these allegations against the chief and had since contacted the District Attorney's Office requesting an investigation.

I met with the assigned District Attorney investigator and shared our developed information. Yet the district attorney was concerned about a conflict of interest between his office and the police chief due to the ongoing need to interact and work together. And therefore, he was not interested in conducting an investigation. However, if a significant amount of evidence pointed to the chief's involvement in criminal behavior, they would refer the case to the State Police's Public Integrity Unit for an investigation. The district attorney wanted a "smoking gun," and if it existed, they would be comfortable referring the case to the state police. Without it, they were not volunteering to do much else. How did they think they would find a smoking gun without conducting some sort of investigation? The District Attorney's Office was worried about a conflict of interest. I understood that considering my own involvement was a conflict of interest I was trying to eliminate.

A decision had to be made. And the loneliness kicked in as I pondered how to proceed. We tried to do the right thing. We reported the information to an agency responsible for this type of case, but they balked. At that moment, we could have quit, told ourselves we did our best and saved ourselves from potential future harm to our careers. But what if? What if the allegations were true? What else would someone capable of this type of behavior do? What might happen to the credibility of the police department and the community's trust? How about the good men and women inside the police department? What might happen to them in the future?

I met with the other two people familiar with the case and allegations. I asked them what they wanted to do and reminded them of the risk we would take by continuing our investigation. To many, this would be career suicide. However, they agreed to continue the investigation was the right thing to do. From a personal standpoint, I was proud of these two people. Many, if not most, would not have made the decision they made. They knew what was right, and it was worth the risk to their families and careers to stand up for doing what was right. That's what we swear to when we take the oath of office and have that badge pinned on us. Part of the Law Enforcement Code of Ethics states, "I recognize the badge of my office as a symbol of public faith, and I accept it as a public trust to be held so long as I am true to the ethics of police service. I will never engage in acts of corruption or bribery, nor will I condone such acts by other police officers."

I left the decision to proceed and continue their involvement in the investigation up to them. And they made the decision I had hoped they would. Talk about leadership. These two went where they did not have to go. They were willing to face the loneliness with me to stand up for that which was good, proper, and right, personally sacrificing themselves and their interests, another principle of true leadership. These were not angry people, just out to get the chief. These were people putting the interests of the organization, the organization's people, the community, and justice above their well-being. I will always admire them for that.

I was the highest-ranking individual involved in this investigation. If it went wrong, I would be the one to take the biggest hit from it. I told the others I would support them and try to protect them the best I could, but there was no guarantee. If this investigation came to light prematurely, before we were ready, it would probably get ugly fast. So it was paramount that the investigation remained confidential and that no one else in the organization needed to know about it. And then we went to work.

Much of the investigation took place after regular working hours. No one was getting paid for these extra hours, again emphasizing the integrity and leadership of those working with me. We would meet away from the police department to review the investigation results. We spent months pouring over phone records and Facebook accounts, documents obtained via court orders. We were looking for connections, and when we found something that looked suspicious, that meant more court orders and records to submit for and dissect. The results were not getting any better. The more information we looked at, the worse it looked for the chief and his involvement in the case. And that led to a more significant state of loneliness as I pondered my future and what that might be.

During the months of our investigation, city government officials put more pressure on the District Attorney's Office. They wanted answers to these allegations. As a result, I would end up having frequent contact with the District Attorney's Office investigator. This arrangement worked out quite well, and he became an asset and benefit to us. The city government was under the impression that the District Attorney's Office was the one running the investigation. I fed the District Attorney's Office bits and pieces of information from the investigation, which they forwarded to the city government officials. We gave them just enough information to ensure them an investigation was ongoing, which bought us more time to work at our pace.

Eventually, we went as far as we could with the analysis of records. From the analysis of these records, we identified potential witnesses, identified connections between those involved, and formulated supplementary theories to the chief's involvement. We also located the primary offender, who had relocated shortly after the investigation commenced. We had known the primary offender frequently traveled between Chicago and Florida but only recently identified where in Chicago he would stay.

It was time to move to the next and probably final stage of this investigation. We needed to get into the field and start rounding up offenders and witnesses.

But if the allegations against the chief were true, once we started interviewing people, we knew it wouldn't take long for someone to inform him of the investigation. At that point, the investigation's existence would no longer be a secret.

We wanted to hit the streets and round up as many witnesses as possible before the word was out. We received help from other investigators who were given minimal amounts of information. They were helping us make arrests and conduct searches, but they never really knew for what we were searching. Even on the day this investigation came to fruition, these two dedicated public servants kept this investigation confidential and performed admirably with complete integrity. And so, out we went, not knowing what our careers would look like at the end of the day. We arrested the primary offender and took him to another police jurisdiction for interrogation, trying to keep him from having any contact with our police chief. We located numerous other witnesses and interviewed them.

By day's end, we sat there looking at each other, wholly exhausted not only from the long day of work but from the months of stress and secrecy, from the loneliness of being leaders, from setting a silent example for others and being responsible to the oath we took. We were whipped, but we were smiling. It was over. And when it was all said and done, we determined that the chief was NOT involved AT ALL.

We had poured over mass amounts of information. Most of which did not look favorably for the chief. It was, however, circumstantial evidence and nothing direct. There was enough circumstantial evidence to warrant the investigation, and we needed to be sure our chief was honorable. As previously said, the investigation from day one was all about doing what was best for the law enforcement organization, the people of that organization, and the community it served. It was never personal. It was never a witch hunt. None of us thought it would end this way, but we were smiling when it was over, I believe because deep down, we wanted it to end this way. After talking to the primary offender, examining additional evidence, and interviewing the various witnesses, the circumstantial evidence began to make sense and get explained away. The chief was innocent and not involved. A great outcome, but it was not over for me.

The city government was still looking for answers. They had received these same allegations and also needed to ensure the chief was in no way involved in this case. I reached out to the District Attorney investigator I had been working with and updated him on our investigation's conclusion. At this point, we considered the case closed. No one else in the department, including the chief, knew that we had conducted this investigation. We considered it a win and tried to get back to business as usual.

The District Attorney's investigator called me back, stating he needed details. The city government, rightly so, was not going to accept a blanket, "the chief was not involved, and the allegations were false" type of response. The District Attorney's Office needed details to convince the city officials. The city officials were threatening to send their outside attorney, whom they hired, to investigate if information was not provided. I started giving the investigator details that he could forward to the city government, as he had been doing for months. As I was feeding him these details, it dawned on me that there was no way I could provide the requisite amount of further information without the city government getting suspicious. The District Attorney's investigator supported me greatly and tried to keep my name and involvement from being revealed. But finally, it was getting too complicated, as they needed many details only I could give. I thanked the investigator for his attempt to maintain my involvement confidential but allowed him to inform the city officials that I had been in charge of the investigation.

Fifteen minutes later, I received a phone call from the city manager, who ordered me to his office. Alone, my mind wandered as I walked the block and a half from my office to his. First, I explained the entire investigation to the city manager. Thankfully, his primary concern was to ensure I was confident the chief was innocent of the allegations. So, of course, I told him I was. Next, I explained how and why I was satisfied that the allegations were unfounded. Next, I was instructed to meet with the chief to explain my involvement, including, what I had done, why I had done it, and what my conclusions were. This was the more challenging conversation. Afterward, I had to meet with the city's outside attorney to give him a detailed presentation of the investigation, including how we derived at our conclusion, which exonerated the chief.

I have had many lonely experiences as a supervisor within a law enforcement agency. Some of which were brought on by poor decisions I made. Others were good decisions that received unjust criticism. Others maybe received no criticism but caused someone I cared about some pain. As a street supervisor, I have received calls from my subordinates who were at a traffic crash involving an intoxicated driver, and the driver was a child of one of our officers. Responding to those situations, I took over the investigations to relieve the officer of the stress and burden of such an ordeal. I made the arrest and then called the parent officer, someone I cared for, knowing I was about to break their heart and ruin their day, at a minimum. I have taken a duty weapon away from an intoxicated off-duty police officer, who was also acting unbecoming within our community and initiated an investigation that led to significant consequences for that officer. I've had to initiate and complete investigations of misconduct against people I considered my friends, which ultimately led to their dismissal from the police department.

All lonely moments, but probably the most desolate and memorable, were the months-long investigation of the police chief. This could have gone bad for me in many ways, but I do not regret it. I, as well as those working with me, did it in good conscience, trying to do the right thing not for ourselves but for others.

It would not be appropriate for me to conclude this text portion without pointing out how the chief responded to this. I am grateful and proud to say he handled it like a champ. I think it gave him some relief knowing that it was over and could be put behind him. But he informed me that he was proud of how I handled it and that I did exactly what he would have wanted me to do. The days, weeks, and months that followed were as if nothing ever happened. We got back to business, and he never, at least outwardly, held it against me or acted any differently towards me, and for that, I'm grateful.

The following quote is attributed to police chiefs, but the same dynamics hold true for police leaders in general. "Leaders report experiencing aloneness, weariness, and abandonment. These three overlapping experiences operate together, multiplying their impact, and if to be survived by a chief [leader] require incredible strength of character. Having the ability to see something that no one else sees, the vision to imagine or create in the mind's eye something that does not exist can be very lonely, isolating and arduous business. It's not just the energy required to translate the vision into reality but the energy to convince others of its value to them. People resist change, especially change that they do not understand or that will require them to experience some discomfort. The more they resist the more alone, abandoned and sometimes exhausted the leader can feel. . . . Leaders have been known to pay the price of leadership in the form of loss of friends over disciplinary issues, making unpopular decisions that cost them pain and anguish and still others who paid the supreme price, the loss of their jobs because they refused to violate their own long held personal ethical and moral principles and stood their ground."[1] But hey, it's lonely at the top if you're a true leader. It comes with the territory.

[1] Used with permission of Charles C Thomas Publisher, from *Police Chief: How to Attain and Succeed in this Critical Position* by Daniel D. McDevitt and Mark W. Field, copyright © 2010, p. 37. Permission conveyed through Copyright Clearance Center, Inc.

Chapter 3

THE LEADERSHIP PIPELINE

Based on my experience and observations, another void frequently found within the leadership of police agencies is the failure to understand the leadership pipeline or the failure to unclog the leadership pipeline when applicable. The term leadership pipeline and the accompanying concept come from a book titled *The Leadership Pipeline, How to Build the Leadership Powered Company* by Ram Charan, Stephen Drotter, and James Noel.[1] The book is not a law enforcement-related text but a book about leadership within the business world. It appears the void left by not adhering to the leadership pipeline concepts, as explained in the book, is prevalent in the business world. The same principles are just as true for law enforcement, and I have seen the deficiency that comes from not ensuring the leadership pipeline is in place and not hindered by clogs again and again. So, what is the leadership pipeline?

This chapter will provide a rudimentary explanation of the leadership pipeline and relevant examples related to law enforcement. Then, I would refer you to the text for a more detailed understanding and description of managing the leadership pipeline to optimize success.

In summary, the leadership pipeline involves clearly understanding the different roles and job expectations as individuals move from one position within the organization to the next and ensuring the person chosen for that position appropriately meets those expectations. More specifically, it requires that an officer promoted within a law enforcement agency make the appropriate changes in acquiring the new skills necessary, refocusing what they invest their time on, and making the correct change in the type of work they value.

The job of the patrol sergeant is not identical to that of the patrol officer. The sergeant must acquire different skills to perform his sergeant duties successfully. He must invest time in activities, such as evaluating members of his patrol shift,

[1] Used with permission of John Wiley & Sons Books, from *The Leadership Pipeline: How to Build the Leadership-Powered Company* by Ram Charan, Stephen Drotter, and James L. Noel, copyright © 2000. Permission conveyed through Copyright Clearance Center, Inc.

that were not required of him previously as an individual contributor. Further, he must learn to value work he may not have previously found significant as an officer. Patrol officers must ensure they respond to their assigned calls, complete a preliminary investigation, make arrests where appropriate, complete reports, patrol their designated area of responsibility, tend to traffic enforcement, attend court when required, etc. Primarily, they must be concerned with themselves and their performance. As an individual contributor, finding time to be available to routinely talk with each member of their patrol shift, having concern for their performance, or evaluating their training needs is probably not an important value for the patrol officer. As a sergeant, however, these tasks become extremely important. The new sergeant must learn to value these new tasks and invest time in them to be successful as a leader.

As you continue to move from one position to the next, each level requires additional changes in skills, time applications, and work values. For example, the job duties of a lieutenant are different from the sergeant, and the captain's job is not the same as the lieutenant. Except for very small departments, the position of the police chief will not closely resemble that of a patrol officer, and it shouldn't. The question is, do the leaders within your organization make the appropriate transition as they move up the organizational hierarchy? If they do not, they are a clog in the pipeline and hinder effectiveness and ability from progressing further.

Frequently we find individual contributors, such as the patrol officer or detective, get promoted to a supervisory position due to their record of excellent performance. They are active employees, supportive of the police mission, responsive to community needs, aggressive enforcers of the law, and fine examples of an officer. We wish we had more officers just like them. So, they are promoted and, in many cases, rightly so. However, without appropriate guidance and coaching, these fine officers will fall back on what they are good at and what got them promoted. They were good at being patrol officers or detectives and enjoyed their assigned duties. That is why they were so good at it. They cherish the skills and values that have made them successful to this point. They enjoy the recognition they have received from their previous performance. This reinforces their behaviors and habits. This work life is what they know, and these behaviors come naturally to them, so they continue valuing the same behaviors. In other words, they try to stay in their comfort zone. If they cannot adjust and transition appropriately to the required skills, time applications, and work values of their new position, the next turn in the pipeline, their leadership potential will be limited.

"To be successful as a first-time manager requires a major transition for which many people are not adequately prepared. Perhaps the most difficult aspect of the transition is that first-time managers are responsible for getting work done through others rather than on their own. While new managers may recognize this transition intellectually, they reject it psychologically, as evidenced by their behaviors."[2]

I had been a patrol officer, undercover tactical officer, and then a detective before being promoted to sergeant of a patrol shift. I found myself reverting to the skills and tasks at which I excelled – the skills for which I was recognized and promoted. I was an active individual contributor. I proactively looked for law violators, specifically those related to possessing illegal drugs. I spent much of my free time making traffic stops and looking for suspicious persons in search of wanted persons and drug offenders. If I had a chance to search a person or vehicle for contraband, I took it. This activity led to many arrests, confiscations of illegal drugs, and people going to jail.

As a new supervisor who still loved the individual contributor's skills, time applications, and work values, I would rush to complete the necessary tasks of a sergeant so I could get back on the street and make arrests. I would start the day determining patrol assignments for the shift and then respond to roll call, handing out said assignments before sending the troops into the field. I would quickly handle any small supervisor-related items that had come up, which I perceived as undesirable and mundane tasks. Then, as soon as possible, I would get into the field and start looking to make arrests. A subsequent consequence of many arrests was a lot of report writing and time spent in court. With this as my priority, when would I find time to do the job of a sergeant?

It took a while for me to figure this out. After several occasions where I found myself in a position where I was unable to render the help, support and assistance my patrol shift needed, I began to think about my responsibilities differently. For example, after "digging up" an arrest, I would find myself in the municipal lockup interrogating or monitoring an offender during the twenty-minute observation period required of a DWI arrest. Then, the emergency tone would go off over the radio; a crime of violence, a potentially dangerous and complex situation for my patrol shift to respond to, and there I was, stuck in the lockup with an arrestee. Oh, yes, if I needed to respond to the emergency, I could and would secure the arrestee as soon as possible. But in crises, seconds are valuable, and securing and dealing with this arrestee would add minutes to my response time.

So as not to lose progress made in an interrogation, there indeed were instances where I did not respond to the emergency. I would maintain the present course of action and hope the officers responding to the emergency would be ok and respond appropriately. In other instances, I would discontinue my interaction with the arrestee to respond to the emergency. However, this would negatively affect the quality of the case and future prosecution. In either

---

[2] Ram Charan, Stephen Drotter and James L. Noel, *The Leadership Pipeline: How to Build the Leadership-Powered Company* by Ram Charan, Stephen Drotter, and James L. Noel, p. 33.

situation, I wasn't there to support and help my patrol shift in a time of need, which didn't sit well with me. After all, as a supervisor, my responsibility was to supervise and lead. The greater the risk and more complex the incident, the greater the need for supervisor involvement, and I let the shift down. To my recollection, the patrol officers managed any crisis during these instances fine, as they were true professionals. For me, however, this was a learning opportunity and a valuable lesson learned.

Do the requisite skills needed to perform in a specific supervisory capacity automatically come when a person is promoted to that position? Does sound performance in one position ensure a person's success in the next? After learning the hard way and accepting the lessons provided from the experiences detailed above, I have come to perceive a promotion as follows:

Having already mastered the necessary skills for the position from which you are promoted, you must now start over in developing yourself to learn the skills needed to excel and be successful in your new role, to master these new skills at some future point. This development will require constant self-reflection ("Where am I now?") and work, as discussed in Chapter 1, "The Number One Rule of Leadership."

This development was the view I took that served me well as I moved up from one position to another. I humbly accepted the promotion, considered myself a new guy again, and got to work asking questions, studying, watching my peers, asking more questions, and learning the new job. Indeed, different people master various positions at different speeds, some excelling and mastering required skills quicker than others. The fact, however, is this: you must make the appropriate changes in acquiring the new skills necessary, refocusing what you invest your time in, and making the correct change in the type of work you value to be successful.

After I retired from a municipal police department in the Chicagoland area as the commander of a detective division, I took a job as the captain of a 37-person criminal investigation division for a sheriff's office. The lack of emphasis on supervision by the division's supervisors became apparent quickly and needed attention. For example, a detective may have seven or eight open investigations being investigated. A corporal of that unit, who I believe they perceived as a "good" detective, may have 10 to 12 open cases. Then, the sergeant of that unit, who I assume was being perceived as a "super duper" detective, would have 15 open cases. My immediate question was if the sergeant has 15 open cases to investigate, who is supervising the unit? This type of supervision was backward. Let the detective be the detective. It is his job to investigate cases. The supervisor needs to do just that, supervise. Jack Welch, in his book *Winning,* suggests that leaders spend the majority of their time and energy evaluating, coaching, and building up the self-confidence of their personnel.[3] In the book *First, Break All the Rules*, Gallup tells us the four basic roles of a great manager: selecting people, setting expectations, motivating people, and developing people.[4]

I am not suggesting that a sergeant should not be assigned or investigate any cases. It is important they set an example of the expected quality of work, and their subordinates know they are competent in the area they supervise. In a small-sized law enforcement agency with minimal resources, there may be no choice but to have the sergeant or police chief assist with investigations. I would assign myself cases from time to time. These were often cases I thought could be handled quickly and might be perceived as a burden or annoyance to the detectives. For example, a case involving a complainant or victim that was known and frequently challenging to deal with, or possibly a case perceived as sensitive due to involving a political person, another law enforcement officer, or maybe a child of one of the agency's employees. However, if the sergeant is investigating 15 cases, who is monitoring the quality of work of their subordinates?

When you are assigned cases, the people involved, specifically the victims, should be a priority. They deserve to have their cases investigated thoroughly and should expect the investigator to be responsive to them. After all, they are community members whom we have sworn an oath to serve and protect. So, the victims become the priority, which places other duties lower in focus. Those additional duties for a sergeant working 15 open cases will include some of their supervisory responsibilities. If their supervisory responsibilities are not being addressed, there is a clog in the leadership pipeline.

To the sergeant carrying 15 open cases, I would ask the following questions: who is reviewing and approving investigative reports? Who is ensuring the quality of work in your unit is good? Who is evaluating your detectives? Who is concerned about your unit's morale? Who is identifying training needs? Who is coaching and mentoring your detectives to enhance their skills and prepare them for future promotion? Who is ensuring the required resources and equipment is available or obtained? Who is recognizing the excellent work of your unit and its contributors? Finally, who is ensuring your unit's needs and capabilities are known and represented by upper command personnel?

When I signed on at the sheriff's office, that is just what I found, inconsistency in the review and approval of the detectives' work. There was no consistent and formal process for ensuring the quality of work by the detectives. Some supervisors reviewed the work and reports of their subordinates, and others

---

[3] Welch, Jack. (2005). From *Winning* by Jack Welch, Suzy Welch. Copyright (c) 2005 by Jack Welch, LLC. Used by permission of HarperCollins Publishers, pp. 55-57.

[4] Used with permission of Gallup, Inc., from *First, Break All the Rules: What the World's Greatest Managers Do Differently* by Gallup, copyright © 1999/2016, p. 58. Permission conveyed through Copyright Clearance Center, Inc.

did not. A supervisor never reviewed some detective reports. As I randomly checked reports or pulled a case file in response to a complaint from a community member regarding handling their case, I found numerous reports and casework deficiencies. There were cases where detectives followed minimal leads. Others lacked any details about the probable cause that led to an arrest, and in one case where an arrest had been made, I found no narrative to document the investigation and arrest. Where was the supervisor of these detectives? My guess would be handling and investigating their 15 cases.

In which scenario would an organization benefit more? Having a sergeant with a personal caseload of 15 cases, which requires most of their time, or having a sergeant with a limited caseload who can spend time strengthening, developing, and building up the unit to increase the unit's future capabilities? An investigative unit with ten detectives would mean less than two additional cases for each detective if this sergeant assigned all of his cases and three more per detective for a unit with only five detectives. Would three more cases break the detectives? It certainly might add some additional work, and the detectives might complain that the extra three cases will overload their already full caseload. If they are overloaded, however, a better conversation might be adding detectives or using solvability factors to assign the right cases to avoid wasting valuable time and resources. But that's a topic for another book.

However, imagine what benefit would come from the sergeant who prioritized the above supervisory skills? To excel as a leader, you must be concerned with quality work, ensuring your personnel knows what is expected and holding them accountable for those expectations. You need to be concerned about morale and teamwork? Invest time with your personnel, helping them with their cases instead of ignoring them while you work your own cases. In doing so, you can lighten their load and, at the same time, set an example and demonstrate your expectations of quality work. You can display your competency level. You can observe their skills and abilities firsthand, conducting more accurate evaluations, identifying areas that need improvement, and recognizing their strengths. The time spent with them in conversation while assisting them with their cases alone will further develop them and prepare them for greater responsibility than you being absent because you are too busy working all your cases.

This concept is certainly not just for the leaders of detective units. I have seen patrol sergeants, including myself, earlier in my tenure as a supervisor, giving superficial attention to their supervisory responsibilities so they can spend as much time in the field performing the tasks of the individual contributor. I have seen other leaders, including higher command team personnel, look for every opportunity to attend the newest and greatest training classes, travel the region teaching, or take on as many specialty assignments as possible. These leaders frequently go missing from the office for long periods while significant organizational performance deficiencies get ignored. Problems ignored grow into more significant issues. These leaders become a clog in the pipeline because they are not effectively carrying out the roles and responsibilities of their position.

I am not suggesting that a police supervisor should not attend training courses or take on specialty assignments that will further enhance the ability to develop the organization and provide services to the community. I did. I was a crisis negotiator, the supervisor of the K-9 Unit, a member of a critical incident stress management team, and a member of terrorist-related associations. It is essential to have various specialty roles filled so the law enforcement agency can accomplish its mission.

I am also not suggesting that a police leader should not participate in the enforcement of the law or make traffic stops or arrests; after all, they are the police. If they observe crime before them, they are responsible for acting. As sworn officers, they should take the appropriate action if they come across a significant risk to the community, such as an intoxicated driver. I am suggesting that before the supervisor invests time in what they want to do, what they enjoy, and what are the tasks of the individual contributor, they need to ensure that the roles and responsibilities of their assigned position are effectively accomplished. The duties of their present position must be the priority and not simply receive whatever time may be left after they do all the fun stuff they enjoy. Remember what we discussed in Chapter 1, "it's not about you; it's about the organization and the people within." The leader needs to know their job and do their job. Not investing the right amount of time and effort into performing the essential functions of their position, no matter what it is, creates a clog in the pipeline and a void in the leadership of that organization.

As people transition to the next level within the organization, their responsibilities change. Some of these changes include:

- From an individual contributor to the first-line supervisor, where one goes from doing the work themselves to getting work done through others. A successful supervisor must be able to delegate. A person who does everything themselves may be a hard worker and very smart, but they aren't a leader. "When first time managers lack the ability to delegate or coach, they'll schedule relatively little time for each activity, preferring to spend as much time as possible on what they are good at."[5]
- From a first-line supervisor to a manager of managers, one must value communication, coaching, and team building among their first-line supervisors. It is not enough to have a good relationship with the

[5] Ram Charan, Stephen Drotter, and James L. Noel, *The Leadership Pipeline: How to Build the Leadership-Powered Company,* p. 48.

> individual first-line supervisors; the manager of managers must ensure the first-line supervisors have a good supportive relationship with each other. For example, I would routinely meet with the supervisors of the various units within the Criminal Investigative Division to open dialogue, thus making each leader aware of the present needs, challenges, and concerns of the other teams so that they could lend support and resources, as necessary. A manager of managers must also be on the lookout for any first-line supervisor who is not transitioning well in their acceptance of managerial work or is clinging to their former skills as an individual contributor. If these behaviors are observed, the first-line supervisor will become a clog in the leadership pipeline if not corrected.

Delegation is equally as necessary during this transition, as the manager of managers cannot do everything themselves. They must rely upon their first-line supervisors. One of the cardinal sins in this transition is usurping the authority of your first-line supervisors by going around them and making assignments directly to the individual contributors. I am not suggesting the manager of managers should not be communicating with individual contributors. On the contrary, they should build relationships and trust and glean information from all personnel up and down the organizational hierarchy. However, suppose the manager of managers routinely ignores their chain of command, going directly to the individual contributors. In that case, those same individual contributors will do the same, returning the favor and ignoring their chain of command, coming straight to the manager of managers. This behavior is inefficient, counterproductive, and disrespectful to the first-line supervisors.

Respecting the chain of command with subordinates was an area I understood and thought I did well. However, I learned otherwise after sending anonymous surveys to all my subordinate personnel, allowing them to evaluate my performance as the division leader. One of the complaints I received was that I would frequently go around the chain of command and assign tasks to a sergeant's subordinates. This response was a shock that took me by surprise, as I again understood the importance of respecting the first-line supervisor, at least intellectually. After some self-reflection, however, I did come to realize that there was room for some improvement in this area. I openly recognized this and shared the complaint in a supervisor meeting and again in an all-division personnel meeting. I informed the troops that I would try to do better. However, I told them, if the first-line supervisor were not available, if having a random five-minute conversation with an individual contributor, whom I pass in the hall or by their office, could solve a problem or make significant progress, I would continue to do so, to include making appropriate requests, as this method was both efficient and got things done promptly. However, I assured them I would follow up with a discussion or email to ensure the first-line supervisor was aware of my conversation with their subordinate and its content. Moving forward, this seemed well received, and I believe I did better to minimize my commitment to this sin.

As a person continues to transition to higher positions within the law enforcement agency, they deal less with the individual contributors, with the detailed minutia of day-to-day operations, and with the need for strong technical skills. Instead, as they continue to progress beyond the manager of managers, they emphasize conceptual skills, big-picture thinking, planning and strategy with a view to the future, the agency's relationship with outside stakeholders, and the need for a broader array of information to assist and direct decision making.

As a division leader, be it the patrol division, investigative division, support division, human resources, etc., the leader here must realize they cannot be experts in all aspects of their function. They must learn to respect and value those functions with which they are unfamiliar. They must build relationships and work-teams with other division leaders. They must expect that meetings and ongoing communication will take on the importance not previously seen at previous levels. They must commit themselves to the overall organization and not just the performance of their specific function. To succeed, the patrol division leader realizes their division's role in adding value to the detective division and vice versa. Both division leaders must know they are limited in effectiveness if not for the support they obtain from the agency's administration, support, or human resources division. If a person transitions from one level of the organization to another without making the appropriate changes that go with the position, they will become a clog in the pipeline.

What happens when there is a clog in the pipeline? Typically, required work, such as developing subordinates for future growth and advancement, will not occur, or someone else will have to fill the gap. If a supervisor is not investing time in areas of his assigned position, their leader or supervisor often has to come down and compensate for that. Going back to the complaint I received about going around the sergeant, usurping the chain of command, and giving his subordinates assignments, I am confident that I made errors of judgment in doing so from time to time. Just as often, however, I went around that sergeant to get work accomplished that the sergeant should have been doing himself but was not. My actual error in judgment was probably not assigning tasks to their subordinates, as much as not holding the sergeant accountable for their work and responsibility.

Other examples I've seen are new supervisors excited about the positive attributes of their new leadership role, such as team building, improving morale, recognizing good work, giving their personnel a pat on the back for a good job well done, and getting their personnel exciting new equipment. Of course, all of this is important and the supervisor's responsibility.

Unfortunately, however, I've seen these same supervisors shy away from other duties that are not so fun and exciting. For example, when handling citizen complaints, evaluating and taking corrective action against poor performers, or applying discipline, they try to defer those perceived negative activities to upper management or simply ignore them.

How about the supervisor who spends time dealing with minor details that distract them from other responsibilities instead of delegating those details to subordinates? Supervisors often worry about their subordinates not having the skills, know-how, or commitment to the organization's mission to make appropriate decisions, leading the supervisor to make all the decisions. This attitude about one's subordinates likely leads to the often-heard accusation of being a "micro-manager." Regardless of the accuracy of the supervisor's attitude and opinion, if a supervisor is not doing their job, then either their job doesn't get done, or someone else has to do it. If someone has to do the supervisor's job, then more than likely, their job isn't completed. Know your job and do your job.

No one expects that a newly promoted person transitioning to a new leadership role will walk in the front door on their first day an expert on all things in their new leadership position. To eliminate a void in leadership among the ranks of our law enforcement agencies, however, we need to start looking at these leadership positions differently.

The newly promoted person needs immediate communication and coaching by their supervisor. The skills, time applications, and work values necessary for success in the newly acquired position must be spelled out. The new leader needs to know and understand the expectations for which they will be evaluated. And then they need to be held accountable for those results or moved out.

We may consider assigning a mentor or creating a field training program for newly promoted supervisors, like the FTO programs provided to new law enforcement recruits. Immediately after my promotion to sergeant, I received only a few days of riding with another patrol sergeant. I considered him an outstanding supervisor and law enforcement officer; however, I was alone and in charge after only three or four days. It was a Sunday, and I was the highest-ranking officer (higher ranks were off for the weekend); I was in charge of the city and all police department operations. I was scared to death and ran "what if" scenarios through my mind trying to be prepared for anything that could go wrong. I got through that day and many more like it after that. However, could it have been better? Is there a better process out there? Are we preparing our new supervisors for success? Often, I believe we fail our best performers, promoting them to new levels of leadership while assuming they will excel without the training and coaching needed to be successful. If this is the case, it isn't their fault but the organization's fault. Either way, it creates a clog in the pipeline and a void in the agency's leadership.

Chapter 4

CONTROL WITHOUT COMPETENCE IS CHAOS

The void in leadership addressed in this chapter shares many similarities with the failure to adhere to the leadership pipeline. In the context of the leadership pipeline, for example, a newly promoted sergeant, who is competent and possesses the technical skills needed for success in their new position, is neither held accountable for carrying out the responsibilities of their new leadership level within the organization nor for the subsequent results. Thus, instead of fulfilling their supervisory duties, the sergeant invests much of their time carrying out tasks that should be assigned to their subordinates. They have not yet learned the importance and need of valuing those required skills; thus, they don't make the corresponding change in their behavior regarding the type of activities in which they invest their time and energy. The newly promoted sergeant's immediate supervisor may need to take various steps to ensure the sergeant is accountable to his new role, which will help the sergeant make a successful transition. These may include coaching, training, and ongoing monitoring and reinforcement. Of course, the same holds true of any new leadership position within the organization, be it a sergeant, a lieutenant, a captain, or a chief. Someone in an authority position, preferably their direct supervisor, must ensure the newly promoted leader is accountable for performing their new job's duties acceptably.

Promoting someone without the necessary competence, however, may resemble someone struggling to transition to the next level of the organization's pipeline who fails to achieve positive results. But in this case, the person is promoted to a leadership position lacking the experience and skills necessary to be successful and thus should never have been promoted in the first place.

For this chapter, the idea of competence refers to an individual's ability to be successful in a given position, precisely one of leadership and supervision, which incorporates the person's attitude, experience, and technical and emotional skills and abilities.

The phrase "control without competence is chaos" was taken from the book; *Turn that Ship Around: A true story of turning followers into leaders.*[1] by L. David Marquet. The premise for the purpose of the present text is two pronged. First, as control is delegated, competence (experience, technical knowhow, and emotional intelligence) is required to make the appropriate decisions that go along with that delegation. Secondly, this competence requires an understanding and support of the organization's mission, to ensure their decision making is consistent with the mission.

Just because a person excels in one position does not automatically mean they will be successful in another. A person who consistently excels in performance should undoubtedly be considered for leadership positions. Still, it can be a mistake to make their past performance in a different position the only criterion for promotion. A concept that has come to be known as "the peter principle," taken from the work of Dr. Laurence J. Peter, refers to the idea that many people within an organization's hierarchy will continue to be promoted to one level above their competence and ability. Their sound performance wins them one promotion after another until they reach the point where they are no longer performing acceptably. We have all seen this – where an outstanding and well-respected individual contributor, whether a patrol officer, a detective or an undercover drug agent, is promoted, only to be a terrible boss. One may be a great sergeant but a terrible commander. They may be a great lieutenant but a horrible police chief. "Organizational police management is beginning to realize that its most performance-skilled or productive workers will not always be the better person to promote into a leadership position."[2]

Organizations often assume if an individual has performed well in one position, they will do so in another. Instead of making such an assumption, the organization must assess each leadership level's job duties and responsibilities. Then the organization needs to ensure that a potential candidate has the necessary technical and leadership skills and, just as critically, the values and appropriate attitude to go with them.

I have seen successful patrol officers who were very proactive, high producers in the area of enforcement, and active in the community. Yet they were quick to criticize and insult the agency's leaders openly. On the other hand, I've seen outstanding detectives with investigation skills that stand far above any I've possessed. Still, in the hallways of the organization, they

---

[1] Excerpt from TURN THE SHIP AROUND! A TRUE STORY OF TURNING FOLLOWERS INTO LEADERS by L. David Marquet, copyright © 2012 by L. David Marquet. Used by permission of Portfolio, an imprint of Penguin Publishing Group, a division of Penguin Random House LLC. All rights reserved.

[2] Used with permission of Charles C. Thomas Publisher, from *Police Assessment Training: An Assessment Center Handbook for Law Enforcement Personnel* by John L. Coleman, copyright © 2010, p. 7. Permission conveyed through Copyright Clearance Center, Inc.

spread poison with their poor attitudes and "I'm better than you" arrogance. To promote one of these to a leadership position is like introducing cancer to the body. Yet, it happens because someone is looking at the hard facts of their performance as seen on paper and ignoring the soft attributes and personality characteristics of a would-be leader and team player.

In his book *Winning*, Jack Welch, the former CEO of GE, writes some of your high performers, "[your] stars can become monsters if you let them." He says, he has seen high-performing individuals think they are so great that they can ignore the company's values.[3] The attributes and potential of a candidate for a new leadership position must be assessed and determined before selecting them, not after they have created havoc and clogged the organization's leadership pipeline.

By promoting an inexperienced or unprepared individual to a leadership position, we set up both that individual and the organization for failure. What does this look like?

Because of the present culture in law enforcement, the strong egos, and "type A" personalities frequently found in law enforcement, it is rare that a "would be" leader in this category will admit to their deficiencies. In his book *Leadership Strategy and Tactics*, Navy Seal Jocko Willink references an inexperienced platoon commander that transferred into his platoon. Although he was the least experienced member of the platoon, he wanted to make all decisions and refused to take advice from others. When the performance of the platoon eventually declined, the platoon commander took no responsibility for the decline, nor did he change his attitude or habit of making all the decisions. "When we failed a training mission, he blamed others. He would never recognize or admit that perhaps his plan wasn't the best or maybe the decisions he'd made in the field weren't good calls. Looking back, it is obvious that what this officer lacked in experience, he made up for with a massive ego."[4] Have you seen this leader before? I think most of us have experienced one or two, or maybe more, of these leaders. What do they bring to the table, chaos?

Instead of admitting their lack of confidence or competence and seeking assistance in developing themselves appropriately, they often fake their way through it, which leads to them staying in their comfort zone in hopes of not being found out. They struggle with difficult decisions, often stalling for time, hoping for a better scenario or someone else will decide for them. They may seek out approval for all decisions of any complexity from their supervisor in fear of being second-guessed for making a less-than-perfect decision. Delays

---

[3] Welch, Jack. (2005). From *Winning* by Jack Welch, Suzy Welch. Copyright (c) 2005 by Jack Welch, LLC. Used by permission of HarperCollins Publishers, p. 111.

[4] Willink, Jocko. (2020). *Leadership Strategy and Tactics Field Manual.* St. Martin's Publishing Group, New York, NY, pp. 20-21.

in necessary action and decision-making can lead to devastating results when talking about urgent and unfolding events that occur at a moment's notice in the risky business of policing. For example, suppose a leader's supervisor is spending excessive time making decisions that should be left to the incompetent leader; this distracts them from their work and snowballs into the organization-wide inefficiency, as explained in Chapter 3 on the "The Leadership Pipeline."

Rather than seeking innovative and creative ways to improve the organization's ability to serve its communities, a "would be" leader works to maintain the status quo where they are most comfortable. As a result, they may not take advantage of learning opportunities for themselves and not value training for their personnel, fearing their subordinates may become more competent than they are.

A lack of competence among leaders may further manifest itself by the leader promoting and surrounding themselves with friends and "yes" men who will further insulate them, reinforce the status quo, and protect the leader's image of themself. This lack of competence does nothing to progress the organization but instead demonstrates the leader's selfish act of putting themself before the organization. "The better [more competent] the people who are closest to you in responsibility, the more effectively you will lead the organization. Promotion of cronies or promotion for the sake of being perceived as a nice guy is destructive to the organization and, of course, to your ability to lead. Promoting people on any basis other than demonstrated ability is at best an act of unwarranted faith and, at worst, one of vain stupidity."[5] In the words of Jack Welch, former CEO of General Electric, "It is true that some companies are corrupted by cronyism and favoritism. The top 20 percent are the boss's head-nodders and buddies. . . . That happens, and it stinks, and it is a function of a leadership team lacking in brains or integrity or both." He further says, "rewarding those who deserve it only annoys the underperformers. To everyone else it is fair, and a fair environment promotes teamwork and motivates people."[6]

GET DOWN AND DIRTY

I had an officer who had worked for me as an individual contributor before being promoted to patrol sergeant. As an individual contributor, he had a great attitude, was supportive, and was committed to the organization's mission.

---

[5] Used with permission of John Wiley & Sons Books, from *Eisenhower on Leadership: Ike's Enduring Lessons in Total Victory Management* by Alan Axelrod, copyright © 2006, p. 87 Permission conveyed through Copyright Clearance Center, Inc.

[6] Jack Welch, *Winning,* pp. 43, 47.

He volunteered for extra duties and worked on projects as needed. He was respected and liked by all and was a valued team member. However, he was not ready for the promotion, as he had not yet gained the experience and skill set needed to be a successful patrol sergeant. Ask anyone who worked with and knew him well, as they would say the same thing – a great guy but not supervisor material, at least not yet. Would he ever have reached the competence level to be ready for such a promotion? We will never know, as he won't have that chance. He was promoted when he should not have been.

This officer was a "yes" man. He did as he was asked but did not ask questions and was not necessarily a free thinker. Is it possible the organization's top leaders promoted this officer because of his "yes" man attitude?

There was a promotional process, and one could argue that this officer fared well in the testing process and deserved the promotion. The promotional process consisted of a written test worth 40% of an applicant's score, an interview worth 40%, and what was called "chief's points," where the police chief, at his discretion, could allocate from 0 to 20 points to each candidate based upon the chief's personal preference. Allocating points appropriately gave the chief input on the promotional process based upon his opinion of the candidates, who he believed would support his vision, had the appropriate character, the work performance he sought, etc. In theory, a candidate could score the highest on both the written and interview portions of the process but still have a lower overall score than another. Or a candidate could obtain a score lower than other candidates but be the top candidate on the promotional list by receiving 20 "chief's points."

In addition to the police chief's prerogative of assigning a maximum of 20 points, by law, once the promotional list was posted, the police chief could choose to promote any of the top three candidates.

Regardless of where this officer fell on that promotional list, the department's leadership, specifically the police chief, had influence in selecting and promoting the person most competent for the position, which affected the organization's ability to succeed. This officer, as nice of a guy as he is, was promoted to the organization's detriment. He received control of a patrol shift without the needed competence, and chaos ensued. He made poor and wrong decisions, which his personnel knew were terrible. The confidence of his troops in his leadership ability fell and fell hard. There was talk of a "no confidence vote" against him. His actions caused damage to the organization and its people; this good man may never rebound from it. Was it his fault? He might carry some of the blame, but the organization's leadership did him no favors; they let him and the organization down by failing to recognize this void in leadership – control without competence is chaos.

The prior administration handled promotions differently. The police chief would meet with the command team and all supervisors as a group, at which point we would discuss all the candidates that had passed the promotional process. I was part of this process. We discussed the candidates' work performances, evaluations, strengths and weaknesses, and abilities to be good supervisors. We would get down and dirty into the mud of details. We would debate and disagree with each other, often passionately, to ensure incidents like what occurred to this good officer did not occur. At the end of the meeting and the robust dialogue about each candidate, all present supervisory and command personnel ranked the candidates individually and confidentially. Before we left the room, we gave our rankings to the police chief, which he used in determining how many "chief's points" to provide each candidate.

In this present incident, no such meeting or robust dialogue occurred. With minimal input from those who knew this officer best, the police chief instead decided what points to give each candidate and who to promote. Indeed, that was his right and prerogative to do as he pleased, but one must be prepared to live with the consequences. And, in this instance, chaos ensued.

While working at the sheriff's office, we had a similar process for transfers and promotions. There were written tests and an interview board where peers, or would-be peers of the rank the candidate was testing for, sat in and provided feedback on the candidate's qualifications and competence for said position. Once candidates successfully passed the testing process, their names were added to a list. This list was then put forward to the command team, who met and engaged in dialogue concerning the various candidates and their ability to be successful in the position for which they tested. "When several people who've watched the same person over time pool their observations in robust dialogue, subjective reviews become objective. You'd be amazed at how accurately, thoroughly, and quickly a group can pinpoint the critical issues."[7]

I went one step further and requested feedback from members of the division in which the candidate was hoping to work. Any feedback I received was kept confidential. I didn't share who provided the specific information. When the criminal investigation division was promoting a candidate to sergeant, I was interested in the other sergeants' opinions. I also encouraged the sergeants to seek out the input of their personnel, who may become subordinate to the candidate if they were chosen for promotion. Ultimately, they would have to work with or for this individual. They would have to communicate with this person, support them, and expect support from them. Questions needed to be answered, such as: Is the candidate a team player? Does he support the agency's mission? On most occasions, members of a division had already worked with the candidates, had established personal

---

[7] Excerpt from EXECUTION: THE DISCIPLINE OF GETTING THINGS DONE by Larry Bossidy and Ram Charan, copyright © 2002 by Larry Bossidy and Ram Charan, p. 159. Used by permission of Crown Business, an imprint of Random House, a division of Penguin Random House LLC. All rights reserved.

relationships with them, and had opportunities to view and assess their strengths and weaknesses and how those strengths and weaknesses might help in the new position. In sum, a significant amount of information is available to evaluate a candidate's competence level if the time and effort are taken to retrieve the information. The information and feedback gathered in this fashion were collected, reoccurring themes were identified, and then shared and discussed during command team meetings. See Appendix A for an example of a Request for Feedback Survey.

I solicited feedback from those expected to be affected by the final decision, which allowed them to be involved in the process, and ensured their opinions were heard. I received positive input referencing this process from those who provided solicited feedback. Those affected often have information crucial to promoting the right person, which is the ultimate goal. This process occasionally altered my decisions regarding who to promote. For example, I may have thought Candidate A was best suited for the job during a promotional process. However, I had to conceive that it was possible Candidate A had been on his best behavior during our interactions and less than genuine regarding what he said or did when away from administration or command team members. And others, who saw and worked with Candidate A daily, may know more about Candidate A's actual and consistent performance and leadership abilities than me.

On the other hand, I had to realize I might be completely overlooking a sound candidate who would best serve the organization. I have had negative preconceived notions about a promotional candidate on multiple occasions. And the candidate would end up selected for promotion and turn out to be an outstanding leader and the right choice for the promotion. This further reinforced the importance of taking the time to assess in every way possible the competence level of your would-be leaders. Left to me and my personal bias and superficial opinion, the best person for the job and organization would have been missed and filled with someone less competent.

As part of this request for feedback, I would ask those providing feedback to rank the candidates in numerical order. For example, if we were promoting a sergeant, I would request feedback and rankings from the other sergeants in the division (i.e., patrol, detective, etc.). Hopefully, the sergeants would use input obtained from their personnel to help determine their chosen rankings. Then, after averaging the submitted rankings, I got the final overall rankings. I admit I received both criticism and concern over the feedback request's numerical ranking portion. The primary complaint was that the ranking was a popularity contest demonstrating how well others liked a candidate versus how well a candidate would perform at a given position. This valid point must be seriously considered, as people will naturally "vote" for those they most like or with whom they share similarities. So how do we combat that?

First, recognize the requested feedback, including any numerical ranking, is used to provide insight and help decision-makers and in no way changes a candidate's status on a current promotional list, as determined through the official promotional process held.

Secondly, ranking candidates as part of the requested feedback should be accompanied by additional information/feedback provided to support a person's opinion. Once averaged, the ranking gives an overall picture of the views of others on the various candidates. For example, it very well might demonstrate that two or more candidates are very closely perceived as qualified candidates or two or more candidates are consistently perceived as weak candidates.

Finally, the requested feedback is only information and is not binding on the final decision. Having worked closely with the candidates, other agency members may possess important considerations unknown to the command team that may provide valuable insight worth considering. Ultimately, however, the agency's leader, complying with related laws, maintains the authority and discretion in promotions, and any requests for feedback about the candidates do not alter that.

The magic behind the numeric ranking of candidates is that it can assist in taking qualitative characteristics of a candidate, which are hard to measure and see, and changes them into a quantitative piece of information, where patterns become visible. In staying with the complaint that ranking candidates lead to a popularity vote, whereupon those liked get promoted over those most qualified, consider the below example:

Evaluator 1	Evaluator 2	Evaluator 3	Evaluator 4	Evaluator 5
1 Candidate A	1 Candidate A	1 Candidate A	1 Candidate B	1 Candidate B
2 Candidate B	2 Candidate B	2 Candidate D	2 Candidate D	2 Candidate D
3 Candidate D	3 Candidate D	3 Candidate E	3 Candidate C	3 Candidate C
4 Candidate C	4 Candidate C	4 Candidate B	4 Candidate E	4 Candidate A
5 Candidate E	5 Candidate E	5 Candidate C	5 Candidate A	5 Candidate E

Final Ranking	
Candidate A = 12	12/5=2.4
Candidate B = 10	**10/5=2.0**
Candidate C = 19	19/5=3.8
Candidate D = 12	12/5=2.4
Candidate E = 22	22/5=4.4

This example involves five candidates, identified as candidate A through candidate E. They are participating in the promotional process for the position of sergeant. Five evaluators, who are presently sergeants in the division where the newly promoted sergeant will be assigned, have been asked to evaluate and rank the candidates from one to five in order of their perceived ability to be successful in the open sergeant position. A ranking of one means this candidate is most qualified for the position, and a ranking of five means they are least qualified. The rankings of each candidate are totaled and then divided by the number of evaluators, in this example, divided by five. The result is the candidates overall average (ranking).

In the data provided, we see that three evaluators ranked Candidate A as the most qualified. However, two evaluators ranked this same Candidate A towards the bottom of the scale, not the top. Looking over the additional feedback you have requested and received referencing these candidates, you find that Candidate A is a "go-getter"; he is active, gets things done, and his performance is outstanding. Those three evaluators who ranked Candidate A as number one, the most qualified, know of Candidate A's ability to perform successfully. They may also be friends of Candidate A, have things in common, and enjoy working with him. Does this give credence to the complaint that ranking candidates turns the process into a popularity vote?

Now, let's consider the final two evaluators who have ranked this same candidate toward the bottom of the rankings. Although these two evaluators would agree that Candidate A has been successful in his performance, they share concerns about his arrogance, lack of teamwork, and inability to get along well with others. They feel that this would inhibit him from being a successful leader within the division. He likes to get things done but enjoys being the guy who gets the credit for success, and this isn't necessarily the message the organization wants its leaders to send.

One could argue that maybe the opposite is true. Candidate A is the best person for the job, but the last two evaluators do not like him and have it out for him for some reason; perhaps something previously occurred. The argument would be that he is unfairly being rated down by the two evaluators who don't like him. But, again, the ranking is just one aspect and should be supported by additional information and feedback. Furthermore, unless the entire leadership pool of evaluators is unethical and not concerned with the organization's success, which would be a problem in itself, it is vital to look for reoccurring themes about a candidate's character and performance. Looking for reoccurring themes reinforces the rankings received, as the qualitative feedback about Candidate A's alleged arrogance and weak teamwork ability did in the above example. Also, more evaluators providing feedback will result in more consistent and reliable results.

If we look further at the data, we will see Candidate B, although ranked number one only twice compared to Candidate A's three times, has been more consistently ranked towards the top. In fact, when you average all the rankings together, Candidate B has the best score among all the candidates.

Considering Candidate D, we can see that this candidate was never ranked number one by any evaluator. However, he consistently ranked toward the top with a number two or three ranking; his actual score tied with Candidate A, even though he never received a number one ranking, where Candidate A received three. Looking at Candidates C and E, we find they are more consistently located and ranked towards the bottom, and their scores consistently reflect that.

So, just by looking at the rankings provided, Candidates B and D might be the better choice to consider for promotion. Although Candidate A received a number one ranking more than any other candidate, because two evaluators rated him so low should cause concern. I would seek additional information to explain the more significant variance in his scores. Candidates B and D are perceived more consistently as strong candidates by all evaluators. These patterns become more observant when qualitative behaviors and characteristics can be numerically quantified. These behaviors can then be questioned and acted upon more accurately.

I'm not suggesting that the process and procedures I've used and explained in this book are the best or only way to proceed. As you read further in the book, you will find other processes used to achieve various organizational improvements or performance enhancements. These processes and tactics are provided for consideration and use if appropriate. However, some of them might not work well for your organization.

I found going from a municipal police department in the Chicago area to a sheriff's office in North Carolina, that a lot of the procedures and attitudes I was accustomed to, and that had worked well for my organization and me, were not going to work well at the sheriff's office, at least not in any short period of time. However, with some innovation and creativity, there are processes out there that can and will help your organization progress. To not try or sit back and do nothing is not leadership. I desire that some of the ideas and concepts I share will get your creative juices flowing, so the best processes and procedures for your organization will be found.

Plain and simple, the critical point of explaining some of the promotional processes used is that we must ensure our law enforcement leaders are chosen for their competence and ability to succeed for the organization's benefit. Hiring and promoting the best and brightest requires a thought-out and planned process.

In today's world, professionalism involves meeting a set of standards and an ongoing commitment to identify and incorporate best practices from the field of policing. This involves creating appropriate hiring and promotional standards and processes. To promote someone into a leadership position out of selfishness is not leadership. To promote someone because they are your friend or will insulate you from bad news, protect your job, or help you maintain your comfort zone is chaos waiting to happen. There is plenty of research available that supports the use of promotional processes, including structured interviews and assessment centers to identify your best candidates. "Most promotional processes involve some type of written examination, some type of interview process, an assessment center or similar segment, or some other testing/evaluation component or mechanism aimed at determining the best person to promote."[8]

HOW IMPORTANT IS COMPETENCE IN LAW ENFORCEMENT LEADERSHIP?

What are you willing to accept in your organization? A 95% competence level among your leaders? How about 75%, or maybe 50%? You are running a high-liability organization. People's lives depend on you and your personnel. Your personnel's lives depend on you and those chosen to lead your law enforcement organization, a high-risk and dangerous profession. So, let's ask again – what level of competence are you willing to accept?

The larger the organization, the greater the need for confident and competent leaders and an ongoing commitment to developing said leaders, so their competence remains solid in an ever-changing environment. If you are the police chief of a ten-man department, your competence and leadership abilities may suffice. With only ten employees, you can interact and communicate with all of them, consistently sharing your vision, ensuring the quality of the performance is up to standards, personally reinforcing the appropriate behaviors, and taking corrective action as needed.

When your organization grows, the need for additional layers of leadership and supervision also grows. For example, if you are now the police chief of a thirty-man department, more supervisors will be required. If you have five supervisors in your thirty-man department, but only four are appropriately competent for the position, that's an 80% competence level. Will that make a difference?

You can expect performance to be weaker for those supervised by the incompetent leader and services to their area of responsibility to be diminished. Essential values and desired behaviors of the organization will start to slip. Their assigned area will begin to crumble, maybe ever so slightly

---

[8] Used with permission of Charles C Thomas Publisher, from *Police Chief: How to Attain and Succeed in this Critical Position* by Daniel D. McDevitt and Mark W. Field, copyright © 2010, p. 18. Permission conveyed through Copyright Clearance Center, Inc.

and slowly, or possibly significantly and quickly, under the stress and urgent conditions created by unpredictable situations that often arise in policing. The five employees supervised by the incompetent leader will not receive the same development and opportunities for learning as those managed by competent leaders. Essentially, these five employees are not receiving the same positive benefits and opportunities from being led by "true leaders," those with the correct competence level for their position.

How about if you are the police chief of a one-hundred-man department with twelve supervisors, and only eight are competent for their position? With a 66% competence level, approximately thirty of your employees are led by an incompetent leader. These thirty employees may be spread out in different areas of the organization, delivering less than appropriate services to the community and organization. The impact of their performance puts more pressure and responsibility on competent people, who will likely be called upon to pick up the slack or clean up the mess left behind by those not appropriately completing their duties.

Does this affect your organization? The lack of competence leads to chaos! No good will come from it. Don't hire or promote your friends unless they are the most competent and best fit for the job. In his book titled *Lincoln on Leadership*, the author says of Abraham Lincoln, "he had enough confidence in himself that he was not threatened by skillful generals or able cabinet officials. Rather than surround himself with "yes" men, he associated with people who really knew their business, people from whom he could learn something, whether they were antagonistic or not."[9] In his book titled *Winning*, Jack Welch writes, "a good leader has the courage to put together a team of people who sometimes make him look like the dumbest person in the room."[10] I have never hesitated to surround myself with people more intelligent and talented than myself. It is my goal to search them out. These people have consistently made me look good again and again. With some of them, I've had little in common. Others I may not have liked very well personally, and would never have invited them over to the house for dinner, yet they were the most competent for the job; they were the best for the organization and accomplished the right things. They are the people we need to lead the organization.

---

[9] From *Lincoln on Leadership* by Donald T. Phillips, copyright © 1991, p. 138. Reprinted by permission of Grand Central Publishing, an imprint of Hachette Book Group, Inc.
[10] Jack Welch, *Winning*, p. 90.

COMPETENCE PART TWO

The second aspect of competence requires leaders to understand and support the organization's mission to ensure their decision-making is consistent with its mission. As stated previously, I have seen people with outstanding skills capable of performing their job functions. However, they are cancer to the organization because they possess a poisonous attitude that they spread or attempt to spread throughout the organization, just like cancer does to the body. Therefore, competence requires an understanding and support of the organization's mission, which must consistently be preached and repeated to the organization's members.

Understandingly, there will be occasions where a leader in the organization has a difference of opinion or will not agree wholeheartedly with the course of action decided upon by their supervisor or the organization's chief executive. This type of disagreement can and should be positive if we hire and promote competent people. If shared and vetted in a healthy environment, the difference in ideas and opinions will lead to innovation, problem-solving, and better results. However, if someone in a leadership position subverts the organization's mission, they will only create confusion and a lack of direction for their subordinates.

All law enforcement agency employees need to see and understand the big picture. They deserve to know what they are striving for, to see that they are making a positive difference, and are personally involved in improving the quality of life for community members. How can we expect "buy-in" and support from the organization's members if they don't know for what they are fighting? A competent leader will preach, measure, and reward adherence to the organization's mission. To openly and intentionally subvert or show disdain towards the mission is selfish and neither helps the progress of the organization nor their own subordinates. Selfishness is not leadership.

When a promotional opportunity became available, I recall being approached by an individual who told me I should give them the promotion. The promotion was for supervisory responsibilities of a particular unit, which was in dire need of leadership at the time. They told me they would get busy and make needed improvements. This individual was a talented law enforcement officer with a lot of experience. When I pointed out, however, that there was a known promotional process they would have to participate in, they expressed displeasure, refusing to go through the process. This individual previously told me they never wanted to attend another leadership course because they didn't believe leadership could be taught. Their attitude was that "you either have it, or you don't." Do we want to promote this person? Do they possess the support for the agency required to be competent in a leadership position?

For a moment, let's assume this individual is the most qualified for the position. What if we completely ignore the promotional process the organization has in place, which others have been required to participate in, and promote this person outright? How will that affect the other employees who also think of themselves as qualified for the position? How is this going to affect the morale of the organization? Will the promotional process be supported and respected in the future or just be viewed as a sham? And how about this individual who gets promoted without adhering to the process set in place? What will happen the next time they don't get their way or don't share the organization's leader's opinion? Will they support the process or subvert it again?

I have known other people who believed they were qualified for a supervisory position and thought they should be a supervisor but refused to participate in the established promotional process. Why?

I can think of three potential reasons. First, they may not want to go through all the effort required to pass the promotional testing process successfully. Written tests may require reading various books on policing, supervision, applicable law, organizational policies, procedures, etc. Then there may be multiple interviews or an assessment center. Therefore, putting forth an effort to prepare and study may be required. I've both participated in and helped facilitate these types of tests, and they typically require some effort to pass.

Secondly, you may have an individual who fears stepping out of their comfort zone. For example, they would like to be a supervisor and have that promotion but possibly fear failure. They fear not passing the promotional testing process and how failure might affect their self-esteem, especially if co-workers and peers learn they could not successfully pass the assessment or at least could not obtain a high enough score for promotional consideration.

Finally, some will refuse to participate in any promotional process entirely out of principle because they don't support the promotional process or the organization's mission and leadership.

Do you want a person who would fall into any of these three scenarios as part of your leadership team? None of these individuals possess the competence required for true leadership. You do not want an individual unwilling to do the needed work. If they aren't going to do the work to be successful in the testing process, they aren't going to do it as a supervisor. If they fear failure during the testing process, they will fear failure as a supervisor. They will stay in their comfort zone, second guess their decisions, not make the hard ones, and wear out a path to their boss' office, where they will seek approval for all serious matters they should decide. If they publicly shun the organization's promotional process because they disagree, they will do the same in the future on other issues of disagreement. Promoting one of these invites chaos and a sure void in leadership.

"All leaders should realize they can't do everything on their own. They simply must have [competent] people below them who will do what is necessary to ensure success. Those subordinates who will take risks, act without waiting for direction, and ask for responsibility rather than reject it, should be treated as your most prized possessions... Executives can possess great vision and be able to provide all the direction in the world, but they can't succeed without people like U.S. Grant to carry out the company's mission,"[11] and get things accomplished.

[11] From *Lincoln on Leadership* by Donald T. Phillips, copyright © 1991, p. 135. Reprinted by permission of Grand Central Publishing, an imprint of Hachette Book Group, Inc.

Chapter 5

SMALL THINGS MATTER

When it comes to leadership and your ability to drive the performance of your work group to its highest capacity, do small things matter? Can little things lead to big results? The tendency to overlook small things as unimportant and trivial when considering the big picture and purpose of the law enforcement organization is another void in leadership capable of holding us back from true success as a leader. Thinking of it presently, it just makes sense. Small things, extra efforts, kind gestures, consideration for others, giving those few additional minutes of your valuable time, etc., can make a difference. These small "extras" often improve morale within your organization or work group. Likewise, these small "extras" often make the difference between community members, be they a resident, business owners, a victim, or offenders, being satisfied or dissatisfied with the service they have received.

We were involved in an incident involving a foot pursuit of an individual wanted on a warrant. After losing sight of the offender, a police K-9 was summoned to assist. The offender was again located, and another foot pursuit ensued, leading to the eventual apprehension of the offender, who was bitten in the leg by the K-9 in the process. As a detective, I was contacted to speak with this offender because his name had come up as a possible suspect involved in two overnight burglaries at a local service station. The offender's name came up because he was a prior employee of the service station and was known to have recently developed a drug addiction problem. Other than those two factors, no witnesses or physical evidence connected him to the crimes. I interviewed this offender, who confessed to both crimes despite no evidence directly linking him. He would receive an eight-year sentence in prison for these burglaries.

Two things stand out in my mind about this incident. First, even though both the offender and I knew our interaction and his confession would cost him years of his life in prison, he wanted to shake my hand and thank me for treating him with respect. At the time of this interaction, I marveled at how weird that was. "Why is he thanking me? I just ruined his life." Looking back on it today, the "small things" made the difference. When I met this man, I showed interest and concern for his bleeding leg where the dog had bitten him. I provided him with a bottle of water. I offered him something to eat. I heard his side of the story regarding the great chase that led to his capture. I spent a few extra minutes with this man, but it paid for itself when he decided to tell the truth and confess to his crimes.

Secondly, the other part of this story that sticks with me involves a conversation with another officer involved in this offender's foot pursuit and apprehension. When I went to retrieve the bottle of water for the offender, this officer confronted me angrily at the thought that I would give this "piece of s_ _ _" a bottle of water. After the chase they had, after fighting with this man, he was undeserving of water in this officer's opinion, and he had some choice words for me. Ultimately, this offender would have also probably preferred this officer's plan. If I had come in and stuck my finger in his leg wound, cussed him out, and told him how worthless he was, it might not have felt good to him at the time, but certainly better than the eight years in prison he was going to receive. For me, that might have felt good too, but that wouldn't have gotten the positive results, being the confession and eight years of prison deserved for his crimes.

Looking back at it today, it makes sense; those small things made a difference in this case. I have seen that work many times over, and I know law enforcement professionals worldwide get positive results when they tend to the small stuff daily. However, do they consciously comprehend what might be making the difference in their success? I didn't. At the time of the story, I thought it weird and was thankful and excited for the confession and positive outcome. Unfortunately, it would take me several more years before I put any real significant thought into the importance of tending to "small things."

It was 2012. I was a commander and had been a supervisor for many years already. A new police chief had just been appointed from outside the agency. There was a new and unknown boss to lead the agency. I arrived at work one day and headed to the locker room to adorn my uniform. Just before entering the locker room, I looked down the hallway and noticed the door to the administration's offices, consisting of the offices of the police chief, two deputy chiefs, and their administrative assistants, was propped open. I had worked at this agency for almost twenty years, and that door was routinely closed. "Huh, what's going on in there," I thought. I entered the locker room preparing for duty, wondering, "What's going on? Why is that door open?" After exiting the locker room, I looked down the hallway again. "Yep, it was still open," I told myself. It was calling me, inviting me, and I had to find out what was going on and why the door was open. I entered and began speaking with the administrative assistants. They informed me that the new police chief wanted the door open. He wanted people to feel welcome to come inside and believed the closed door signaled isolation, sending the message that the administration was not available or approachable.

It wasn't just me. As the days went on, everyone was talking about that open door. People were excited. They believed positive change was coming and the new chief would be approachable and show concern for the feelings and needs of the people in the organization. And I was thinking, "really, an open door can cause this much commotion, interest, and excitement?" This very small gesture and the overwhelming response that came with it caused me to ponder the importance and difference small things can make.

But that is just the beginning of the story. After seeing the attention and discussion this open door was generating, I thought of the possibility of an article on the topic of leadership. I would title it, "An Open Door – how little things lead to big results." But unfortunately, this article would never get written. Why? Because small things matter and the results were not what we hoped for.

Let me explain as I provide a word of caution. Small things can have negative implications as quickly and easily as positive. When small things are improperly tended to or ignored, devastating results can occur. People can become de-motivated, morale can suffer, performance can suffer, and an increase in turnover may occur.

This same new chief made other "small" decisions that reversed the positive effects of that open door. He quickly removed a sign that said "roll call" on the wall directly outside the roll call room and replaced it with a sign that said "squad room." It doesn't sound like a big deal, does it? But there were over 100 employees in this organization, all of whom called this room the roll call room. This is where patrol shifts met before going into the field, holding roll calls, reviewing all police-related activities from the last 24 hours, receiving their assignments, patrol cars, etc. The time spent in roll call was the one opportunity each day where the patrol shift could be together, sharing stories, laughing a bit, and fellowshipping before being sent into the field to chase radio calls.

This change upset people. This room had always been known as "roll call." This was their home, the organization they took pride in, and he was making changes that affected their home without consulting the masses on their thoughts. This was not sitting well with people. People were no longer talking about that open door but about the change in the name of the roll call room. Supervisors would explain this dynamic to the new police chief and ask if he would consider putting the old roll call sign back up. His response was, "Roll call is what takes place inside the room, but the room itself is called the squad room." He was ignoring the culture of his new police department and holding fast to his personal culture or that of his previous department, which he had since left.

Shortly after that, he began to talk about changes to the uniform and badges. We always had tan over black uniforms. This was a unique uniform, and no one close had one similar. When I was new to the department, I had been told that the uniform was chosen so our police department would stand out and people would know who we were. We were a professional organization, progressive compared to many in the area, and we didn't want people confusing us with other departments. I took a lot of pride in the organization and the uniform that represented it. The new chief thought police uniforms should be blue (the color of his old department).

The new chief also changed the design of our badge. Some supported and were excited about these new changes. Some always disliked the tan uniforms and wanted to be in blue, believing police should wear blue uniforms. Others were also happy with the new badge design. It was a good-looking badge, but that wasn't the point. Overall, the masses were unhappy, mostly about not being considered or included in the decisions regarding these changes, which left many in a growing state of decreasing morale.

Then there was "the rock!" It was a natural rock about the size of your standard computer mouse and had been a part of the police department's history and culture. This rock sat at the front desk of the police department. Whenever an officer would turn in paperwork requiring a supervisor's review and signature, he would put it under the rock. You would typically find a pile of paper sitting under this rock. As a supervisor, I would come into the front desk area, look at the rock, and any paperwork below it required my review. This procedure would occur numerous times a day, but everyone knew what the rock meant – put your paperwork under the rock for review.

This rock had been painted many times (most frequently with whiteout) and had the words "the rock" written on the top of it in marker. This rock had been used in this fashion since I started working there. It was a part of the police department's culture. That rock sat at the front desk for over twenty years, maybe much longer, as I'm not sure anyone still around would remember where and when it first came to be. The new chief talked about the rock. He thought it was silly and demeaned its use. It got to the point where people feared he would take "the rock" away. Out of fear the new chief was planning on confiscating the rock, it was taken into protective custody for a while and replaced with another rock. Did he really contemplate taking it? Who knows, but people perceived that he might. It was a talking point, and the chief's lack of respect for its place in the organization had a negative effect.

So, what does a door, a wall sign, the color of uniforms, or a rock have to do with being a successful leader or having a high-performing organization?

It's not about the door, the sign, the color of the uniforms, or the rock. It is about genuinely caring about the people that make up your organization. It's about symbolism, the organization's culture, and caring enough to find out and understand the "small stuff" in your organization. What's important? It can and will be different in every organization and among various people within every organization. Are you willing to put in the time and energy to understand and respect the small stuff in your organization? I believe that too often we get busy tending to what we perceive as the crucial and essential aspects and tasks of our position as a leader that we don't think we have time for the small things. We want people to get on with doing the job, and we forget that they are people who come with varying emotions, perspectives, and values.

The new chief did not recognize the importance of these "small things." And he made other decisions that further exasperated the morale of the organization. As a result, complaints about the administration increased, morale and performance decreased, and people started talking about leaving what had always been a professional organization, a department that officers came to, not left. Research has demonstrated that people don't leave companies; they leave managers.[1] And I believe the failure of a leader to tend to the small things can frequently evolve into disenchantment among the work group.

This is further demonstrated when we see various units or work groups within the same organization doing similar work, making the same pay, and receiving the same benefits. Yet, the morale in some groups is good, and in others, it suffers. In such cases, look to the leaders of that group, and the answer as to why is probably there.

MAKE THOSE "SMALL THING" DEPOSITS

Stephen Covey refers to the Emotional Bank Account, which he explains as a "metaphor that describes the amount of trust that's been built up in a relationship. It's the feeling of safeness you have with another person. You make deposits into this Emotional Bank Account through being courteous, kind, honest, and honoring your commitments. In doing so, you build up a reserve. As trust between people become higher, the reserve increases, and we can call upon that trust many times, even when making mistakes."[2] The

---

[1] Used with permission of Gallup, Inc., from *First, Break All the Rules: What the World's Greatest Managers Do Differently* by Gallup, copyright © 1999/2016. Permission conveyed through Copyright Clearance Center, Inc.

[2] Covey, Stephen R. (1989). The Seven Habits of Highly Effective People; Powerful Lessons in Personal Change. Free Press, New York, NY, p. 188.

leaders of law enforcement organizations should be making deposits into this Emotional Bank Account. If the deposits far outweigh the withdrawals, our personnel, in most cases, will be willing to compensate for or overlook our occasional failings, mistakes, and inadequate judgment calls that will occur from time to time. On the other hand, suppose there is no reserve or balance in the Emotional Bank Account. In that case, trust is not present, and our mistakes and misjudgments will likely come with a much greater cost, being decreased morale, performance, and downright disgruntled employees.

Notice I said that deposits made must "far" outweigh the withdrawals from the reserve. It isn't a one-for-one proposition. It would be nice and more straightforward if that were the case. However, humans frequently focus more on the negative than the positive. I believe our organizations and society would be much better if we could maintain a more positive focus, but in my experience, that isn't the case. We tend to migrate towards the negative more easily.

Look at the news media; what gets the attention, positive or negative stories? What are people in your organization talking about, positive events or negative events? Are they excessively talking about the extraordinary work a co-worker has done or focusing on the screw-ups made by other officers, such as who has the drinking problem or who's cheating on whom?

Consider this and see if it sounds familiar. I have been blessed to work for some great leaders who have treated me well, helped me develop, and given me great opportunities. If I were to stop and try to list all the support and good things they have done for me, I wouldn't be able to because there is just too much good stuff they have done. However, what do we do when those same leaders make a "bad call"? When the police chief makes a decision that doesn't make sense to us? When the sheriff selects a direction for the organization that seems opposite to where you think it should go? If you are like most, we immediately go to the negative. I cannot believe he is doing this! That is a terrible decision! That's the dumbest thing I've heard! What are they thinking? We start talking about the clueless people in the ivory tower. Admit it!

I do; I have been there and done that. But, unfortunately, those same great people, who have supported and helped me, make one bad call and it's easy to forget the good they have done. Our leaders screw up and immediately become clueless, and the agency is falling apart. That is, if the Emotional Bank Account is dry, overdrawn, and depleted of trust. However, if the bank account has a high balance, the leaders are more willing to be given the benefit of the doubt, trusted, and forgiven for their errors.

The previous police chief I referred to made a quick deposit with his "open door policy" but then quickly began to make withdrawals that he couldn't cover. His overdrawn account led to distrust, decreased performance, and struggling morale. I am going to suggest, and this is an arbitrary number for demonstration purposes, that leaders of our law enforcement agencies need to make about ten deposits to every withdrawal to make sure they maintain the appropriate balance in their Emotional Bank Accounts. This may sound like a lot, but don't fear; tending to the small things that matter is an easy way to make those deposits. So, let's get busy making those deposits.

In this chapter, I won't try to identify all the "small things" our leaders need to attend to. There are just too many possibilities that vary among organizations and people. However, I will provide one concept taken from a book written by Rudy Giuliani called *Leadership*, located within the chapter called "Weddings Discretionary, Funerals Mandatory." The premise of this chapter, as it relates to leaders, is that celebrating the good things with your people, such as weddings, parties, recognitions, etc., is good. However, being available and supportive of your people during struggles and challenging times, such as losing a loved one, is more important for leaders to involve themselves in.[3] Being available and supportive of your personnel during tough times, even when those tough times are personal in nature and unrelated to the workplace, is a small gesture and consideration that will go a long way.

Other examples include some leaders who do a great job at getting to know and remember the names of their personnel's spouses or children and asking about them occasionally. I think that sends a strong message that the leader cares for them as a person. I have never done well with that. Others do a great job of remembering and recognizing the birthdays of all their personnel, in some way, again demonstrating they care. I have tried this several times and have done pretty well, making it a point to recognize them at roll call with a birthday cake or maybe buy them lunch for the day. Still, inevitably, at some point, I will forget or miss one or two birthdays. Then the perception that I favor or am treating some of my subordinates differently than others can potentially arise and have a negative effect. So, I struggled with that as well. But I can still find, as all of us can, many behaviors and actions to make investments into the Emotional Bank Account and demonstrate to our people that we care about them.

Rather than list as many so-called "small things," extra efforts, gestures, consideration, etc., that I believe can make a big difference, I will identify two that I believe to be most crucial. Following these two general practices will open the door and give you what you need to meet the "small things matter" threshold. The first is setting aside time to be available and get to know your personnel. This in and of itself will help you identify the small things that you, as a leader, need to be conscious of in your organization. What is important to those you lead, and how do those important things fit your leadership style?

---

[3] Giuliani, Rudolph W. (2002). *Leadership*. Hyperion, New York, NY, pp. 253-264.

The second is recognizing good work! Refrain from thinking of yourself as too busy or important to stop and acknowledge the positive performance of others. Again, it is a small gesture that leads to big results, being more positive performance.

GET OUT AND ABOUT

In the 1982 book *In Search of Excellence*, authors Tom Peters and Robert Waterman introduced the frequently used phrase today, Managing by Wandering Around (MBWA). The concept involves the leader getting out of the office and among their personnel and troops. Having genuine interaction and communication with your subordinates has many benefits. This may seem obvious and taught in most leadership training courses, but my experience has been that many of us struggle with this.

Operationally, the benefits of managing by walking around and interacting with your personnel are huge. Your people are closer to the action, to the work that gets done, which is the primary purpose of the law enforcement agency. The individual front-line contributor has the information and details needed for your agency's success. You, as a leader, require this information if your work group and organization are to be successful. Knowing your people and being close to them ensures access to this information, which is used to make more accurate and appropriate decisions. This will be emphasized further in future chapters on driving performance and utilizing a modern and proper leadership style for today's policing. For now, however, the concept of walking or wandering around and making yourself available to your subordinates, as it relates to the idea that "small things matter," will be considered.

Is it essential that people believe their leader cares for them as a person? Is it important that they trust their leader? How about having respect for their leader? Does trust and respect for a leader affect a person's commitment to the leader and the organization?

Many times throughout my career, an officer would enter my office and shut the door. This usually isn't a good sign. Many of these officers didn't even work for me but worked for other supervisors. They would then share with me personal events going on in their lives. Nine out of ten times, these would not be good events but problems, such as severe issues with their children, drug addiction, or problems with their spouse, whether they were contemplating a divorce or maybe learned their spouse was cheating on them. There were physical or mental health issues affecting their lives or work performance. There were officers struggling with a specific call that they were involved in. I would think to myself, "Why is this person telling me this? They don't even work for me?" But I think they recognized that I did care for the organization's people and people in general. I had spent my career serving others where I could, trying to tend to the small things that make a difference. These officers knew I would listen to them and help them where possible. They trusted that I would not gossip behind their backs and share their story with others. These were small efforts, just being available to them, validating them as someone of value, and maintaining their confidence when I could.

I am grateful to have been able to help and support many of these officers. Indeed, there were some issues where I could do nothing more than be a listening ear and include them in my prayers. However, because of my relationship with these officers, I could count on their commitment and would receive high-performance levels from them. Sometimes this commitment included them being honest with me and telling me when I was wrong, when my ideas or direction were off and not going to work. Someone will rarely tell his boss he is wrong unless a relationship of trust and respect exists.

We must understand that commitment is different from compliance. As leaders in a law enforcement agency, we can force compliance. We can enforce rules and regulations. We create policies that employees must adhere to. If they don't do their job as ascribed by the organization's rules and regulations, they don't get a paycheck and end up without a job. But we can never force commitment. An individual commits voluntarily. To have a high-performing work group or organization requires people committed to the cause.

How do we demonstrate genuine concern for our people, build trust, and earn their respect and commitment? It requires making a sufficient number of deposits into your Emotional Bank Account, which comes from personal involvement with your personnel. Don't lose touch with your people. Instead, listen to them, understand them, and get out and about among them.

In short, you want committed people. You want to be respected because people commit to the leader they respect. They will be compliant, at best, to the leader they don't respect. Your people need to know you care. They will only be convinced of this by personal interaction with you.

What will you, the leader, gain from these interactions? First, you get to know your people, what makes them tick, how they think, their personalities, and how they best work. Is this good information for you to have? Are all employees created equal? Certainly not! There are gender, generational, and personality differences, as well as differences in upbringing and values. Spending time getting to know the personal side of your people will help you better understand how to manage them, and they will be grateful for the effort you put into it.

You may learn that they are suffering through some personal problems in their life. There may be something you can do to ease their burden or just be that sounding board, someone there to listen. They may be having difficulties with a co-worker, and some small action or adjustment on your part might make all the difference. You may find they are overworked and carrying a significantly high caseload, and you can relieve them of some of their burdens. There may be a small piece of equipment that would make their jobs more efficient that you could obtain with minimal cost. Maybe they don't completely understand the systems and processes that might be helpful but are embarrassed to ask. Perhaps they have ideas on enhancing the systems in place to make them work better. Maybe they just have great ideas to help you and the organization be more successful. Perhaps the name of the roll call room, the color of the uniform, the badge design, and that silly rock are important to them and the culture of the agency. But you will never know unless you make time for your people to understand them and what is important to them. What are those small things that matter to each of your personnel?

So, get out and spend some informal time with your people. You are not micromanaging their work or providing every direction and detail, but supporting them, listening to them, and validating them as people with unique opinions and feelings. This can be accomplished by having an open-door policy and meaning it. If my door is open, that means come on in. If it is closed, I'm busy and shouldn't be interrupted but for something urgent. But my door stays open 99% of the time. And when someone comes to my office or frequently sticks their head in, not wanting to disturb me, I invite them in and give them my attention. I'll admit this can be challenging, especially when you are in the middle of something and your mind is going in one direction and you risk losing your train of thought. Or, some people don't know how to have a short conversation, and thus you know you have to hunker down because once they get your attention, you will be there for a while. However, fight the urge to look at your watch, cell phone, or computer screen; fight it the best you can, stop what you are doing, and give your people your full attention.

Besides maintaining an "open door" when I commanded the detective division, I would take frequent trips through the hallways, past the detectives' offices, and check in with those present. I would do this at least once a day unless committed to meetings or pulled from the office on urgent matters in the field. During these daily strolls, I would provide everyone an opportunity for discussion, interaction, and one-on-one conversation to tell me or ask me anything they wanted. Sometimes, the detective was busy, and the conversation would end in seconds and not go much beyond the general "how you doing?" type discussion. Other times a conversation would ensue, and I may end up with a detective for an hour, or a group of investigative personnel might assemble for a group discussion. And, then, there was everything in between. These discussions allowed them to share their opinions and what they thought was important and allowed me to reinforce the mission and the expectations I had of them, but to do so informally, often with an example or story to emphasize the level of performance we were aiming for.

I have been told detectives cringed when they saw other supervisors coming down the hall towards them or their office because they knew those supervisors would either criticize their work or assign them more work. However, when detectives saw me walking down the hall, they perceived my presence differently. They knew there was a 50/50 chance that I would either talk about business and work or just check in with them and see how they were generally doing, which I learned they appreciated. Therefore, they frequently enjoyed my visits and didn't dread seeing me from afar.

As a patrol supervisor, I would utilize roll call as a forum for discussion. We would cover the required materials for roll call, such as beat assignments, car assignments, special assignments, public relations events, wanted persons we were looking for, etc. But then I would take some extra minutes to have a genuine conversation with the group, maybe debrief a good or bad call the shift may have responded to, sharing some stories and even some laughs (usually at another shift mates' expense).

As a patrol shift that spent most of its time in the field responding to calls, this was the one time the entire shift was together. There was no telling what they might experience and be confronted with in the shift that lay before them. Likely they would see some ugly things – people at their worst, violence, child abuse, death, and people who hold them in contempt. So, this time together in roll call, before facing the unknown, was important to me.

I have heard supervisors, including some of my co-workers, insist that this time of fellowship during roll call was wasteful and that officers needed to get into the field as quickly as possible. They would blow through the required information as soon as possible, almost as if competing to see who could hold roll call in the shortest time. And then they'd push their people out of the building and into their assigned beat to start handling calls. Their arguments, at least in theory, made sense; the officers needed to be in the field as much as possible, where they could respond more rapidly to calls for service and patrol the neighborhood to deter crime. Indeed, there are limits to the amount of time that should be spent on roll call. Of course, you don't want the officers in roll call half of their shift, but I think those supervisors who denied their people anytime together missed great opportunities.

First, research has demonstrated that random patrol isn't as effective as we thought. Secondly, if officers believe they need time together or have something important to share with another officer, they will find a way to make that happen. Police officers complete most of their work unsupervised.

We have all driven down the street and seen two police cars side-by-side, with the officers talking to each other. Are we to believe they are always talking business or just concluding a call together? Of course not; that is an unrealistic view. Again, I have been there and done that. Finally, by not creating some time for the work group to be together, these supervisors missed an opportunity to gather information that was beneficial to the organization and their ability to make the best decisions for the organization.

I took advantage of the time in roll call. If a call came out that needed immediate attention, it would get covered because committed officers would ensure that. I used this time as part of my long-term plan to develop a work group of supportive, competent, and committed officers. If they are going to support each other, there needs to be some personal investment in each other. Those few minutes together in roll call provided some of that investment. Sometimes, delicious treats put together by Wendy, my lovely wife, were also part of this time in roll call, a parting gift, a way to say thank you or we care about you before sending them out into the unknown. Often, I would just sit and listen to others talking about what they were experiencing on various calls for service in the field. Usually, the conversation would turn to what was happening in their assigned areas and who the problem people – the criminals – were; which of them was selling drugs, where they were living, who they hung out with, etc. This was information the entire patrol shift could use to make them more effective during their tour of duty.

Conversations would also turn to department policy and procedure, equipment wants and needs, and what was working and what wasn't. And, of course, every police officer knows what is needed to solve all the world's problems, both inside and outside the department. But, again, most of this was good information to understand the perceived working conditions and opinions of those working for me. Indeed, there were varying opinions, and I didn't agree with everything I heard. However, listening and making myself available to the officers gave me information I needed to make better decisions and understand my people and what was important to them. I will admit there were many times I wanted to leap over the roll call table and strangle an officer or two after hearing, and passionately disagreeing with, what they had to say. But, to do that would have shut the entire group down, and I wouldn't have been receiving the needed information any longer. So, as long as the conversations remained respectful and didn't cross the line of professionalism, roll call was a safe place to share your opinions. This short time in roll call, maybe fifteen or twenty minutes, was one of those small things that I believe significantly impacted the morale of the work group (see Figure 3).

Figure 3. Roll call is a good opportunity to share vital information, while increasing camaraderie, and identifying what the "small things" are that mattered to your people.

Another opportunity to interact with your personnel occurs when you show up on their calls. For example, respond to a scene of a crime with them but don't show up and take over, micromanage, or direct the investigation. Instead, let them do their job but play a supporting role. Offer to help them. "Small things" will significantly impact your people, such as your personnel seeing the police chief or sheriff directing traffic, interviewing a witness, offering to conduct neighborhood interviews, or canvassing the area of a crime. This not only relieves some of the burdens from the assigned officer or detective but demonstrates care for them and their work. It also allows the law enforcement leader to see the conditions their people are working under firsthand. Do they have the right tools and equipment for the job? Is their equipment in good condition? Is there better equipment out there? Are there any observable training needs that would help them perform more favorably? Are the right systems, processes, and procedures in place?

I spent some time informally conversing with the officers assigned to the front desk area of the police department. Like walking the halls of the detective division, this was a practice and routine once or twice a shift. During the discussion, the topic came around to the front desk officer's responsibility of taking all the bar sheets from all patrol officers and transferring the information, rewriting all the data onto one Master Bar Sheet, as it was called. The information from the master sheet would then be entered into a spreadsheet on the computer.

Patrol officers were responsible for checking the drinking establishments in their assigned areas. They were to conduct bar checks where they would enter the establishment and look for any violations, such as underage drinkers, overserved patrons, etc. After closing time, the officers were required to check and confirm that said bars were in fact closed, if call volume allowed them to do so. They would then turn in a "bar sheet" listing the bars they checked and the time they checked them.

The officers at the front desk could easily end up with twenty separate bar sheets or more. The midnight shift front desk officer would take all those sheets, transfer the information onto the Master Bar Sheet, and then enter the same information into the computer. This task would take thirty to forty-five minutes. I don't recall if I asked or if they did, but the question was posed, "What do they do with this information?" No one present at the discussion, including myself, knew. The front desk officer said the Records Division had instructed them to collect and enter this data into the computer. Still, the front desk officer didn't know what was done with the data once it was collected and documented. I didn't see any benefit to completing this task, especially the redundancy of putting it on paper as the Master Bar Sheet and entering it again in the computer. I instructed the officers to stop and postpone this practice until I could ask questions and determine why it was required.

My first stop was the Records Division. They confirmed they had instructed the front desk officers to complete the task of collecting the data and entering it into a computer database. Still, they advised that they did nothing with the information. My next question for them was, "If you don't do anything with the information, why are we collecting it?" According to the Records Division, a specifically named deputy chief of the police department had instructed them on the procedure. Unfortunately, this particular deputy chief had retired about a year prior, and no one could answer why this procedure was in place.

My next stop was the following staff meeting. I inquired about this procedure before the command team, including the chief and present deputy chiefs. I asked about this procedure, specifically the spreadsheet where the data was collected and saved. No member of the command team in the department at this time was even aware that said spreadsheet existed, let alone any knowledge of why it existed. Consequently, the use of the spreadsheet ceased from that point forward.

I tell this story to emphasize this point – the officers wasted thirty to forty-five minutes daily on entirely irrelevant and unnecessary tasks for over a year.

We're talking about thirty to forty-five minutes and a silly bar sheet. It doesn't take much effort to recopy information from one paper to another and then type it into the computer, right? I mean, this is just small stuff. So why bother with it? Who cares, right?

That is thirty to forty-five minutes a day, equal to approximately 180 to 270 hours a year. The time could have been spent doing something beneficial to the community and moving the organization forward instead of wasting taxpayer resources. For a moment, just consider the cost. At $20 an hour, which is probably less than what the officers were making at the time, $3,600 to $5,400 a year was wasted on that procedure. These small things do add up and lead to big things.

Had it not been for a casual and informal conversation, who knows for how long that practice would have continued? But unfortunately, most law enforcement agencies have these types of stories of busy work and tasks that probably serve no reasonable purpose. So how do you find them? You make yourself available, get out among your people, watch, listen, and ask questions. Be open to their input, opinions, and what is important in their lives.

I recognize that all this is easier said than done. Frequently, as supervisors and leaders, our plates are so full, and we have so much on our "to-do" list, projects we are behind on, etc., that it can seem wasteful to spend time in informal and casual conversations with our personnel. As I try to accept my advice of getting out and spending time with the troops, I can think of countless examples where I failed. I have started days with good intentions, such as planning to go out into the field and respond to calls with the officers, until I arrived at the office and saw all the work I was behind on. Other times, I would choose to get into the field, where I'd start patrolling, waiting for some good radio calls to respond to so I could back up and support the officers. Then, as I was driving around the city, I would start thinking of all the projects and other tasks needing my attention and would cut my time in the field with the troops short to head back to the office. There have been times while working in my office I realized I should take a break and wander the halls to check in with the officers or detectives, but I didn't do so, not wanting to interrupt my train of thought. Sometimes, I started walking through the halls and found myself in a conversation, but rather than giving my full attention to the one I was speaking with, my mind kept wandering back to the office and what I could be accomplishing there. I've talked with other supervisors who have expressed similar concerns; they know they should get out and spend more time with their subordinates but are too busy.

As supervisors, managers, and administrators, we are busy with numerous responsibilities, programs, projects, and tasks that need our attention. Taking valuable time away for casual and informal conversations can seem wasteful. However, at a minimum, committing and devoting that short period, be it daily or weekly, will be a small investment that pays enormous dividends in the long run. You will better know and understand your personnel and what they, as individuals, need to succeed. And, if you are listening and available to them, you might also learn some things about yourself and how you can be a better leader.

IS THERE SOMEONE WHO NEEDS RECOGNIZED TODAY?

Another "small thing" that makes a big difference to those you lead is recognizing positive performance. We are probably reasonably good, at least I hope, at recognizing the significant events and accomplishments, such as: stopping an armed robbery in progress and taking the offender into custody; negotiating with a deranged man holding his family captive and obtaining a peaceful resolution; jumping into a freezing body of water to find the car that submerged moments before, after which the elderly driver is rescued, and his life saved. These types of occurrences occur, and again I believe we do well at recognizing this type of officer performance, as we should. However, I am not as confident that we sufficiently recognize the excellent work our personnel do day in and day out to keep the organization moving forward in a positive direction.

I have heard supervisors say they will not reward people for doing their job. Instead, they save their "thank you" and recognition for the extraordinary events. Unfortunately, those supervisors are missing great opportunities to reinforce positive behaviors. The everyday performance of law enforcement's men and women determines whether a given law enforcement agency achieves its mission. Furthermore, what we may consider small or insignificant tasks can hold great significance in successfully accomplishing the mission.

When I was new on the police force, we responded to a burglary in progress at a residence. This residence was within my assigned beat; therefore, my call. Based upon the information received and witness accounts, we were confident the burglar was still in the house. We surrounded the house. We made numerous attempts to call out the offender to no avail. Finally, the decision was made to assemble a team to enter the home and look for the offender.

I was assigned to cover the front door, so I positioned myself behind a large tree where I could monitor it. I heard the supervisor calling various officers on the radio and putting his entry team together. I was frustrated, as I wanted to be part of that team. After all, this was my beat and assigned call. And being new to the department, I was young and excited, wanting to be where the action was. I didn't want to be stuck behind some stupid tree where nothing was happening and miss all the fun that I expected would occur inside once they found the burglar. The team entered without me and eventually found the burglar hiding behind a wall in a crawl space.

In my immaturity, I vented some of my frustration about why I did not get to go inside the house as part of the team. After all, it was my call; I was the primary assigned officer. Setting aside the fact that I was new, lacked any real experience or training, even maybe lacked some maturity, and had no business being a part of the entry team, I was instructed on the fundamental importance of my assignment behind that tree. Someone had to cover the front door and windows.

Was this an insignificant assignment? Not at all! If no one was covering the front of the house, our offender may have walked away from the home, into the neighborhood, and into freedom, where he could victimize someone else. That vital role had to be covered for this operation to end successfully.

Is there anything wrong with a supervisor telling the officer assigned behind the tree, "Good job, thank you. I'm glad you were there"? I took this lesson with me and have shared it many times since as I try to convey, specifically to newer officers, how all the parts, including the small tasks, come together to support operations and the big picture.

Directing traffic at the scene of a major crime or crash may seem small or insignificant, but take that person directing traffic away and see what happens. For example, I responded to a case of a barricaded person who had fired shots at responding law enforcement. Unfortunately, appropriate traffic control was not in place, and someone drove a car past the barricades. A police officer had to leave his place of cover to run into the road to try and stop the vehicle before it entered harm's way. In doing so, this officer was shot by the barricaded subject. Fortunately, the officer survived the shooting. Do you think this officer believes that the often-perceived mundane task of directing traffic is essential?

Leaders, thank your people! Let them know you appreciate what they bring to the table. Yes, even when they are just doing their job. If it is done well, done right, make sure you take time to recognize that because they could choose otherwise. Remember, compliance is not the same as commitment.

In his book *Winning,* Jack Welch refers to *differentiation.* He explains differentiation as "a process requiring managers to assess employees and separate them into three categories in terms of performance: top 20 percent, middle 70 percent, and bottom 10 percent." He then explains further how these categories should be responded to differently. The top 20 percent, being your superstars, get a lot of perks, including financial benefits and recognition. The middle 70 percent, the majority of your workforce, is very valuable, and the organization won't be successful without them. Therefore, this group needs to be engaged and motivated continually. Welch then described the bottom 10 percent group as the poor performers that need "to go."[4]

You will find these same categories of employees within a given law enforcement agency. We do great at recognizing our top performers, that 20 percent group. These are our superstars, many of them leaders or future leaders of law enforcement organizations. This group is successful at almost any task, and it is the norm that they give 110% at all they do. They must because this group tends to be motivated intrinsically. They have an internal drive to be successful.

Being that our law enforcement personnel are public officers, the ability to provide financial perks to our superstars might be limited. We can and should, however, continue to recognize this group for its high-performance level.

We do well at recognizing the superstars, but we, as leaders, could do more at recognizing the middle 70 percent group. This is the group that shows up and does its job on a daily basis. They may not be at the same level as our superstars. They may be quiet in their work and not as flashy with their "look at me, in your face" performance, but they do perform and perform appropriately. This is the largest group, a group we need committed to be successful. This group may be the bench players or the second string, but it is essential.

Would the Chicago Bulls have been so successful in winning multiple championships in the 1990s with Michael Jordan as their superstar if not for the outstanding bench players and supporters they had to back him up? It is this group that we sometimes take for granted. Many within this group may be bordering at the upper limits of the 70 percent group, teetering on becoming a superstar. Similarly, some may be at the lower spectrum teetering close to the poor performers. A supervisor's interaction with this group and his ability to encourage its subordinates, helping them recognize their value to the organization, might make the difference in turning them into superstars or keeping them from becoming poor performers. They need to understand their importance in the organization and how we appreciate their contributions, even when they are just assigned to watch the front door from behind a tree.

How about the bottom 10 percent, the poor performers? I would agree with Jack Welch in that if you have employees who aren't doing the job or are completely incompetent on the job and untrainable, they need to go. A plan should be in place for removing this person and limiting the damage they can do to the organization. However, even if all our employees are performing the job's essential functions satisfactorily and firing them is not appropriate or

[4] Welch, Jack. (2005). From *Winning* by Jack Welch, Suzy Welch. Copyright (c) 2005 by Jack Welch, LLC. Used by permission of HarperCollins Publishers., pp. 41-43.

possible, we can still find three distinct levels of performers. We will have to contend with the bottom 10 percent.

The bottom 10 percent might be that group that does their job but is not motivated to do much beyond that. They will do what is expected, but nothing more. These are typically compliant employees, doing enough of what is required to stay out of trouble but not committed. You know who I'm talking about and who those people are in your organization. Although this group is considered our low performers, sending them packing to the unemployment line is not always an option. That can sometimes be a challenge, depending upon your location in the U.S. and the various rules and laws that may apply in a given state. It is not always as easy to fire a public officer as it might be in the private business arena that Jack Welch is familiar with.

However, in most cases, when dealing with your bottom 10 percent, there is something this lower-level performer does well. They have a strength or strengths they can excel at. The key to getting more from your poorer performers is identifying that strength, allowing them to use it, and then recognizing them for it. Unfortunately, recognizing these individuals as poor performers, I believe many supervisors look at them in all matters with the "poor performer filter," a biased perception that can see no good in this person. They write the person off as worthless or no good. In the supervisor's mind, they put this person in a box due to the person's previous mistakes or poor performance and never let them out, even when they may do or have the potential to do something good. If you see no good in a person, what are the chances you will encourage this person to do good?

I'm not suggesting that you will take someone from the "ten percenter" category and turn them into a superstar. It's probably not going to happen! However, we can get some good work and positive performance from them by recognizing and appreciating their good work. Maybe we can get them into the middle 70 percent category with effort and encouragement. I have had some luck with this over the years.

I've had subordinates that were consistently low in productivity regarding uncommitted patrol time. That is when they were not committed or assigned to calls for service and were free to patrol, proactively enforce laws, and initiate service to the community. In one instance, an officer was well-trained and versed in forensics and evidence collection. Recognizing this as a strength and interest of his (by the way, strengths and interests often go hand in hand. as people aren't usually going to have strength in an area they dislike or despise), I acknowledged his skills in this area. I asked if he would be interested in mentoring and training other less experienced evidence technicians. He was willing, and the agency was better because of it. He was also utilized for various public relations educational opportunities, again a benefit to the organization. Yes, this person was not a superstar, and his performance was less than desired in some areas of his patrol officer responsibilities. However, we benefitted the organization more by recognizing and showing appreciation for this officer's strengths, which encouraged him to use said strengths.

I've had similar experiences with other officers who were borderline poor performers but possessed excellent skills and knowledge of tactics. These officers were recognized, encouraged, and used to train others in appropriate tactical responses to crimes in progress, building entry and searches, and other high-risk responses. And, when the going got tough and we needed someone who knew tactics, these were the guys we called upon. Did I say "thank you" and recognize their performance after a successful high-risk call? You bet!

So how do we do this? How do we go about recognizing positive performance? There are numerous easy ways to accomplish this, like taking time to get out among your personnel for some informal interaction. It's not difficult, but it takes a strong commitment. So, we must set time aside for this straightforward and small practice.

Of course, a verbal acknowledgment, person to person, says a lot, as it is more intimate and personal. Here are two examples: "Hey, I appreciated your comments and willingness to share your opinion in roll call yesterday?" and "You were outstanding in how you handled that angry person on the phone. You were very patient." If appropriate, recognizing a person in front of their peers in a group setting, such as a meeting or roll call, can be more encouraging, especially if the group is already familiar with or has witnessed the performance in question. If the person you recognize doesn't work for you, they are either your peer or works for another supervisor, recognizing them in front of their supervisor may be a plus. Just recently, one of my peers lent me great assistance in researching the equipment needed for the agency's budget preparation. In our weekly command staff meeting, I took the time to thank him and tell him how appreciative I was that he took time away from his responsibilities to help me. I recognized his efforts before the entire command staff so they could also recognize them.

You can also recognize positive performance with the written word. This type of recognition can be a quick e-mail to the person in question, thanking them for their efforts. Or you could write the person a note. Although I would send many e-mails due to convenience, I kept an 8 ½ by 5 ½ notepad that I would use to write thank you notes on. Even when personally thanking or recognizing someone verbally in person, I liked to wait a day or two and again follow up with an e-mail or note. As mentioned, I believe personal contact and interaction one on one is significant. Still, there is also something special about a leader taking the time to write down their thanks and appreciation. I had a police chief that would do this routinely. I would come to work and find a note in my mailbox. That was always appreciated and an excellent way to start the workday. Another benefit to recognizing the person in writing is that a copy of this "note of recognition" could be saved and included in their personnel file for future use on their annual evaluation.

A good practice that I used, although certainly not perfect at it, was to take a few moments every week or two and review a list of all the personnel that worked for me. Then, I would ask myself if anyone did something I needed to recognize. If there were, I would get my notepad out and start writing those "notes of appreciation." Then, after considering all the personnel that worked for me, I would run down the list of my peers. Then, I would think about any other agency personnel who, although they might not work for me directly, had rendered assistance or done something positive to support our operations. If so, I took the time to ensure they were recognized personally and ensured their supervisor was informed of the positive performance rendered. This is extremely important in building positive relationships and getting support from people outside your area of responsibility. Below are several examples of notes used to recognize positive work, show appreciation, or say thank you!

Sgt. Smith,
I am writing to commend you for your genuine concern for your personnel, leading to the recent discussion with Officer Jones about the personal problem he is presently enduring. Your desire to help him personally and push all your personnel out of their comfort zone professionally is appreciated. I'm glad you are here.

Officer Smith,
I wanted to thank you for the leadership you've shown during the recent homicide case. I appreciate you jumping right in and taking charge of the evidence/forensic aspect of the case. We knew we were in good hands and could then concentrate on other areas requiring our attention. Thanks again!

Crime Analyst Smith,
Thanks again for your help Saturday and willingness to come in on your day off. You really helped expedite several tasks and relieved the detective division of some responsibilities and stress. I appreciate your attitude and flexibility.

Corporal Smith,
I just wanted to say thanks and let you know that we recognize the excellent work your unit is doing. Your guys are smiling and appear to be having fun. That is important as it makes coming to work and being productive easier. I wanted you to know that your efforts are noted and appreciated.

Sgt. Smith,
In a casual conversation with another detective, I learned you helped the domestic violence unit last week. I thought that was great and wanted to say thanks for stepping up to help even though you weren't required to.

Deputy Smith,
I just wanted to take a moment to thank you for your honest and candid feedback reference the new initiative. Too often, people withhold information needed to make the best decisions. What you demonstrated is what I want from everyone and is truly the only way that leads to excellence. We need commitment reinforced with this type of honesty and robust candid dialogue where we aren't afraid to challenge our thinking. Thanks again!

How hard is it to say thank you? How hard is it to let someone know you appreciate their efforts? When someone holds the door for us, we say, "Thank you!" When we sneeze, and someone says, "God Bless you," we say, "Thank you!" We don't even think about it. It's automatic. It's easy! It takes minimal effort. Yet, we too often take for granted the positive performance going on around us day in and day out, by our superstars, by our solid middle 70 percenters, and yes, even by our lower performers. Some people in leadership positions find it hard to say thank you. Others claim they aren't going to reward people for doing their jobs. But, if you don't recognize good work, you are a void in leadership, missing a great opportunity and limiting your organization's performance. Recognition for positive work reinforces positive work.

Spend time with your personnel, let them know you care and do not withhold praise, recognition, or appreciation when warranted. These are two exceedingly small things. Can these so-called "small things" really make a difference? Small things do matter because these small things are sometimes not so small after all!

Chapter 6

AN OUTDATED LEADERSHIP MODEL

David Marquet, a retired U.S. Navy Captain and author of *Turn the Ship Around!: A True Story of Turning Followers into Leaders,* stated, "When I served in the U.S. Navy, I had firsthand experience with an outdated leadership model. Here's what my Naval Academy leadership book told me about being a leader: 'Leadership is the art, science, or gift by which a person is enabled and privileged to direct the thoughts, plans, and actions of others in such a manner as to obtain and command their obedience, their confidence, their respect, and their loyal cooperation.' In other words, leadership in the Navy, and in most organizations, is about controlling people."[1]

Notice the definition of leadership presented here: the leader is to **direct the thoughts, plans, and actions** of others. Is standing over people, directing and controlling their every move, how we motivate our personnel? Is this from where outstanding performance originates? And notice, as the Naval Academy's definition of leadership concludes, it states it is the directing and controlling that will lead to their troop's loyal cooperation. Is controlling people what brings about their loyalty to their organizations?

How about the law enforcement agency? It is typically a bureaucratic, rule-following, and paramilitary organization too. What kind of leadership model or style do we find prevalent there?

We now find ourselves in the middle of an evolution regarding the leadership style most appropriate for today's law enforcement profession. When I started police work in the early 1990s, most leaders and supervisors probably

Note: Portions of the content for this chapter have been taken from a previous article in *Law Enforcement Executive Forum,* written by the author. Sections of the article have been reprinted with the permission of ILETSBEI. Excerpts from "Community Policing: What Style of Leadership Works?" by Dan D. Terry, 2015, 15(3) Copyright © 2015 by ILETSBEI; all rights reserved.

[1] Excerpt from TURN THE SHIP AROUND! A TRUE STORY OF TURNING FOLLOWERS INTO LEADERS by L. David Marquet, copyright © 2012 by L. David Marquet. Used by permission of Portfolio, an imprint of Penguin Publishing Group, a division of Penguin Random House LLC. All rights reserved.

held fast to the traditional command and control philosophy depicted in the above definition of leadership within the U.S. Navy. If any good work were to get done, it would be accomplished through practicing direct control over personnel and ensuring officers adhered to the numerous rules, regulations, and policies created to keep them under control.

However, during this time, our progressive chief questioned the wisdom of the traditional method of leadership and policing and began to move away from it. With the movement away from traditional policing practices, and our present emphasis on community policing, problem solving, and data-driven policing, we will find more and more leaders turning to a modern and more appropriate leadership style for today's policing environment. We are heading in the right direction, but those who hold fast to the traditional desire to control their people remain. Hence, among these, we will continue to find a leadership void.

David Marquet continues in the introduction to his book to say the following about the control-oriented, leader-follower way of doing business: "it has been so successful that it is both appealing and so hard to give up. But this model was developed during a period when mankind's primary work was physical. Consequently, it's optimized for extracting physical work from humans. In our modern world, the most important work we do is cognitive; so, it's not surprising that a structure developed for physical work isn't optimal for intellectual work. People who are treated as followers have the expectation of followers and act like followers. As followers, they have limited decision-making authority and little incentive to give the utmost of their intellect, energy, and passion. Those who take orders usually run at half speed, underutilizing their imagination and initiative."[2]

Today's policing environment is far too complex and technologically advanced to operate effectively in the outdated model of control and autocratic leadership. In days gone by, authoritarian leadership may have been more appropriate. The job of policing was less complex, the workforce was less educated, and many of the officers were hired by the local police force upon returning from military service in the Vietnam War. Moreover, the highly structured, top-down paramilitary autocratic organization was a comfortable place for many young police recruits to be. But today, we need more than just order takers to be successful. We need thinkers. Police work is different from the work of soldiers. Typically, soldiers work in groups with direct supervision. Police officers, on the other hand, frequently work alone or with a partner. A supervisor may be on duty, but most decisions are made without immediate input from a supervisor.

---

[2] Ibid.

The field of law enforcement needs self-motivated people willing to challenge the status quo to obtain true excellence within our law enforcement organizations. However, those who refuse or find it difficult to change and accept an updated leadership model will undoubtedly be limited in their abilities as a leader and supervisor, thus remaining a void in leadership.

In today's community policing environment, our call is to partner with the community to enhance community safety and problem-solving efforts. Though community policing is not a "one size fits all" strategy, and may look different in various communities, a problem-solving orientation is paramount to a claim of the existence of community policing within a given police organization. Though the evolution and full acceptance of community policing has not occurred overnight, a 2014 study by the Police Executive Research Forum showed that 94% of surveyed police agencies reported using the community policing strategy; 89% reported using problem-oriented policing.

The percentage of agencies reported using community policing and problem solving is encouraging. However, have these agencies made the appropriate corresponding organizational and leadership changes required to fully take advantage of what community policing and problem solving have to offer the police and their communities?

In the same Police Executive Research Forum study, 61% of respondents reported that their agencies would experiment with the traditional command and control organizational structures within the next two to five years.[3] Although it is possible that these reporting agencies were already in various levels of experimentation, it is implied that this 61% still needed to thoroughly examine how their organizational structure supports the more progressive policing strategies of community policing and problem solving. Will a void in leadership be found in these agencies? How effective can community policing be if police organizations are still adhering to the paramilitary hierarchical structure designed to control employees?

GOOD IDEAS; WHERE DO THEY COME FROM?

Where do good ideas come from? Empowered people, not controlled people!

As the police consider new alternatives in response to community problems and concerns, great ideas can be cultivated from both inside and outside the police organization. It is now reasonably clear that the person at the top of

[3] Police Executive Research Forum. (2014). *Future Trends in Policing.* Washington, D.C.: Office of Community Oriented Policing Services, p. 38.

the hierarchical structure cannot successfully make all the required decisions by themself. "The greatest untapped resource within any organization is its people's potential," and empowering employees can lead to more creativity and commitment.[4]

I had separate conversations with two members of my department. One of them was a sworn officer, and the other was a civilian and support employee responsible for the crime analysis function, which included tracking and reporting crime within the jurisdiction. Both individuals understood the importance of community policing and argued how increasing community engagement activities with the public could reduce and prevent crime. We frequently had informal discussions on the subject as they shared their ideas with me. Not only did they believe enhancing the organization's community engagement could reduce crime, but it also would substantially improve the community's satisfaction with the police department. If only we had a strong community engagement or crime prevention program, right? If only there were more support for such an initiative than just these two people, right? Wrong!

What they suggested and encouraged was no more than "Police Work 101." Unfortunately, most law enforcement professionals, especially those just beginning their careers, are typically interested and excited about the law enforcement function. This is the aspect of the job often seen in the media via TV, movies, fiction novels, etc. – the police chasing down and arresting the bad guys. Often, officers develop the mindset that crime prevention and meeting and interacting with the community is the soft stuff, not part of the job, and may show little interest in doing it.

Nonetheless, it is or should be just as much of the job as chasing the bad guys and the slew of other tasks required of the police. Police are required to perform many tasks unrelated to their law enforcement function, such as directing traffic, responding to medical emergencies, taking traffic crash reports, writing various types of reports, and responding to order maintenance type calls for service. So, my advice for these two individuals was to "get out and go do your job," which included creating community engagement and crime prevention opportunities.

At first, they wanted to start a new program. They wanted a program name. They wanted the administration's blessing in recognizing their new program and giving it legitimacy. But I strongly discouraged that. If we were to identify their new tasks and behaviors as a new program, the masses within the department would see it as such. A new program. A new fad. Something the administration was going to try and push down their throats. The masses would certainly think, "If we can just hold out long enough, this program

[4] International Association of Chiefs of Police. (2008). *Police Chiefs Desk Reference: A Guide for Newly Appointed Police Leaders,* 2nd Edition. McGraw Hill Learning Solutions, pp. 39-41.

will fade away, as so many others have done." Furthermore, rather than recognizing community engagement opportunities as part of the everyday police officer's job, they would be more inclined to see it as the job of those who were assigned to, or part of, the new community engagement program, further distancing themselves from the requirement of performing such tasks during their daily activities.

I wanted to avoid this mindset. Instead, I recommended going out and getting busy, quietly increasing the organization's community engagement. That's part of the job, "Police Work 101." Let's create a few successes, build upon those successes, and then have more successes. If we were successful, as I believed we would be, by the time anyone noticed the change in the organization, we would already have momentum in our favor. Slowly and quietly, the idea of enhanced community engagement, partnership, and crime prevention would integrate and evolve within the ranks of the police department. This was about all I did; I made a couple of suggestions. These two professionals took over and just got busy.

So, what can two empowered and committed people do to make positive change in an organization? First, the crime analyst looked at crime numbers every day. She saw what crimes were happening where. Who were the victims? What crimes were increasing? With this information, they both began to target specific community segments for attention.

During her regular patrol, the sworn officer would conduct "walk and talks," taking time to meet with community members and marketing the organization's desire and willingness to hold meetings and give presentations to the various groups, customizing the presentations to the needs of the intended audience (see Figure 4). She started to schedule numerous presentations, beginning with the elderly population, as financial crimes and scams against the elderly were increasing. As they conducted these presentations, other community members would hear of it and reach out to schedule their own crime prevention presentation. And the successes began to add up. Articles started showing up in the local newspaper about the crime prevention presentations. Part of the article included who and where to call if others in the community were interested in a crime prevention meeting with the police department. So, even more presentations were scheduled, and the program, which wasn't really a program to begin with, continued to grow.

Figure 4. The award-winning Neighborhood Roll Call. Another community engagement opportunity where the police meet with residents in their neighborhood to share ideas and information with the goal of addressing the needs of the community.

The elderly population was a big audience that these two employees sought out. Others included college students, young Latino females, bank employees, specific neighborhood groups, church groups, scouting groups, and bike rodeos. Rather than wait for a request to come into the police department about a group desiring a police officer to talk at their event, these two individuals sought out community members for engagement opportunities. In addition, they created numerous crime prevention pamphlets, customizing them for various types of crimes or unique types of crime victims.

During the winter holidays, when we often saw an increase in late-night store robberies, a robbery-specific pamphlet was created, informing would-be victims what to do, what not to do, and how to be a better witness. These pamphlets were then delivered directly to those businesses more likely to be targeted for a robbery, which also provided the opportunity for face-to-face communication.

These two employees also wrote crime prevention articles, which were submitted to the local newspaper and city mailings. In addition, they worked with the city government to include crime prevention pamphlets inside the city water bills mailed to residents. We also began to look for citizens who deserved recognition for their proactive behavior in helping others. For example, someone who went out of their way to help another person, whether they were injured or had a disabled vehicle, or someone who had been a great witness to a crime that occurred. If it was worthy of recognition, we were now paying better attention to ensure citizens were recognized. As a result, letters from the chief were being sent to these citizens, more so than they had been previously. And the community took notice.

The brilliance of this initiative and its success came from the fact that these two employees were empowered to act. This was their initiative. They were allowed to run it and schedule it as they liked. I asked them to keep me informed of the ongoing activities, which were recorded on a spreadsheet. They documented past and upcoming events, which I could monitor on my own time without bothering them. If they could not handle a specific scheduled event, they had the freedom to find another officer to cover it for them. They knew which officers were prone to take this seriously, be interested, and do a good job. They worked with these officers every day. I was solely there as a sounding board and occasionally ran interference if they needed help covering an event or activity. I would work with other supervisors asking for help from their shift or work group if required. I also was the go-to guy when money was needed to finance their activities.

As the initiative grew, they began to raffle off or use prizes for those in the audience who spoke up and participated in the presentation. The chosen prizes were creative and often were representative of the specific crime prevention discussion they were having. For example, some of the prizes consisted of small engraving pens so people could engrave their personal information on their tools in the event their tools were stolen. Another prize was a fanny pack that the older population could wear to keep their identification, money, or credit cards on their person while in the grocery store, instead of having a purse in the shopping cart for a would-be thief to steal.

Other officers began approaching these two employees inquiring about the various extra crime prevention tasks they were involved in. Most of the inquirers believed the administration and supervisors were directing these two to complete the various assignments related to the initiative. Once they discovered that wasn't the case, but instead that these two employees were working on their own initiative, more officers also showed interest in participating in the community engagement initiative. As a result, the core group of involved officers increased, helping the organization engage with more of the community.

So, what did these two empowered, creative, and committed employees accomplish? In the year this community engagement initiative took place, the organization made 92 presentations reaching about 3,000 people. These numbers are specific to group presentations and don't include people who were met one-on-one or those who received pamphlets or recognition letters, etc. In addition, the organizational involvement in the initiative increased, growing from the original two employees to more than 25, who, in one way or another, participated in providing community engagement services during the year.

Did the increase in community engagement reduce or prevent crime? I don't know. There are too many variables on what causes and prevents crime, and unfortunately, the duration of the community engagement initiative was too short to draw any conclusions in that area. However, based on my experience and feedback, the police department was getting noticed and getting positive publicity. In addition, the community was happy with the increased service they were receiving.

Unfortunately, as new leadership took over the organization, the responsibility for community presentations was removed from those two committed employees. As previously stated, the brilliance of this initiative was the ownership and empowerment given to those two employees. People want to have a say so in the work that affects them. Unfortunately, additional steps, red tape, bureaucracy, and control were added, with all community engagement requests having to go through a supervisor first for scheduling and assignment. I encouraged the administration not to do this. They were holding to an outdated leadership model that doesn't work effectively with today's workforce. I predicted that taking away the empowerment and ownership these two committed employees had would be the downfall of the initiative. It had been their initiative. The success and glory were theirs as the initiative grew and more officers participated. I had done nothing besides support them and be their cheerleader.

Being required to get approval for every move and losing initiative over the program, they lost momentum, and their involvement eventually fizzled out. The year following the initiative showed a significant drop in community engagement services, with only 21 presentations reaching about 500 people. Besides the morale of these employees, who suffered? The community did, losing a great resource and relationship with the police. However, I am happy to say that at the time of this writing, several years later, this police department appears to have again enhanced its community engagement activities and programs to an increased level. Hopefully, this will again allow these two employees to utilize their strengths and do what they do best, for the community will be better for it.

As leaders of law enforcement organizations, we cannot take the organization to the next level by ourselves. We need help finding solutions and solving community problems. We need to empower others to help us reach these goals, and that does not happen if we cling to the outdated leadership model meant to control and not empower our people. One of my favorite leadership quotes by D. Michael Abrashoff, another Navy Captain, is, "if all you give are orders, then all you will get are order takers."[5]

PROBLEM SOLVING

We need problem solvers, but problem solvers aren't found in the outdated leadership model that aims at controlling employees. The idea of problem solving implies creativity. A problem must be analyzed, data gathered, alternatives created and considered, and a decision on the best approach made. This may entail trying new approaches, thinking "outside the box," and using non-law enforcement resources and partnerships. When it comes to community problems, officers working in those communities are in a better position to understand the various dynamics of the problem. They may have a more accurate picture of the problem than those higher on the organizational chart. When considering alternatives to a given problem, the input of those closest to the problem, who know of it, should be involved.

It is likely that officers working the street have already responded to and have experience with a given problem under analysis. They may be familiar with the location of a given problem or the people involved. They may also know where they can turn to find information that will help them best analyze and create alternatives to addressing the problem. Community policing involves officers working the streets and becoming creative problem solvers through increased use of discretion and responsibility.

We had a new bar open in the downtown area. This added to the several other drinking establishments in the downtown area, all within walking distance of each other. This new bar, however, was being marketed for a younger crowd, specifically the college-aged group, as there was a college just a couple blocks away. Shortly after this bar opened, we began to receive more calls for service reference fights and disturbances in and around this bar. The bar's surrounding area also began to deteriorate, with increased trash littered about, mostly liquor containers, and some signs of drug use. Reports of drug use in vehicles and calls of people urinating in the neighborhood were being made. The most significant complaints about the activities of this bar came from residents of a condominium building that sat directly across the street. The residents were increasingly calling about noise and disturbances from the bar. We were not getting the same number of calls and complaints about the other bars in the downtown area as frequently as this bar. There was a

[5] From *It's Your Ship by* D. M. Abrashoff, copyright © 2002. Reprinted by permission of Grand Central Publishing, an imprint of Hachette Book Group, Inc., p. 107.

new problem in our community that would fall on the police for intervention, like other problems that creep up in communities nationwide.

The solution to this problem would require a coordinated and cooperative approach involving multiple persons in and outside the law enforcement organization. This was not something the police chief or even the patrol sergeant in charge of policing activities in the area of this bar would resolve alone. They would need the minds and commitment of those officers assigned to the area familiar with the various dynamics involved, having responded to the numerous calls at this location. They knew and saw what the issues were. As time went on, they would better understand what responses or interventions would work and what would not. There were also outside stakeholders whose input and assistance were important to the issue.

Law enforcement met with the bar management so they understood the issues and complaints. A cooperative relationship would be a win-win for both sides. The bar management and employees could help law enforcement solve the problem, demonstrating themselves as good stewards of their liquor license while preventing any necessity for additional attention from law enforcement and the city liquor commission by an unwillingness to cooperate.

The bar management was given contact information, which enabled them to report any issues or concerns and ask questions directly to the midnight shift patrol supervisor. The bar reorganized the physical structure and plan for the bar. The main entrance and outside beer garden had been in front of the bar, directly facing the condominiums across the street. The primary entrance and beer garden were moved to the rear of the building, utilizing the front door as a fire exit only. This would reduce the significant amount of noise heard by the residents of the condominium complex. The bar management also agreed to install and utilize sound reduction windows, which would reduce the sound and music heard by the neighborhood.

Law enforcement began increased bar checks on the establishment. They also increased patrols of the area utilizing traditional marked and unmarked police vehicles and undercover and bicycle officers who could quickly get into more secluded and challenging areas without detection. As a result, arrests in and around the bar increased, including for the following offenses: driving while intoxicated, open alcohol, being drunk in public, consumption of alcohol by minors, minors on licensed premises, drugs, damage to property, disorderly conduct for fights and disturbances, and charges for public urination.

At first, arrests were being made constantly. They were easy, like taking candy from a baby or fishing from a barrel. But, as the word spread of the numerous arrests and the increased police presence around the bar, crime, and arrests dropped, demonstrating some level of success.

This first phase of minimizing problems in the neighborhood during open bar hours was successful. However, the second phase of problems was found to be more challenging. The calls of service for disturbances and excess noise at the closing time increased, and the patience of the complaining residents from the condominiums across the street decreased. At closing time, it was not uncommon for a couple of hundred people to pile out of the bar into the streets. Intoxicated, they yelled and talked loudly as each drunken individual, wanting to be heard, tried to speak over the next person. Not wanting to call it a night, many tried to hang out on the sidewalk and keep their evening going as long as possible. Then there would be the revving of car engines, honking of horns, and squealing of tires. Some would try to leave the bar with a drink in hand, and the occasional fight in the street would also start.

Initially, we found that having an officer presence outside the bar at closing time was the best way to keep order. When officers were present, they would remind bar patrons to be quiet, keep them out of the roadway, keep them moving and not congregating outside the bar, and were a deterrent for potential fights. If patrons wouldn't go with the program or insist on yelling, screaming, or participating in other law violations, officers would take enforcement action, as required.

We learned that one of the dynamics that kept these loud drunken patrons congregating in the area after closing time was the insufficient amount of taxi cabs. There just were not enough of them. As a result, we would see the same taxi driver pick up a patron, leave, and return for additional patrons, who would still be standing around, being loud and a nuisance to the community. In addition, patrons were competing for the same taxi. The winters in Chicago can be brutally cold. Combine that with fifty drunks standing outside waiting for a few cabs. One person might call and schedule a taxi, but upon seeing the approaching taxi from blocks away, the masses would make a mad rush down the street to get to the taxi first. This culminated in many drunks impeding traffic while yelling at the taxi driver and fighting each other over who got to leave first.

We worked with the city to create a taxi stand outside the bar on a side street. Signs were posted, designating the area as only for taxi cabs during this time of the night. We maintained our police presence at closing time and limited taxi pickups to this area only. They were not allowed to load or unload passengers in the middle of the street. Patrons were not allowed to walk in the roadway or down the street and sidewalk to flag down a taxi. The only way to get a taxi was to line up and wait at the newly created taxi stand. The taxi drivers didn't take long to catch on and follow the new procedures. The intoxicated patrons took a little longer to comprehend the new system. But after waiting out in the cold for an extended time or being the last person to get a taxi, they understood what was in their best interest, which was following the rules.

After contacting the various taxi companies and explaining the problems and concerns, more taxis were dispatched to the bar area at closing. This was a win-win situation, as we got the intoxicated patrons off the street quicker, and the taxi companies obtained more fares. So, as closing time approached, taxi cabs started to line up at the taxi stand, awaiting the crowd to pour out of the bar. As a result, we were able to move a significant number of people from the area quicker, thus increasing the bar patrons' safety while at the same time reducing the noise and nuisance for the residents living in the area.

As part of this problem-solving effort, I would routinely meet with the identified liaison from the condominium association representing the concerns of the residents living there. He was given my direct contact information to contact me with questions or concerns. In addition, he would frequently update me on the various problem nights and behaviors he observed from intoxicated bar patrons. Just as often, he would also recognize and acknowledge the efforts of the police trying to reduce or eliminate the nuisance behavior stemming from the bar. Unfortunately, we could not successfully eradicate all of the noise and inappropriate behavior associated with the bar. However, we did make a significant difference and reduced crime and disturbances related to the bar. In addition, the residents saw their police force present and trying hard to improve their quality of life, promoting a positive community-police relationship.

The point of this story is that no one person could have done this alone. It required multiple members of the police department, supervisors, and the rank and file responsible for getting the job done. The problem-solving efforts also involved bar employees and management, neighborhood residents who were the customers we were trying to serve, and who possessed needed information referencing the characteristics of the problem at hand. In addition, the city government, the liquor commission, and the city's streets division were necessary, as were the taxi cab companies and their drivers.

When numerous minds, experiences, and perceptions come together to share the responsibility for community policing, the potential for enhancing an organization's problem-solving capabilities is present. Community policing and problem solving require experimenting and trying the non-traditional to find the best solution to a given community's crime and quality of life issues. These multiple minds coming together to analyze and look for solutions to the community problems of the day are more likely to find the right and lasting solutions. We need thinkers, the minds and hearts of our personnel giving to the cause willingly and not out of the fear or intimidation often displayed among the leaders practicing tight control of all aspects of the job.

You want an organization full of something other than Daniel Terrys. Indeed, I believe I have some strengths that make a difference in the law enforcement community. However, there are multiple areas where my knowledge and skills could be stronger. If you have an organization full of Daniel Terrys, your organization will fail. Required competence, skills, and know-how needed for success in today's complex and high-tech law enforcement organization will be lacking. No one person can excel or master all aspects of policing. Therefore, tapping into the strengths, experiences, and resources of others is a must. Today's most significant problems in society, such as homelessness, drug addiction, mental illness, and domestic violence, require multiple perspectives from both inside and outside the police organization if there is to be any chance for success in resolving these complex issues.

Not only does empowering employees lead to more creativity, but also greater commitment. Employee commitment is an essential component in effectively responding to the communities they serve. The success of today's policing strategies does not rely solely on the quality of the decisions made but also upon execution and how well decisions are implemented. Unfortunately, many good plans have failed due to poor implementation that resulted from the lack of employee commitment. Are employees afraid to make decisions for fear of making mistakes and suffering belittlement or discipline from their leader? Are mistakes made in good faith allowed? Are employees comfortable speaking up and sharing dissenting views? Can they disagree with their leader, or is blind compliance of the "yes man" rewarded? How an organization answers these questions can significantly affect employee commitment and, subsequently, how successful their policing efforts will be. Additionally, the leadership style utilized within the law enforcement agency may dramatically affect how the organization answers those questions.

The police are typically individuals who come to the job with personal characteristics consistent with that required to carry out the police function in society. They are strong-willed, passionate, action and control oriented. Take their passion for control and action away by refusing to acknowledge and appreciate their ideas and contributions, and you eliminate their sense of value and worth, leading to the unfortunate frustration and cynicism too frequently found in the police culture. Commitment to decisions and the decision-making process can be increased when other's viewpoints are considered. The traditional autocratic organizational structure can stifle rather than encourage open communication and problem solving.

I have been blessed to have worked with some great professionals. They have made me look good again and again. The truth is I've often found myself standing around during a significant or critical event doing not much of anything. The personnel who worked for me would routinely show up, take charge of a given incident, make appropriate decisions and get the job done well. I would look like a superstar, my supervisors would commend me later on a job well done, and I reaped the benefits of working with intelligent, professional, competent people. This was frequently the case because I would routinely give everyone a voice. I strived to create an environment where people could share their ideas and opinions and even disagree with the boss if done respectfully. Because I tried to practice this daily under normal non-stressful operations, it often carried over into emergency situations.

Now make no mistake, although I ascribe to the participatory leadership model in most environments, there isn't always time for consensus or getting everyone's opinion in an emergency. It can be appropriate to use a more autocratic controlling leadership style during a critical incident, as these emergency conditions are more consistent with military operations where life and death are at stake. Decisions must be made quickly, and there isn't always time for explanation. Therefore, we must have personnel who will do what is necessary to accomplish the mission without delay. However, when you allow and encourage everyone to have a voice and to share their ideas, and then give credit to them for their excellent ideas and problem-solving efforts during typical day-to-day operations, it has been my experience that they will respond more confidently during times of stress.

Suppose you start barking orders at your personnel during a critical incident, such as responding to an officer-involved shooting or a barricaded person shooting from their home. In that case, your personnel will read your behavior, demeanor, speech, and body language and decide appropriately whether they need to take orders and act without question or whether it is safe to share their thoughts and ideas or ask questions. This response from your personnel works if you have already made the appropriate number of investments into the Emotional Bank Account with your people. In other words, you, the leader, are trusted by your personnel. They may, even under emergency conditions, have something important to contribute. I've always told those working for me, "If you see I'm about to drive the ship into the iceberg, I want you to speak up. Don't just stand there or quietly tip-toe away for your life jacket as I sink the ship." If this is routinely reinforced through your leadership style, your personnel will be more comfortable and confident to speak up when appropriate. This does not work for the leader practicing the outdated autocratic leadership style that controls people and wants people to do what is ordered without question.

There have been countless incidents where I have taken charge of a critical or at least a serious event. I have generated a plan, made assignments, given orders, and then a subordinate came up with a better idea or something I hadn't considered. For example, I may be sitting at the command post working on setting up a perimeter around a residential neighborhood where a burglar is running loose and hiding when an officer sends me a suggestion on my patrol car's Mobile Data Terminal (MDT). It is a brilliant suggestion that I immediately put into action, and it gets us results. I have had tactical thinking officers provide recommendations in the early moments of a barricaded person call of putting a react team together in case the barricaded person decided to walk out on their own without notice. "Great idea, that slipped my mind." Realistically, when under stress, one person isn't going to think of or remember everything. I might even tell that tactical-minded officer with the good idea to put the react team together himself. "Identify who will be on the team, devise a plan, and report back," I may tell him. I have given him credit for the great idea and empowered him to give even more. I've had officers come up to me during an operation and say, "I know you said we were going to do 'A, B, & C,' and we will do that, but what do you think about D & E?" And, I immediately say, "No, D & E is a better idea. Scratch my plan; we are doing it your way." And again, I get positive results.

Unfortunately, I have also seen just the opposite. Officers with great ideas that might get positive results and end an incident successfully. Still, they say nothing because they fear the response they might get from the supervisor who routinely practices the outdated autocratic leadership model.

Today's employee desires more input into their work. They seek involvement and challenges, are more likely to question decisions, and are less prone to accept orders just for the sake of them being orders. Ironically, the characteristics of the new employee may be more conducive to community and problem-solving policing. They are independent, desire responsibility, seek challenges, and want to be involved in the decisions that affect them. The challenge is for police leaders to inspire this group towards commitment to the organization by realigning and stepping away from the autocratic leadership of the past towards a leadership style more consistent with the principles of community and problem-solving policing, one of participation, facilitating, and coaching.

One of the most significant challenges to community policing is transitioning from the traditional leadership style designed to control employees to a more participatory leadership style. Modern police strategies, such as community policing and problem solving, are better suited with an employee-oriented participatory leadership style versus the autocratic controlling style of the past. However, this is easier said than done. Like a child who grows to accept and demonstrate the same values and behaviors as those of their parents, those of us who came up in the law enforcement organization practicing the autocratic "Do it because I said so" mentality are likely to follow through and continue with those same leadership tactics. After all, this is what we know!

But remember, compliance is not the same as commitment. The behavior of committed employees will differ from merely compliant employees. The police leader can force compliance. The autocratic leader can demand that tasks be carried out. They can further ensure that such tasks are carried out by force, coercion, punishment, discipline, and even termination. The committed employee, however, voluntarily gives their heart and mind to the good of the organization. Their choice is to truly accept the organization's mission, go above and beyond, and sacrifice for the organization. Commitment cannot be forced.

To foster a climate where proactive problem solving and creativity flourish requires an organizational environment conducive to such. Therefore, leaders must actively look for and encourage employees to speak up and participate in dialogue concerning department matters, specifically regarding an officer's duties and interaction with the community. In other words, the leader must emphasize a more participatory leadership style. In addition, leaders must support the idea of "psychological safety," a climate where a group believes it is safe for interpersonal risk-taking, speaking up, and not being punished. When such a belief exists, employees are more likely to share their knowledge and experience and commit themselves to the organization's mission and community policing and problem-solving efforts.

Those in leadership/supervisory positions are responsible for growing, developing, and motivating those beneath them in the organizational hierarchy. Therefore, they must set a suitable climate to motivate employees. Unfortunately, the traditional autocratic leadership style frequently found within police organizations can have the opposite effect and is contrary to what is required to carry out the community policing strategy. The autocratic leader who closely directs, controls, and does not allow decision-making by officers can lead to an environment where motivation and hence responsiveness to the community is lacking. Whether the majority considers you a good or poor leader is primarily determined by your leadership style. Are you holding to the outdated autocratic leadership model meant to control people or a modern one meant to empower and get the best from people?

We will continue exploring this idea in the next section on Driving Performance, starting with the importance of creating an environment for success.

Section Two

DRIVING PERFORMANCE

I have titled Section Two of this book, Driving Performance. Such a goal is certainly worthwhile, if not an expectation, for any law enforcement leader, whether chief or sheriff, responsible for an entire organization or first-line supervisor overseeing a single work group. A quality performance is essential; the greater the performance, the better off the agency or community will be.

This section follows that of "The Leadership Void" for a simple reason, not understanding the traps found in the leadership void and not eliminating, or at least minimizing, those voids will directly interfere with one's ability to drive performance. The ideas and suggestions made in Section Two do not work well, and are virtually impossible to achieve, if a leader has not first examined themself and committed to being a true leader, a person who puts the organization and its people above themself.

So, you have committed to being the best leader you can be. You recognize you are not perfect and will struggle with leadership voids occasionally, but you are prepared to re-examine yourself, improve continuously, and recognize and avoid the traps that hold back your effectiveness as a leader. Now what?

Based on my experience and observations, several concepts and behaviors will significantly increase the ability of your organization or work group to perform better. These include:

- Creating a work environment more conducive to success. An environment where people are the priority and commitment is the norm versus mere compliance.
- Making the effort to get to know your people – those you lead, their strengths, weaknesses, and interests, and then give them opportunities to do what they do best.

- Recognizing the importance of relationships and building the positive relationships needed for success. You cannot do it alone. The job is just too complex.
- Identify what is important to the organization, ensure everyone knows it, and reward those who get it done.
- Do not assume the things that are supposed to be done are getting done. Instead, stay involved, follow up relentlessly, and create processes that reinforce accountability.

Chapter 7

AN ENVIRONMENT FOR SUCCESS

I was fortunate to work with and supervise many great work groups, including patrol shifts, detective divisions, and specialty groups. Of course, as personnel come and go from a given work group through new hires, retirement, transfers, and promotions, the dynamics of said groups tend to change also, even if only so slightly. Nevertheless, I appreciate and am proud of the relationships built within all those groups and their performance. However, probably the most successful work group I've supervised so far, in terms of high levels of performance and positive attitudes about their performance and service provided, was the detective division I ran in 2016. They were a fun and effective group that seemed to get things done, made it look easy, and shared many laughs along the way.

After a successful 2016, I met with this group of detectives in January 2017 to review the previous year's results and performance. My first question was, "Were we effective in 2016?" I already knew the answer. We had a great year. I believe that in 2016 we successfully cleared every robbery case we had, which was almost unheard of, and there were many other highlights to go along with that. I believed I knew the answer but wanted to hear from them. What did they think? They concurred and gave numerous examples of why we were effective in 2016.

The next question, however, was the important one. The why? I had some instinctual gut-feeling ideas about why we might have succeeded but did not necessarily have a solid understanding. Why were we effective? Why were we so successful that year? Why did the performance of this group stand above that of other groups I had supervised, those I would also characterize as successful? I took notes as we discussed, and the detectives responded to that question by providing me with their opinions on what made them successful. At the end of the meeting, having documented their feedback, I wrote **"Dynamics of Success and Effectiveness"** at the top of my page of notes.

I never imagined I'd ever use those notes in the future for a book such as this. But here it is! The title I gave my page of notes, Dynamics of Success and Effectiveness, evolves into the foundation and title for this chapter, An Environment for Success. These are the words of those detectives when asked "why we were successful in 2016." These are their words, not mine:

- The group had diverse talents and experiences.
- They worked towards each other's strengths and compensated for each other's weaknesses.
- They had a good blend of experience.
- They had a good amount of workplace antics and humor.
- The unit (group) came before the individual.
- They possessed a "low ego" amongst each other (versus with members of other groups where their ego could be much more robust).
- All cases were unit cases, not just individual detective cases. Therefore, solving every case was important to all members of the unit.
- They possessed a common drive to do the right thing and remember what they were in business for.
- They possessed self-discipline, addressing deficiencies among themselves (rather than relying on supervisors and command to solve and handle their problems).
- The more experienced investigators took responsibility for developing the less experienced/skilled investigators.

Compare this list to the characteristics business executives and managers have identified as those possessed by high-performing teams that have "caught fire" and "outdone themselves" regarding their collaborated performance:[1]

- daunting challenge or noble mission
- intense group loyalty
- diverse range of talents
- trust and selfless collaboration
- focus and passion
- intrinsically fun and rewarding work

Sound familiar? Let's look again at the list provided by the detectives of 2016 and see how they compare, as they just may have been on to something:

[1] Excerpt(s) from *Working with Emotional Intelligence* by Daniel Goleman, copyright © 1998 by Daniel Goleman, pp. 227-229. Used by permission of Bantam Books, an imprint of Random House, a division of Penguin Random House LLC. All rights reserved.

- The group had diverse talents and experiences **(diverse range of talents)**.
- They worked towards each other's strengths and compensated for each other's weaknesses **(diverse range of talents)**.
- They had a good blend of experience **(diverse range of talents)**.
- They had a good amount of workplace antics and humor **(intrinsically fun and rewarding work)**.
- The unit (group) came before the individual **(intense group loyalty)**.
- They possessed a "low ego" amongst each other (versus with members of other groups where their ego could be much more robust) **(trust and selfless collaboration)**.
- All cases were unit cases, not just individual detective cases. Solving every case was important to all members of the unit. **(daunting challenge or noble mission)**.
- They possessed a common drive to do the right thing and remember what they were in business for **(focus and passion)**.
- They possessed self-discipline, addressing deficiencies among themselves (rather than relying on supervisors and command to solve and handle their problems) **(trust and selfless collaboration)**.
- The more experienced investigators took responsibility for developing the less experienced/skilled investigators **(trust and selfless collaboration)**.

Looking at this list provided by this group of detectives, these attitudes and behaviors are more likely the result and positive consequences of working in an environment created for success rather than the actual characteristics or elements that caused success. This is what it looks like when you have a successful environment, but how do you get there? What causes this successful environment?

It is the duty of a supervisor, manager, chief executive, the leader to reflect upon and seek out the factors and leadership behaviors that will foster the type of environment that will result in this level of performance. What decisions or changes can a leader make to develop and encourage positive behavior and attitudes like those exhibited by the detectives of 2016?

We are not going to identify all the possibilities and answers to that question in this chapter. However, I think we can consider the above list and glean some insight into some characteristics that would lead to this type of effective behavior and attitude, at least characteristics that have worked well for me in most instances.

This group of detectives came up with this list to explain their success and effectiveness and summarized their success as that of **team chemistry**.

The rest of this chapter will explore several suggestions to enhance the work environment and **team chemistry**. These are my opinions on the above list, why this group of detectives was effective, and why they performed as they did. These same suggestions have also served me well in achieving positive levels of performance in other work groups I've had the opportunity to work with. So why did the detectives answer the question the way they did?

If I had to summarize the remainder of this chapter and the success of this group of detectives, it would be to remind all leaders that **we are dealing with human beings, so let them be human!**

We are all human, not programmable robots. We have feelings and emotions. Although we have different values, interests, and characteristics that make us unique, we all desire to do well, to be liked and accepted, to feel valued and important, and make a difference.

DIVERSE TALENTS, STRENGTHS, AND WEAKNESSES

The first two comments on the list were having diverse talents and experiences and being mindful of how you utilize and compensate for personnel's strengths and weaknesses. These are important in a leader's desire to drive performance. This topic will be temporarily put on hold as it will be covered in greater detail in the next chapter.

HAVING ALL BASES COVERED

Having a good blend of experience is also essential. Having people with various abilities and strengths that complement each other will strengthen a work group. For a detective division, it is nice to have some detectives who are experts and skilled in interrogation and others well versed in forensic services or information technology. Then there are financial, cyber, and sex crimes that take a particular type of person with a mind for these investigations to excel. Some detective personalities make them prone to like hot calls. They jump on a hot case, maybe a violent crime, work it hard and heavily when the leads are fresh, hopefully make an arrest, and then move on to the next big case. They get bored quickly.

Enjoying the work of hot calls was the habit of one of the best detectives I have known. However, he didn't enjoy the longer detailed work of financial crimes, which included: following the money, submitting various court orders, waiting months for the results, and then scouring over the records trying to make sense of them. His mind didn't work well that way. So, having that detailed person who enjoys such investigations on your team is undoubtedly a blessing.

The same might be said for homicide and sex cases. Some people do not have the stomach for those but are great at investigating and solving property cases. Of course, it does not mean that you won't be involved in these types of cases from time to time. Still, it does make a difference when you have a diverse group of personnel with skill sets that complement each other and can effectively cover all, or at least most, of the roles required within a detective division. "A strong team brings to the collaboration skills, knowledge, and experience to deliver...and in any team, you need a mix of people with different strengths and characteristics."[2]

How might this look in other areas of the law enforcement organization? First, there are SWAT officers, and then there are good officers who perform well in some environments but should never be SWAT officers. I always believed the D.A.R.E. Program (Drug Abuse Resistance Education) was good. Regardless of whether it reduced drug use, I thought it was an excellent opportunity for the police to interact and build positive relationships with the community, especially with our youth. However, as much as I supported the program, I was grateful other officers enjoyed and lived for that work because I didn't want anything to do with it. I did not have the patience to teach young children. My skills were better used in the field, finding bad guys and making arrests.

As the captain of investigations, I preferred dealing with people and people problems, trying to coach and motivate personnel, help them excel, and see a greater vision of what could be with the right attitude and effort. I didn't get excited about ordering cars and uniforms or researching equipment. Fortunately, the lieutenant I worked with was incredibly detailed and didn't mind such work. He would create spreadsheets and keep track of everything, including assigned equipment, car assignments, training, forfeiture cases, the use of division funds, etc. Together we got things done and made a good team, as his strengths and interests complemented my weaknesses. Today, as the chief of police, I'm again grateful to have such a person on my team that compensates for my weaknesses.

As a leader, if you can choose your personnel and fill capability gaps in your work group with people possessing the skills and experiences needed to complete your work group, this certainly can increase the effectiveness of the group or organization. But there are other keys to success.

I would caution you; leaders should always look for performance gaps and means of filling them, but it isn't enough. You may have a group with a great

---

[2] Excerpt(s) from *Collaborate Or Perish! Reaching Across Boundaries in A Networked* World by William Bratton, 2012 by William Bratton and Zachary Tumin, p. 171. Used by permission of Crown Business, an imprint of Random House, a division of Penguin Random House LLC. All rights reserved.

blend of experiences, but having a significant amount of knowledge and skills is just the first part of the equation.

The second required part, and most important, comes down to attitude, teamwork, and a person's commitment to use said experiences and skills for the common good of the organization. This is clearly seen in the detectives' list describing their success. I have known officers with excellent skills, but their egos were so strong that they couldn't get along with others. If they weren't in the spotlight or getting recognition for a significant arrest or case, they wanted nothing to do with the matter.

For example, I was involved in a situation in which I located a car wanted for its involvement in a crime just minutes prior. I announced over the radio that I had found the car and was following it, but I was waiting for backup and looking for the best and safest location to make the stop. As I continued following the vehicle and calling out my location, another officer, whose priority was personal recognition over teamwork and bringing this criminal to justice, quickly and abruptly pulled out of a parking lot in front of me, cutting me off. The officer squeezed his patrol car between mine and the wanted vehicle so he could immediately make the traffic stop and arrest him. It was so important to this officer that he gets the "collar" (good arrest) that he was willing to risk an accident between two patrol vehicles, not to mention the unsafe maneuver carried out in a heavily traveled area for the public to see. This officer wanted to be number one, and no other place was acceptable to them. Who wants to work with this guy?

These egomaniacs, even with their incredible skills and potential, isolate themselves and limit their capabilities. We can often train, teach skills, and provide personnel experiences. Still, it is difficult to change a person's negative attitude and almost impossible to fix someone with poor ethics and integrity. Hire, select, and promote those with the right attitude and work ethic. And then, if their experience and skill sets are correct, use them to fill your capability gaps, and you will strengthen the environment that leads towards success. A well-versed organization full of personnel with complementary skills and experiences can help, but it isn't enough. What else is needed?

SMILE AND HAVE SOME FUN

The group of detectives I talked to about their success and effectiveness identified "workplace antics and humor" as one of the characteristics of their success. At first, you might think, what does this have to do with being effective at their work? But I think it deserves at least some consideration. If people enjoy coming to work, you will get better work out of them. If they enjoy their work group, like their peers, and get to have some fun at work, this will be reflected in their performance. Compare that to the person who hates work, hates the people they work with, and dreads getting up and going to the office every day. Do you expect to find a successful and effective environment in a group of these people?

The group of detectives I supervised in 2016, much like most of the groups I had the opportunity to work with, took some time for a bit of fun and shared some laughs. Practical jokes were the norm. I am not encouraging any joking that would be considered racist, sexist, or harassing, as this should never be accepted or tolerated within a professional law enforcement agency. But over the years, I have been on both sides of many practical jokes, the victim of some and the originator of others. There are enough good ones that I could fill up a few extra chapters of this book (see Figure 5).

Figure 5. Midnight shift patrol – what a great group of officers. Probably the most fun on the job I ever had.

The detectives I supervised would often start their day over coffee and share some laughs by telling old war stories, kidding around, or playing jokes on each other. However, these fun encounters, informal discussions, and meetings over coffee were also peppered with much good work, ideas on handling cases, and problem solving. Unfortunately, the leaders practicing the old, outdated leadership model might frown on encouraging personnel to take some time for fun and laughs. They may see it as wasted time that could be spent in the field working cases or patrolling the neighborhood.

Indeed, there are limits to the time spent in fun and folly. Of course, we must be responsive and respectful of the resources, time, and money the taxpayers provide. But we miss an excellent opportunity for building teamwork and camaraderie within our organizations, trying to outlaw any fun. Still today, a day of work doesn't go by where I don't get a good laugh, often at my expense or that of my peers.

Laughter lightens the day. It makes the difficulties and challenges of work easier to cope with. It fosters a stronger and more positive relationship with my peers, which may help when at any given moment, one of us may be called to jeopardize our life for the other. Law enforcement gets to deal with the ugly side of life, and a smile and laugh with your work group here and there reminds you that you are not alone; you are surrounded by law enforcement brothers and sisters who care, and that can make the ugliness a little more palatable. "Groups that have fun together, enjoy being in each other's company, can joke together and share good times, have the emotional capital [Emotional Bank Account] not just to excel during good times, but to get through hard times too. Groups that don't share this emotional bond are more likely to become paralyzed, dysfunctional, or disintegrate under pressure."[3] (see Figure 6)

When I arrived at the sheriff's office, I found a sterile environment within the Criminal Investigation Division. This was one of the first significant observations that told me the working environment needed improvement. I was used to daily laughter and banter back and forth between detectives because they were having fun and enjoyed working with one another. At the police department, it had not been unusual to come into the office to find someone had somehow tampered with your office. Being an Alabama Crimson Tide fan, I showed up for work the day after the Clemson Tigers beat Alabama in the National Championship Game in January 2017 to find my office decorated heavily with Clemson Tiger paw prints. Someone, or several people, took the time and energy to print, cut out and then decorate my office with those paw prints. Why would they do that? Because the work group liked each other, it was fun. It would be even funnier when they saw my face when I walked into the office the day after my team, which I was so proud of, took a beating (for the record, it wasn't much of a beating, Alabama lost 35-31).

More recently, I arrived to work to find a poster-sized canvas print of me hanging on the wall of the police department. It was a photograph taken from

[3] Daniel Goleman, *Working with Emotional Intelligence,* p. 212.

Figure 6. The detectives of 2016 often took time for fun and laughter. But when it was time to get down to business, make no mistake, they took care of business, and they did it well.

a TV crime show I appeared in during the 90s. They had learned of my TV appearance from someone other than myself and thought it would be funny and somewhat of a surprise when I found it gracing the department wall. Who would do these things?

Would someone who hated work, disliked their work group, or dreaded coming into the office have done this? I don't think so! It takes tremendous energy for those who dislike their job just to get to work. Then once there, they will be more inclined to participate in grumbling and complaining. I do not see this person taking extra personal time to cut out Clemson Tiger paw prints and arrive to work early enough to get them posted in the boss's office before his arrival. Or search the internet for the correct episode of the TV show I appeared in, then order and spend their money to pay for such a significant print. Will enjoying your work and having fun make a difference in the level of performance you get from your personnel? I think so!

So, I saw none of this as the new captain of the Criminal Investigation Division. The halls were empty. The division was quiet. I didn't hear anyone laughing, or yelling at each other, no joking around, nothing! I'm confident members of the various units (i.e., Property Crime Unit, Violent Crime Unit, Drug Enforcement Team) probably met from time to time in their individual offices and shared some laughs, but as far as between units and division-wide, nothing; a quiet, serious, sterile environment.

There was no doubt in my mind that this lack of any fun and laughter, and the lack of positive interaction among division members, affected how well they supported and worked together. I tried to loosen up the environment and get people talking and laughing together. I would make my daily rounds around the office, try to joke around with people, and let them know they could joke with me. I tried to lighten division meetings by looking for opportunities for some laughter, many times at my own expense. I would highlight a screw-up of mine, again letting the group know I was not off limits, could take a joke, and was open to them like anyone else. The lieutenant and I would throw friendly shots (insults) back and forth at each other in public to let our personnel know it was ok to loosen up and have some fun. As time passed, I saw the environment changing for the better. People would gather in the hallways for informal discussions, laughter could be heard throughout the division, and yes, the practical joking and pranks against each other increased.

I heard one detective was the victim of a "Nerf gun" drive-by shooting. Several other detectives had walked by his office, shooting him with "Nerf darts" before fleeing the scene. Hearing of this incident, and knowing my son had what would amount to a "Nerf machine gun" that fired about 50 rounds of "Nerf darts" within seconds, I snuck his machine gun into the office unseen and brought it to the victim detective. "The next time they show up with their small 'Nerf pistols,' you pull this baby from under your desk and let them have it," I told him. And he did. Unfortunately, the victim detective ratted me out about where the machine gun came from, and I became a victim while exiting the men's room a few days later, shot up with "Nerf darts" from numerous directions. In a later conversation with one of the culprits who shot me with the "Nerf gun," he described how nervous and unsure they were about shooting at me because they feared getting in trouble for shooting the boss. They took the risk anyway, and I am glad they did. I can and should be able to take a clean and good-hearted joke like the rest of them. Yes, I hold a higher rank in the organization, but am I more important than them?

Do you think demonstrating yourself as open and approachable in a situation like this might pay itself forward in terms of personnel being comfortable interacting with and providing their leader information that may be sensitive and detrimental to the organization's well-being? On the other hand, if they fear the leader, if he is harsh, doesn't take bad news well, kills the messenger, or has no sense of humor, they may just decide to withhold that needed information to the leader's detriment.

Here are excerpts from a letter forwarded to my supervisor and then shared with me. I received it about a year after I took over the Criminal Investigation Division at the sheriff's office. "I can say that the overall picture of CID has improved immensely. . .. In general, I have noticed a marked difference in CID over the past year. For example, before Terry and [lieutenant], detectives rarely attended the weekly CID meetings. There was a feeling of disrespect. Now the meetings are well attended, and members are relating more, not only among themselves but with the captain and lieutenant. I no longer sense an undercurrent of disgruntled employees. Of course, there will be employees who will always be disgruntled, but I'm not talking about them. I refer to the BIG PICTURE. In the hallways, I see more verbal articulation among employees. They are laughing and interacting more . . . a good sign that they just may be a little happier in their work. . .."

I cannot say I remember ever reading any police management or leadership literature on encouraging fun and playfulness within the law enforcement organization. Some may disagree with me and believe this topic should have been omitted. Therefore, I pondered whether to include a discussion on this topic. However, the truth is that well-performing teams are engaged in "workplace antics and humor" within our law enforcement organizations worldwide. They enjoy working together, and it shows through their humor.

We could ignore and leave the topic out, but it will still be a part of the police culture. I am also aware that there is a risk, if left unchecked, that work-related fun can get out of hand and lead to dysfunctional behaviors. Furthermore, there is a significant risk, which I have personally seen, to any law enforcement leader who gets caught up in the idea of promoting fun in the workplace as a primary purpose or function. With such behavior, a supervisor may start seeing themself as "one of the guys" instead of the supervisor/leader with very specific responsibilities to ensure proper performance of the work group. We cannot let the lines between supervisor and subordinate get blurred. There must always be respect for the chain of command with appropriate limits between supervisor and subordinate behavior.

Our job as law enforcement is to provide our communities with a high level of service. We are getting paid to perform a job rather than to spend our day playing. And it is undoubtedly the leader's job to ensure the fun and joking stay within appropriate limits and doesn't lead to inappropriate behavior or hurt feelings, which would have the opposite effect of what we are trying to accomplish. But, if a person enjoys their work, is happy performing it, and feels liked, valued, and treated as a vital team member, you will get a higher level of performance from them. I guarantee it!

TEAM FOCUSED

The remaining behaviors and attitudes making the detectives of 2016 list are:

- The unit (group) came before the individual.
- They possessed a "low ego" among each other.
- All cases were unit cases, not just individual detective cases. Therefore, solving every case was important to all members of the unit.
- They possessed a common drive to do the right thing and remember what they were in business for.
- They possessed self-discipline, addressing deficiencies among themselves.
- The more experienced investigators took responsibility for developing the less experienced/skilled investigators.

This group of detectives deserves the credit for their successes. It would be inappropriate and inaccurate to suggest that I played any significant role in their success. This unique group of people and personalities came together at this one point of time in history that made the team work so well. They demonstrated value for each other. Each member of the team was valued and equally important, even when their talents and skills were not equal. When it came to their interaction with each another, they didn't take themselves too seriously and didn't present themselves as being better or more important than another. Instead, they humbled themselves and gave their time, talents, and energy to see the others succeed. The level of competition among this group of detectives was low, but the level of collaboration was high. They committed first to each other and then to the organization. They cared about each other and made personal decisions that helped develop the individual first, strengthening the team and ultimately positively affecting the organization.

Where did the positive attributes of this group come from? Was their behavior natural? Or was it learned? Naturally, people are selfish. From the very beginning of life, human behavior is self-seeking. A newborn baby isn't concerned about others' feelings. They know when they are hungry and want to eat. They know when they are tired and need to sleep. They don't necessarily care about those around them and how they are feeling. If people are left to their natural instincts, they will look out for "number one," themselves. And unfortunately, many adults in society, and even some members of our law enforcement profession, still possess the "look out for number one" attitude.

However, the behaviors this group of detectives demonstrated were not natural instincts. Instead, they deliberately chose to commit themselves to doing the "right thing," to value and support other group members, and to put others first. This is learned behavior where the environment or, more accurately, environments (home, school, church, peer group, workplace, etc.) have the potential to transform us into whom we are and who we choose to be.

By the time I arrived and had the opportunity to work with this group, their attitude and sound work ethic were already in place. They already had what they needed for success. However, the environment created by leaders of an organization can support and foster the attributes exemplified by these detectives, or they can create a negative environment that stifles and limits creativity, energy, and, ultimately, positive performance. "Some bosses...put a cap on creativity and encourage people under them to underachieve. 'This is what he wants...I'm giving him this and not one iota more.'"[4] This is where leadership and the environment they create and support play a crucial role.

I'm going to suggest that to further maintain a positive work environment for your organization or work group, the leader needs to consider what worked for this group of detectives. The leader needs to focus on the team in the following areas personally: value everybody as a person who wants to do good and feel good about themselves; not take every set back personally; demonstrate humility in their interactions with personnel; and create an environment where communication is opened up, accepted, and appreciated from everyone, regardless of their rank and skill set.

VALUE EVERYBODY

Roger Pearman, Founder and CEO of Leadership Performance Systems, stated, "Executives and managers who have better relationships with people are exposed to more thorough information. As a result, they can make better informed decisions. . . . People want to be around, work for, and walk through hell for people who give them regard, respect, recognition, and appreciation."[5]

Value everybody in your organization or work group, and I mean everybody. The detectives of 2016 valued every member of the unit. The unit came before the individual. They had synergy. The combined effect of all its members was greater than the sum of the skills and talents of its individual members. Their ego, as it related to each other, was low. Certainly, there were detectives with more significant strengths than others. Everyone knew it. But they used these strengths to benefit the unit rather than for personal recognition or gain. It didn't matter whose case it was. If a detective weak in interrogation skills had a significant interrogation to conduct, there was no hesitation to reach out to a more skilled detective. That detective would not only set aside what he was

---

[4] Bratton, William. (1998). *Turnaround: How America's Top Cop Reversed the Crime Epidemic.* Random House Inc., New York, NY, p. 127.

[5] Human Capital Institute. (2013). *Leadership and Emotional Intelligence: The Keys to Driving ROI and Organizational Performance,* p. 5. Retrieved from https://www.sog.unc.edu.

working on and humbly assist but would use that opportunity to develop the weaker detective further, understanding that the greater the strength of each individual, the greater the strength of the detective unit as a whole. It was common to see detectives conducting an impromptu training session with less experienced detectives after such an interrogation. The same could be said for preparing search warrants and court orders, as they would proofread each other's work and provide suggestions. The same dynamics would be found in the field conducting operations.

They relied upon one another, as it was not an "every man for himself" mentality. They were in it together. There were several civilian members of this unit, all of whom were treated as respected and valued members of the team. Say something bad about their civilian crime analyst, and the fight would be on. This crime analyst was worth her weight in gold; neither those detectives nor I would give her up voluntarily for anything. The detectives of 2016 were successful partially because of the value and integrity they placed on their "team." Leaders would be served well to understand the importance of valuing every member of their team. If poor performance prevents a leader from valuing an individual team member, then that person needs to be removed and should not be there.

"Every role performed at a level of excellence is valuable."[6] We are all human. People want to be valued and feel good about the work they perform. Knowing and understanding that their performance, regardless of how menial it may seem, benefits the organization's mission is a motivator. It will encourage continued performance at a level of excellence. Every law enforcement organization has its superstars, its middle seventy percenters, and its bottom 10 percent. Even most of those "ten percenters" have value. Like the example of the evidence technician in chapter five, there is something they can do that adds depth and benefit to the organization, and they should be recognized for those areas where they excel. When they do a good job, acknowledge them, and let them know they are appreciated and valued for what they bring to the table.

If a supervisor needs to address non-performance or deficiencies with an employee, address them. If they don't raise their performance to a level acceptable to the organization, get rid of them. Just don't put a person who has capabilities or potential for success in a box and ignore them, labeling them as worthless or no good because they aren't perfect in your eyes. I think we are often blinded to the strengths of others when they do not perform or carry out tasks precisely how we would. "The hardest thing about being a manager is realizing that your people will not do things as you would. But get

[6] Used with permission of Gallup, Inc., from *First, Break All the Rules: What The World's Greatest Managers Do Differently* by Gallup, copyright © 1999/2016, p. 205. Permission conveyed through Copyright Clearance Center, Inc.

used to it. If you try to force them to, then two things happen. They become resentful – they don't want to do it. And they become dependent – they can't do it. Neither of these are productive."[7]

This was one of the first hard lessons I needed to learn upon my promotion to patrol sergeant. Every report I read and reviewed from the officers on my shift was terrible. So, I had to ask myself whether the report was really bad or just different than how I would have written it. As I began to ask myself this question while I reviewed various reports, I came to find that most reports were sufficient. They contained the required detail and elements of the reported offense; it was just that the format or the word selection differed from my writing. The last time I checked, I was not the sole authority on report writing, and thus their reports didn't have to be like mine. Yet, I believe this is a trap that supervisors fall into that creates resentment instead of value. We must learn to value and appreciate differences and diversity.

Remember, "every role performed at a level of excellence is valuable." We may be talking about personnel responsible for janitorial or clerical work or non-sworn employees in a law enforcement agency. What they do matters, and they should be valued for such.

Imagine if the janitorial staff quit performing or scaled back on their efforts. Would that make a difference to your organization? Would that affect the environment? Might morale suffer if the floors of the station house were filthy with mud and dried up spilled coffee, or you routinely ran out of toilet paper, or the garbage can was not emptied? Would you notice if the service provided by the janitorial staff suffered? Upon my arrival to work, I often saw the janitor cleaning the courthouse early in the morning. I didn't do this daily, but I occasionally got him a cup of coffee and told him I appreciated his work. Do you think he isn't going to remember those cups of coffee or kind words of appreciation when I have a need that he can fill? Of course, he is. Value them, spend time with them, and get to know them. It's the kind and right thing to do, and it affects performance.

In 1998, the International Association of Chiefs of Police came together to discuss and formulate plans for successful police leadership in the approaching new century (21st Century). One of the requirements for future success was the need to recognize the importance of, and investment in, civilian employees of the law enforcement agency. They suggested ensuring civilian employees understand their role and its importance to achieving the organization's mission, that agencies invest in finding ways to increase the morale of civilian employees, and that the "21st century leader accord equal respect for the

7 Gallup, *First, break all the Rules: what the world's greatest managers do differently* by Gallup, p. 122.

views of civilian employees, even in regard to issues traditionally considered as the province of sworn staff."[8]

In today's complex environment, civilian staff plays a more significant role than ever, supplementing and supporting sworn law enforcement officers. Today's policing strategies and tactics, such as community policing, COMPSTAT, data-driven policing, intelligence-led policing, predictive policing, and problem-oriented policing, require employees with the experience and skills to function at a high level with technology. All these modern policing strategies require collecting, analyzing, and reporting significant amounts of data. Civilian personnel with the requisite skills and training are the right people for the job. Most sworn officers are not trained or prepared for such a task. Even if they possess the appropriate skills, tasking them with the job as the agency's crime analysis or records clerk may be seen as an inappropriate use of resources, as it takes sworn officers out of the field where they are most needed. Other administrative support positions within law enforcement, such as information technology, evidence handling and processing, and training responsibilities, are being served by civilian employees in many agencies. However, a culture remains within police departments, a traditional view that civilian personnel are somehow second-class citizens compared to their sworn counterparts.

I have personally seen this; however, I have never understood it. It makes no logical sense. When I worked at the police department in Chicagoland, we had service officers. They were unarmed, non-sworn employees. However, they wore a uniform and handled minor service-type calls in the community, such as animal complaints, vehicle lockouts, assisting with traffic control, school crossings, etc. The purpose was to keep sworn officers free to handle more serious calls for service and address community problems. These civilian employees were a great asset to the organization, carrying out tasks desired by the community while keeping sworn officers available for other calls for service. Yet, some of the sworn personnel would treat these civilian employees as if they were somehow lesser beings. Ironically, these same sworn officers would be the first to complain if a service officer was unavailable and the sworn officer was required to handle an animal complaint or lockout, a call they perceived as distasteful and not worthy of their precious energy. Instead of appreciating those who freed them from having to perform what they perceived as undesirable and "unworthy" work, they treated them poorly. That never made sense to me!

The aforementioned crime analyst, a civilian and part of the 2016 detective division, was worth at least two sworn officers by herself. She was responsible

[8] International Association of Chiefs of Police. (1999). *Police Leadership in the 21st Century: Achieving & Sustaining Executive Success.* Recommendations from the IACP President's First Leadership Conference, pp. 31-32

for multiple arrests and successful case closures without leaving her desk. When a detective gave her a lead, whether a vehicle make, vehicle color, or just a partial license plate, she was like a hound dog, mining social media sites and searching every available computer database. She knew the criminals in each area, their crime of choice, and their unique M.O. She would also frequently provide a detective with a viable and often accurate suspect before the detective asked.

She not only stayed current on the crime trends of our jurisdiction, but knowing that criminals travel, she was well versed in what was happening in other jurisdictions. She frequently solved crimes for other jurisdictions and received multiple recognitions for doing so.

In major cases, as detectives responded to the scene, the crime analyst received pertinent information by phone. Before the detectives could make it back to the office, she would not only have the offender identified but have identified their probable whereabouts. Should we value an employee such as this? Absolutely! Civilian or not, personnel such as this should never doubt whether they are appreciated or valued by the organization. Of course, this analyst will never make what she is worth in pay. But we, as leaders, can ensure she is valued and appreciated for what she brings to the table. The former police chief of San Diego, California, William Lansdowne, said, "It is a simple thing [for the law enforcement leader] to walk into the Records Department and say hello, to Communications, to the Information Technologies Unit, and check on everybody. It makes people feel very valuable.... That relationship-building is important. You've got to make people understand that they are important, whatever their job is, and to understand how they fit into the entire process"[9] (see Figure 7).

More recently, I had sworn personnel tell me that more information would be shared in the department meetings if the civilian employees were absent. That is nonsense and not the environment that will breed success and effectiveness. This is an outdated and ineffective mindset, and those complaining about the presence of civilians are hung up on their oversized egos. Remove the civilians from the meetings, and the complainers will find another excuse for not sharing information with others. They believe hoarding information gives them power. What it does is inhibit synergy and progress.

---

[9] Police Executive Research Forum. (2009). *Leadership Matters: Police Chiefs Talk About Their Careers.* Washington, D.C.: Police Executive Research Forum, p. 11.

Figure 7. One of the best Administrative Assistants and Crime Analysts a manager could ask for. Pictured here with Dennis Franz – actor in the best cop show ever, "Hill Street Blues" and later "NYPD Blue."

I was working on a homicide case. We knew who the offender was but didn't have enough solid evidence to obtain a conviction. Another detective told me he had an informant that could get into our offender. Great, I said. Who is the informant? This detective refused to tell me who his informant was. How would we work this case if I did not know who the informant was? Is the informant credible? Reliable? Did this detective expect I would hand over the entire case to him and he would work it alone? The conversation didn't go further than that, and the informant was never identified or used. Possibly a good opportunity lost.

Indeed, there are sensitive cases where information must be limited to those with a "need to know." I have worked on many of those. Remember my investigation of the chief from chapter two? Only three people in the entire organization knew about that case, and rightly so. And certainly, an agency's leaders will possess information related to personnel or other matters of sensitivity that cannot be shared. However, sharing information on a routine basis gives you more eyes and ears, people who may possess the information or be able to add value to your investigations or problem solving. While working on a robbery case, detectives contacted other department members for help, as they needed additional manpower to help locate the offender. Lo and behold, another department member called in for assistance had an informant related to the offender. Moments later, we had the offender's location, all because the information was shared with others.

Many of our civilian employees work in positions such as the records division or as crime analysts. They have access to a significant amount of data and often see reports from across the agency. As a result, they can often make connections missed by others. If they can't be trusted, they should be removed. But absent that, we must get passed these information silos and value all personnel if we are going to be the best we can be.

Typically, civilian employees have passed a background check like sworn officers. They are hired not to replace sworn officers but to perform specific and crucial organizational roles. I have had administrative assistants, crime analysts, and clerks that have kept me in business, handling various tasks for the division and me. Is it essential to have needed equipment when you need it? Is it necessary that your computer works when you want it to? Is it essential to have the information necessary for prompt and accurate decision making? Is it important to have the proper training available for personnel? Is it important that garbage cans are emptied, and that toilet paper is in the restroom? Absolutely!

Having civilian personnel as part of the team keeps management and sworn officers focused on doing their job and what they were hired to do. Take time to recognize everyone in your organization who adds value. We can find people in our organization doing good work daily. It just takes our energy and time to stop, look up from our busy schedule and see them. Once you do, tell them you appreciate them, write notes, or send emails expressing your appreciation, make positive examples out of them, and you might be surprised when they take their performance to the next level.

CHECK YOUR EGO AT THE DOOR

Bernard Melekian, former police chief of Pasadena, California, says, "the real work is done by the young men and women who drive the radio cars, who answer the phone, who talk to the public. Our job is to make their job possible. I'm not diminishing the chief's role, but it's important to remember that it's not about you; it's about the officers who do the real work."[10] In context, this quote refers to the police chief, the chief executive of the law

[10] Police Executive Research Forum, *Leadership Matters: Police Chiefs Talk About Their Careers*, p. 13.

enforcement organization. The point, however, is equally essential to all supervisors and leaders within the organization. In the very first chapter of this book, we talked about the "Number One Rule of Leadership: it's not about you." This is a lesson every law enforcement leader needs to take to heart. There are going to be difficult times. Things are not always going to go your way. There will be personnel, disciplinary, and performance issues, not to mention any personal issues you may bring to the workplace. Subordinates will have personal problems possibly related to their marriage, children, finances, health, or an addiction. Yes, these can all affect their on-duty work performance, which you will have to deal with. How you manage these issues and how they are presented to your work group will go a long way to fostering a positive environment for your personnel, or creating a negative one. To again quote John Maxwell, "No matter what kind of situation you face, remember that your responsibilities to people come in the following order: to the organization, to the team, and then to the individual. Your interests and comfort come last."[11]

Your personnel know you are the boss. They understand you have the power and authority to direct their performance and make decisions that affect them. You don't have to go out of your way to remind them of that. Instead, I'm going to suggest you take the opportunity to de-emphasize your role of power as often as you can. Use power judiciously and share it when possible.

In Chapter 6, "Control without Competence is Chaos," I referenced Navy Seal and author Jocko Willink and his description of a platoon commander with poor leadership skills. Due to this platoon commander's "massive ego," he accepted no advice from others, even those with skills and experience to share. He made all the decisions yet took no responsibility when those decisions ended poorly. In contrast, listen to Willink's description of the new platoon commander who took over after the first one was removed. "Under the original platoon commander, our world was miserable. When the new commander came in and took over, almost instantly, our world was good. . . . The core of what the new commander taught me was the importance of humility. He had all the experience and all the knowledge and the rank and the position; he had every reason to elevate himself above us, and every reason to look down on us, every reason to act as if he was better than everyone else. Still, he never looked down on us at all. The fact that he didn't is what made us respect him and want, truly want, to follow him."[12] This leader had his ego in check.

---

[11] From The 17 Indisputable Laws of Teamwork by John C. Maxwell, copyright © 2001, p. 72. Used by permission of Thomas Nelson Publishing, a division of HarperCollins Focus LLC. https://www.harpercollinsfocus.com/

[12] Willink, Jocko. (2020). *Leadership Strategy and Tactics Field Manual.* St. Martin's Publishing Group, New York, NY, p. 31.

Unfortunately, some so-called leaders abuse the authority given to them and seem to think they cannot do their job if they are not barking orders and looking for someone to direct or, worse, constantly seeking out someone to discipline. They see themselves in the most favorable light and everyone else negatively. This is not the sign of a leader but of one trying to feed their ego and personal needs over that of the organization.

In his book *Good to Great*, Jim Collins identifies Level 5 leaders as the most capable leaders who take good companies and lead them to great company status. These Level 5 leaders possess a strong will and drive for success but do so with personal humility. "They channel their ego needs away from themselves and into the larger goal of building a great company."[13] When things go well for the organization, they recognize others for success. However, when performance isn't what it is supposed to be, results are poor, great leaders accept responsibility looking inwardly to themselves first.

What do you do when things don't go as planned? When a subordinate does not perform as expected? When they divert from a course of action directed by you? When mistakes are made? Indeed, in the police environment, urgent matters will arise, where delay or inaction can lead to devastating and worsening effects. However, in most instances, no such urgency exists. Therefore, during non-urgent circumstances, I recommend leaders pause and think through their response to such setbacks rather than act impulsively.

As a crisis negotiator, one of the premises negotiators work off of is that rationality is low when emotions are high. Therefore, it is the job of the crisis negotiator to open dialogue wherein the negotiator actively listens, shows empathy, and builds rapport with a person in crisis. The goal of this dialogue is to lower the person's emotions so they are at a level where they can think more rationally. Once at a rational level, problem solving and decision making can occur. This same dynamic works within personal and work relationships. Consider an argument with your spouse or significant other. How much problem solving gets done during a heated argument when emotions are intense; probably very little. During these times of intense emotions, we often say or do things hurtful that can have long-term consequences.

The same thing can happen within our work groups. When a leader responds impulsively to a setback or mistake made by a subordinate, significant consequence can occur that may be impossible to undo. As a leader, allow time for emotions to settle so the decision on how to handle the setback best can be made. That relationship should not be permanently tarnished just because you, the boss, are upset or did not get your way. Leaders must manage their emotions wisely.

---

[13] Collins, Jim. (2001). *Good to Great* by Jim Collins, copyright © 2001 by James Collins, p. 21. Reprinted by permission of Cuertis Brown, Ltd. All rights reserved.

A detective entered my office to inform me of his and another detective's plans regarding a case they were working on. I disapproved of the plans and told the detective of my reasons. A few moments later, I exited my office just as the second detective walked into the detective division. I walked out just in time to see detective one look at the second detective just entering and roll his eyes. It was apparent that this "eye rolling" was due to my unpopular decision. I was offended and somewhat hurt by the gesture as this detective was someone I thought highly of and was a sound and committed employee. My only response was, "Did you just roll your eyes at me?" I continued past him, saying no more, though inside, thinking of much more I wanted to say. Fortunately, my self-control took over, and I did not say anything further that I may have regretted later. Although hurt and wanting to lash out further and to justify my position and decision, thus rewarding that detective with some disrespect, as I felt I had received, I let it go. The following day, I arrived at work to find a division full of detectives wearing blacked-out sunglasses in the office, so I could not see anybody's eyes. That led to a good laugh by all, including myself, who was now past the hurt. No relationships were harmed, and that incident remained a funny story, even being repeated at my retirement celebration. Had I let my ego get out of control and lashed out, it could have damaged a good relationship and gone another direction, not one that would encourage an environment for success.

On another occasion, a subordinate had been instructed to complete some follow-up regarding a case he was working on. The employee had been reminded several times to complete the assignment, and I had been under the impression it was already accomplished. After a couple of weeks, I learned it had not been completed, and it put me in an embarrassing position with one of my superiors. I was embarrassed and angry.

When I learned this, the subordinate happened to be attending a class at our organization. It was a multi-day class that he was excited to participate in and had been waiting for in anticipation. I decided to go and pull him out of the class in the middle of the course until he completed what he had been asked to do a couple of weeks earlier. Fortunately, I shared my intentions with a superior who rightly talked me off the ledge. Unfortunately, I was about to make an emotional decision based on my wounded pride and ego. I was about to make a drastic and impulsive decision that would embarrass this subordinate and probably ruin our long-term relationship. His lack of performance needed to be addressed, but not by a personal attack. Not by publicly embarrassing him. He was a good detective who routinely performed exceptionally. Why would I consider handling his performance deficiency this way? Because I was allowing my emotions to dictate my decision making. Fortunately, my supervisor had talked me down from a highly emotional state where I could think more rationally and thus avoided making such a drastic mistake.

As a leader of an organization or work group, we are obligated to respond to and correct performance deficiencies among our personnel. We would be negligent not to. However, we must focus on the behavior and deficient performance, not the person. I was tempted to attack the person in the previous examples instead of the behavior. I had taken their behavior as a personal attack against me without their input or trying to understand why they did what they did. Think about the "eye rolling" incident. How often have I gone home to vent or talked with a peer about a decision my boss had made that I disagreed with, misunderstood, or didn't make sense to me? Is it ok for me to sigh, roll my eyes, shake my head, and vent in frustration, but don't you dare do that when I'm talking? Who says that, the person who takes himself too seriously? Now ask yourself the same question. How many times do you find yourself doing the same thing? But you are a little more forgiving of yourself. This leads to the next point of checking your ego at the door.

"We judge ourselves by our motives [or intentions], and we judge others by their actions."[14] For example, how many times have you procrastinated in completing a task or project at work? As a supervisor, maybe you intended to recognize some good work performed by one of your subordinates and perhaps even planned on writing up an official commendation. Or maybe you plan on putting together some training for personnel on an important topic. Or maybe set time aside to get away from your desk to: host a coaching session with one of your supervisor subordinates; roam the halls creating opportunities to interact with personnel and find out what is important to them in their world; ride along with an officer; or meet officers in the field to support them, and come to understand their needs better as it pertains to them successfully performing their job in the community. And we could list many other worthwhile goals we, as leaders, come up with. Now, ask yourself, "How often does my busy work, such as ongoing projects, the new crisis of the day, and new requests for my attention, keep me from following through with some of these worthwhile goals?" Maybe we will eventually get to them, but we often procrastinate and put them off, not handling them promptly where we might achieve the best return for our investment if we did. And when this happens, what do we do? Do we immediately report our deficiency to our supervisor? Do we discipline ourselves? Do we think less of ourselves? Usually, we will probably be quite forgiving of ourselves. Why? Because we know our hearts. We know our intentions are good. We know we want to do those good things for the people of our organization, but we get too busy. There are not enough hours in the day. And so, we are patient with ourselves, making excuses and justifications again because we know we are genuinely

---

[14] Enter, Jack E. (2006). *Challenging the Law Enforcement Organization: Proactive Leadership Strategies.* Narrow Road Press, Dacula, GA, p. 48.

good and would do these good things if we had more time or resources. We judge ourselves by our intentions. After all, they are good.

But how do we judge others when they do not complete their tasks precisely as we wish, within the timeframe we have instructed, when they make mistakes, or when their performance might differ from what we would have done?

I'm afraid leaders are frequently less forgiving and patient with others than they are with themselves. They cannot see the heart of their personnel, so they judge them solely by their actions and what they did or did not do. Can you see the problem in this type of thinking and how it can hurt the work environment a leader is trying to create? We feel so busy and overwhelmed, but we assume others are not as busy as we are. Therefore, we make demands or hold others accountable for their actions when we don't want to be responsible for ours.

When a personnel issue arises, a mistake, a lapse of judgment, or a clear example of poor performance, a supervisor must react and deal with that. Ignoring poor performance is not what a good leader does, nor will ignoring bad work foster a successful environment. However, in addressing issues with personnel, the leader should pause and think through what they are trying to accomplish. Don't take it personally; remember it isn't about you, and allow time for your emotions to settle if they are in a heightened state. Also, remember to allow personnel to explain their actions. You may be surprised at what you hear. It may not be as bad as you initially thought, and you may be able to turn something bad into something good that advances the organization's mission. At a minimum, how you handle these issues may determine whether you can maintain the proper environment needed for success. Problems occur, and bad things do happen. In my experience, when problems arise and are handled successfully, the relationship with involved personnel often ends stronger than before the problem occurred.

When keeping our emotions in check while dealing with setbacks, I have found it helpful to delay my response to them when possible. Indeed, there are times when immediate action must be taken. For example, if an officer's performance involves serious misconduct or criminal behavior, or their present performance will negatively affect department operations, the issues may need to be dealt with immediately. The officer may need to be removed from the field to protect the interests of the community and the organization. However, in cases where the setback has affected me emotionally, I have succeeded when I intentionally insert a slight delay between the discovered performance deficiency and my response to it.

Returning to the previous example of the subordinate who failed to carry out a task after a couple of weeks of being reminded, I did not heed my own advice there. My emotions were high; I had been embarrassed, so I took it personally. Had I taken my advice, I'm sure the following day, when emotions simmered, I would have chosen a different course of action. Fortunately, I passed by my supervisor en route to find this subordinate, shared my intentions with my supervisor, and was saved from myself and the negative consequences that would have followed. In many other instances, I have recognized when my disappointment or anger in a subordinate was at an unhealthy level. As a result, I would intentionally allow myself time to think through the issue, my goal in handling the problem, and how to best get there. Often, I would consciously choose to wait until the following day, or maybe even several days, so I had time for reflection and to get my emotions and ego in check. An intentional delay also allowed time to gather pertinent information to ensure I accurately understood the facts and didn't respond based on impulsive assumptions.

During World War II, General Eisenhower had a subordinate general who caused him significant stress on multiple occasions and one he considered a "problem child." This problem child was General Patton. After one considerable deficiency in performance, Eisenhower, outraged by Patton's behavior, contemplated removing Patton from command and sending him home. Eisenhower sent for Patton. However, after a few days had passed and Eisenhower met with Patton, he refrained from allowing his feelings of outrage to dictate his decision on handling Patton. Ultimately, Patton was retained and went on to serve admirably and to help lead America to victory. It is unknown if it were the passage of time that allowed Eisenhower's emotion to lower so he could think more clearly, or if meeting with Patton, and getting his input and side of the story, was more influential in the decision to keep Patton on. It may have been a combination of both, and both factors provide a lesson for leaders today.

For a leader, the worst way to provide feedback or discuss performance issues is during times of overwhelming emotionality. This method leads to attacks on a person's character instead of dealing directly with performance. Giving appropriate time for emotions to settle puts leaders in a better position to focus on issues, not people. Sometimes your most challenging people are also your most talented, and leaders must find a way to harness and reinforce that talent, which may prove difficult if the leader is being led by their ego.

There was a supervisor I worked with that would get so fired up and angry at one of his officers. I remember this supervisor stating that he was going to "break him," referring to forcing this officer into compliance. What was wrong with this officer? This officer was deeply passionate about the job. His integrity was sound. He was one of the best street officers and later detectives I was privileged to work with and supervise. He had terrific instincts. In the field, he could quickly ascertain if suspects were lying to him or were involved in criminal activity. He had outstanding interview skills, obtaining confessions frequently. He was proactive, never hesitating to act when needed. He was involved in extracurricular activities and service projects related to the police department and community beyond his required duties. His problem: he cared too much. He lacked self-control when it came to filtering his thoughts.

Frustrated with department members with poor attitudes, lazy officers, or department decisions he thought were unfair or inappropriate, he often voiced his displeasure openly. He was a "cop's cop," a Type A personality; an action junkie; possessing traits that made him very successful in policing the streets, but, if not kept in check, could be problematic for the organization. Did his open criticism and lack of filter require attention and correction? Absolutely. But "break him"? Is that the leader's goal? At what cost? If that supervisor could "break him," what would the cost to the organization have been? It would have possibly cost this officer's commitment and outstanding performance.

We did not need to "break him." That is attacking him as a person instead of dealing with the undesirable behavior. The supervisor allowed his ego and emotions regarding this officer to blur his reasoning regarding decisions involving this officer. He could not see this officer's positive work through his negative perception of the officer. This officer did require some reminders from time to time when his emotions got fired up, but he came to understand there were appropriate limits to his emotional venting. They needed to be shared in a proper environment. I tried to create an environment where he could respectfully share his opinions, be heard and valued, and eliminate any negative consequences. By the way, this officer was one of the leaders of the 2016 detectives, and I was thrilled to have him as part of my team.

This same dynamic of not providing feedback or discussing performance issues during overwhelming emotionality also holds true for the written word. So much communication today is accomplished via emails and memorandums. If your emotions are heightened on a problem requiring a written response from you, proceed cautiously. People often find it easier to speak harshly, bluntly, directly to the point, and speak their minds without a filter in written form versus a face-to-face conversation. However, harsh words directed at a person can significantly damage relationships and may inflame the issue more than resolve it.

I often start writing my thoughts and response to an emotional issue while the ideas are clear in my mind. This writing could be correspondence to a supervisor as well as a subordinate. For example, I've had supervisors question the actions of an employee and ask that disciplinary action be taken on an event that I approved of and believed the employee acted appropriately on. In an event like this, your emotions can skyrocket quickly, and the impulse is to fire off a quick email to state your position.

If I find the topic to be one like this that carries some emotional weight with me, I will complete the writing but put the correspondence aside and return to it later before sending it. I haven't always done this. This tactic I learned after having to suffer the consequences of sending out impulsive emails without giving them appropriate thought or allowing my emotions to settle until I was thinking more rationally. When an incident of significant importance and emotionality has been involved, without exaggeration, I believe, after having set the written document aside and coming back to it later, I have made changes to the document about 100% of the time. Emotions are just that powerful and affect your reasoning. Therefore, I might soften some language or delete a portion that could hurt feelings or be perceived as disrespectful.

Another tactic would be to share your written document with a trusted companion or associate who will provide honest and appropriate guidance. Both tactics have worked well for me.

Also, taking time to allow personnel to explain and provide their perspective on "why" they performed as they did or made the decision they did may change the entire game. Give your people the benefit of the doubt until the evidence says otherwise. Remember, "we judge ourselves by our intentions and judge others by their actions."[15] Take time to search out and understand your personnel's intentions. You may find them admirable and appropriate.

You may learn that the subordinate diverted from the leader's directed course of action because the situation changed. Those in the field doing the work are closer to the action and can better read the environment. You may find that variables had changed, new information was obtained, and based on what the person involved was confronted with, the changed course of action may have been a wise and appropriate decision. However, jump all over them without allowing them to tell their side of the story because you let your emotions, your ego, and your impulsivity take over, and you may well lose an asset and stifle creative decision making in the future.

There have been several times where I have questioned the decision making of personnel, sometimes angrily, only to learn, after speaking with them and understanding the context of the decision and the process they used to make the decision, that they made an acceptable, if not an exceptional decision.

But might that be a learning opportunity if they did err, made a mistake, or made a poor judgment call? People learn by doing. Allow them to make decisions. Where will our future leaders come from if denied these opportunities? Yes, mistakes will be made. But honest mistakes made with the intention of being responsive to the organization's mission become testing ground for new ideas and solutions. Indeed, some mistakes come with more significant consequences, and officers should be accountable for the decisions

---

[15] Ibid., p. 48

made, but are they allowed to make mistakes in good faith? If we aren't making any mistakes, are we learning anything? History has demonstrated that growth and success often come after struggle and failure in most facets of life. Are we reinforcing and celebrating those employees willing to take some risks in the search for new ideas and innovation? Or does the leader's ego, intolerable of any mistakes, hinder their personnel's self-initiated problem-solving efforts?

The detectives of 2016 handled many of the group's deficiencies and mistakes independently. They utilized mistakes as developmental opportunities that further strengthened the work group and required no intervention from supervisory staff. Many errors, if handled appropriately, provide great learning opportunities. Mistakes are going to happen. Things are not always going to work out and go as planned. From time to time, within the law enforcement organization, crises will occur. A good leader, however, will maintain perspective, check their ego at the door, and remember it's not about them.

COMMUNICATION: KEEP PEOPLE TALKING

The rest of this chapter will continue with a similar thought to the last chapter, "An Outdated Leadership Model." The leadership model suggested in the previous chapter is likely a prerequisite to obtaining the environment prone to success we are exploring in this chapter. The likelihood of creating such an environment while holding to the traditional autocratic leadership model of the past is slim. I suggest you first examine your leadership style and consider any required changes there before expecting to achieve an environment of having a work group that is not only high performing but also doing so with high levels of morale. Once you align yourself with leadership principles conducive to the complex world of law enforcement today, you can start looking at the characteristics of an environment prone to success. What are these characteristics? How can we obtain commitment and not just compliance from our personnel? How can we obtain the necessary feedback and information to achieve our mission? What does an organization that accomplishes these things look like? It is some of these questions that we will examine here.

There have been countless times when someone sitting on the other side of the roll call table had said something I passionately disagreed with. I wanted to jump across the table and grab them by the neck to express my displeasure for their opinion, input, shortsightedness, poor attitude, whatever it may have been. How long would it take before officers in roll call quit sharing their ideas and providing me input had I followed through on those urges? Who would have ultimately suffered had I chosen that path? I would have, as well as the organization. But sometimes, those in leadership positions respond to bad news or information that conflicts with their notions of what is good and proper and do so in such a way as lashing out against the messenger. And then, when personnel quit talking and sharing input, those same leaders perceive no communication or complaints as a sign that people are content and happy, and erroneously conclude everything is going well. They don't hear of conflicts, so they assume things are fine and take no proactive steps to learn otherwise. This conclusion is dangerous and should be a warning to leaders everywhere. If cops aren't talking, there is a problem somewhere.

As previously said, if I am about to steer the ship into an iceberg, I want someone to speak up and warn me. That does not happen if I make it a habit of attacking those who provide input. Instead, people will tiptoe away to retrieve their life jackets, save their own skin, and let me go down with the ship. If you only recognize and accept the good news, you will have a group of "yes-men" who don't tell you the truth, just what you want to hear. Charles Ramsey, former Philadelphia Police Commissioner and Chief of the Metropolitan Police Department of Washington D.C., said, "the troops will do what you say, even if they know you're wrong. If you are too full of yourself and create an environment where your employees are afraid to speak up, you won't get honest feedback."[16]

In Michael Roberto's (2005) book titled *Why Great Leaders Don't Take Yes for an Answer*, he addresses the 1996 tragedy of Mount Everest, during which five climbers died. In this case, the expedition's leader made clear that he would not accept dissension, disagreement, or debate. What followed were several members of the expedition team, including other experienced guides, having reservations about continuing forward with the climb. They knew that best practices and rules pertaining to when and how to make the final ascension were violated but chose to remain silent. Subsequent darkness and bad weather led to five deaths.[17] Had they felt comfortable providing an alternate viewpoint and disagreeing with their leader, perhaps those lives may not have been lost.

A survey of Fortune 500 companies found that the higher in the organization a person went, the lower the perceived risk to an employee [messenger] who delivered bad news. The non-management front-line employees responsible for the day-to-day work perceived a much higher risk for being the deliverer of bad news. Top management was probably not getting all the information

---

[16] Police Executive Research Forum, *Leadership Matters: Police Chiefs Talk About Their Careers*, p. 39.

[17] Roberto, Michael A. (2013). *Why Great Leaders don't take Yes for an Answer.* Pearson Education, Upper Saddle River, NJ, pp. 16-19.

they needed to make decisions because those below them had a much higher perceived risk for providing certain types of information.[18]

The people on the front line, the individual contributors, those completing the work are closer to the action. They possess information and details directly related to the success of any enterprise.

In the world of policing, front-line personnel know where the problems are, both in the community and in the organization. Likely, they have responded to them many times and know the players. They know the problem locations and the problem people. They use department-issued equipment and understand what is working and what isn't. They know the skill levels, strengths, weaknesses, and personal issues that arise with those working beside them. They know where the gaps are, and when it comes to strategy and direction, they have a pretty good idea of what may work in the real world and what currently isn't.

As an individual rises in rank within an organization, they should be able to do the following: understand more of the "big picture;" be able to conceptualize a better future for the organization; think more strategically; and see how the various parts of the organization can work together, and work with outside law enforcement entities, to bring about greater success. However, these same people, those higher in rank who have a better understanding of the whole picture, can lose perspective and the specific details that those on the front line possess, those who are out there in the field, in the community dealing with community issues and problems day after day. This is natural and should be expected.

As previously covered in Chapter 3, "The Leadership Pipeline," as an individual is promoted and moves up the ranks, their skills, values, and time applications should change with the position. The higher rank one obtains, the more significant the gap between their perspective and how they see the world and that of the personnel working for them on the front line. The chief executive, be it a police chief or sheriff, may see the puzzle with all the pieces connected, but it is blurry. The individual contributor on the front line often sees only some of the puzzle. They see their piece of the puzzle, their specific role in the organization, but that piece isn't blurry at all; it is usually quite clear because that is what they spend their working hours doing day in and day out.

I am sure anybody reading this book has experienced an occasion where a supervisor, maybe even the agency head, addressed them on how a problem might be resolved or handled. Perhaps this supervisor was introducing a new program or giving directions on an ongoing program. And as you sat there listening; you knew what the boss was recommending or directing had no

---

[18] Daniel Goleman, *Working with Emotional Intelligence*, p. 286.

chance of success. "It will never work," you found yourself thinking. I've been there, too; a boss had been off the street for so long that he recommended a course of action already ruled unconstitutional by the courts. What the boss suggested was something other than what we could do. It was not going to work in the real world.

It was a standard protocol in the police organization I worked for in the Chicago area. We would put together moving surveillance when we identified a burglar or robbery suspect who was active in the area committing crimes. Numerous detectives in their undercover vehicles would follow the suspect all over Chicagoland until they could catch the suspect committing a burglary, robbery, or other crime. Then, they would move in, make the arrest, and off to jail the suspect went, and "poof," problem solved. So, I retired from the municipal police department in the Chicago area and found myself leading the Criminal Investigation Division at a sheriff's office in a rural area of North Carolina. So, what did I do when we identified a known burglar? I suggested we put together surveillance on the suspect and catch him in the act, all along confused that these experienced detectives had not considered this tactic themselves. "What's wrong with these guys, I thought?" This would later become a running joke, with frequent laughs at my expense.

The group went silent and stared at me like I had three heads when I suggested this. What was the problem? First, there were a few undercover vehicles within the division, but most detective cars were the standard police package black Dodge Chargers, just without markings. They even had government plates on many of them, and MDTs (Mobile Data Terminals) were easily seen inside the window. Secondly, we were in a rural area with country roads that sometimes go on forever with nothing else around but fields and mountains. As I was used to in Chicago, you did not have all the businesses, residences, driveways, parking lots, and multiple congested traffic lanes to blend into. Imagine six or seven black Dodge Chargers following a suspect down a country road for miles and miles; it wouldn't take a rocket scientist to figure out that police were following him. I made assumptions based on my perspective and what I believed to be accurate. But I was wrong and did not have a correct understanding of what was required for success in this situation.

The detectives, those who performed the job daily and understood the real world as it pertained to law enforcement in this area of North Carolina, had the answers. This is normal and should be expected, but it means those in command positions must find ways to tap into their people's information, skills, energies, and motivation. In other words, they need to create an environment for success where their personnel freely commit to the organization and provide management that which is required for success.

"When you are running a unit or division, you rarely think that people aren't speaking up or that they aren't respected. It feels like the people around you certainly are, and your days are filled with visits, calls, and notes from people with strong opinions. But it ends up that what you experience is a skewed sample. The majority of people in most organizations don't say anything because they feel they can't or haven't been asked."[19] Leaders must ask for input and behave in a way that sends a clear message that all opinions, regardless of rank, are welcome. What might this look like? How do we get this commitment, involvement, and the much-needed information that comes from it?

When William Bratton took over the New York Police Department, he "involved people of every rank and formed teams to examine nearly all aspects of the agency. He also "surveyed nearly eight thousand cops and eventually made more than six hundred recommendations, of which 80 percent were eventually accepted".[20]

Bratton was committed to seeking input and ideas from members of all ranks within the department. We can assume that Bratton understood the individual contributors, those responsible for getting the actual work done and those in direct support of them, possessed information pertinent to the success of the organization, information he needed. But that is the NYPD; they have thousands of employees and more people and resources than most law enforcement organizations. What if you are a smaller department lacking in such resources, an organization that may not have the time and people to form multiple committees or teams to research and investigate department operations without sacrificing present service levels to the community?

In previous chapters, we explored creating opportunities for interaction with your personnel, getting out of the office, and meeting informally with subordinates. This involves minimal resources, being an individual leader blocking out time for these informal listening sessions. Most likely, these conversations are already occurring throughout the organization anyway; it's just a matter of the leader consciously taking advantage of and utilizing the already present information. We are talking about cops and Type A personalities. Rest assured, they are talking whether the leader is listening or not. These informal actions, be it walking the halls, going from office to office, spending a few minutes in the communications division, joining officers for roll call, riding along with officers, or joining them in the field on a call, will create listening opportunities. Suppose the leader is sincere about receiving feedback and routinely encourages sharing ideas, even those they disagree with. In that case, these informal contacts will generate much information the leader can use to gauge current operations and the organization's climate.

---

[19] Welch, Jack. (2005). *Winning.* Harper Collins Books, New York, NY, pp. 54-55.
[20] Bratton, *Turnaround: How America's Top Cop Reversed the Crime Epidemic*, p. 215.

Consider the difference between formal meetings and casual interactions. A formal meeting could either be in a group or individual setting where the leader presides. Or, imagine a one-on-one (individual) meeting where a subordinate is summoned to the leader's office and sits in a chair across the desk from the leader while recognizing the leader's attention is solely upon them, requiring their best presentation and behavior. Now compare either of those to a casual-informal interaction. The psychology behind formal and casual-informal interactions is vastly different.

The casual discussion may at times involve topics of a personal nature, such as family, vacation plans, sports, the new car they are planning to buy, the tremendous new pizza joint that just opened up in town, their plans for the holidays, etc. or may be filled with laughter and some joking around. But make no mistake, if appropriately handled by the leader, these discussions will be peppered with information that can benefit the leader and the organization.

In his Book *Thriving on Chaos*, Tom Peters says that these frequent informal meetings and conversations lead to identifying and testing new ideas. Without such encounters, positive changes and opportunities are missed.[21] In their book *Execution*, authors Larry Bossidy and Ram Charan state, "formality suppresses dialogue; informality encourages it."[22] And we know open and candid dialogue leads to information necessary for success.

What are the subordinates' interests? Strengths? Weaknesses? Frustrations? Thoughts on department equipment? Views on department policies? Are there any recent good or bad calls they have responded to; what went well and what didn't? How about their opinions of, or relationships with, co-workers, supervisors, members of other agencies, the district attorney's office, etc.? All good information a proactive leader skilled in listening can use. And the good thing about it, there is nothing manipulative about this tactic. Your people want a good relationship with their leader, and they want you to have this information, to understand their needs and concerns. They want to be successful and feel good about the work they do.

William Bratton also surveyed personnel seeking opinions and recommendations on department matters. Surveys are a simple way to gather information on a variety of topics. They are easy to create and distribute within the organization. It is also an easy way to provide some confidentiality to personnel who may be hesitant to provide feedback directly to you. I have used surveys to keep personnel engaged and invested, demonstrating my

---

[21] Peters, Tom. (1987). *Thriving on Chaos*. Alfred A. Knopf Inc., New York. pp. 169-170.

[22] Excerpt(s) from *Execution: The Discipline of Getting Things* Done by Larry Bossidy and Ram Charan with Charles Burck, copyright © 2002 by Larry Bossidy and Ram Charan, p. 103. Used by permission of Crown Business, an imprint of Random House, a division of Penguin Random House LLC. All rights reserved.

desire for feedback and input. Upon being assigned to a new unit, I would use surveys in conjunction with one-on-one meetings with all team members to help gauge their attitude, morale, and opinions on the present status of operations within the unit. The feedback would then be used for planning and direction in the future.

To assist me in understanding how I was perceived as a leader, which ultimately enabled me to adjust my behaviors or leadership style that might be hindering more effective performance, I gave personnel the opportunity to provide feedback and comment about my leadership skills and abilities. A process was created to ensure confidentiality. To demonstrate to personnel that this was a genuine request for their feedback and that I was also accountable for my performance, I chose to share the information with my supervisor, having him review the surveys before I did. The questions explored in the survey pertained to how well I did in the following areas:

- Recognizes the value of diverse views and opinions
- Shows concern for providing what others need to do their work better
- Defers to others when they have more expertise
- Effectively involves people in decision making
- Ensures people receive the training they need to succeed
- Provides recognition for others' achievement
- Gives people the freedom they need to excel
- Understands his own strengths and weaknesses
- Strives to understand the perspective of others
- Encourages creativity and innovation in others

For those interested in creating a survey of their own, Marshall Goldsmith's book *What Got You Here Won't Get You There* (2007) provides numerous questions that a leader may be interested in utilizing when creating a survey related to their leadership and managerial abilities. A copy of the survey I used to understand the perception of my leadership abilities is included in Appendix B.

To further demonstrate my genuine sincerity and desire for accountability, I shared the three lowest scores from the surveys with my personnel. I committed to some actions I would take to improve in those three areas. Of course, some comments hurt a little, but this was ultimately a good exercise – one I believe true leaders desiring to be their best will welcome. It demonstrates a commitment to the organization, accountability to its members, and another means of engaging personnel and giving them a voice. "An effective leader must remain open to critique and be able to alter his or her leadership model to meet legitimate concerns of staff."[23] Those who refuse to accept feedback fail more frequently.[24]

In charge of detective divisions at two agencies I worked for, I held weekly detective meetings. Although this time was used to keep personnel informed on department matters, ongoing community problems, changes in policy, etc., the primary purpose was to facilitate a group discussion where the detectives would do most of the talking. They would discuss their cases, their investigative plans for the case, and any additional resources or assistance they might need in the upcoming week. This allowed others to provide input, come up with new and creative ideas ("Hey, have you thought about trying this?"), or offer their assistance ("I have a light load this week. If you need help with surveillance, I'm available").

They would further discuss difficulties they may have encountered in a given case, and the group would talk through and work out the problem. As a group leader, I provided suggestions when appropriate. Still, more often than not, I was just a listener absorbing the input provided, which assisted me in making better decisions in the future and in understanding the challenges detectives were facing. In addition, case updates from these meetings offered information that could be forwarded through the chain of command to keep my supervisors informed. In one quick weekly sitting, this meeting allowed me to seek clarification and needed details without constantly or unnecessarily interfering with the busy detectives working in the field. So, it was also efficient.

I used goal-setting sessions to obtain input from staff. I held these sessions as we prepared for the upcoming year. I requested supervisors of the various units to ponder, research, and prepare proposals on the top three goals that they believed should be incorporated and accomplished during the following calendar year. These goals were to align with the organization's mission and would help enhance the organization's capabilities to improve performance in the future. The goals could include equipment that they believed necessary or beneficial but also could involve training, restructuring of the organization, or a change in philosophy and direction. Anything that they thought should be a priority to improve operations. They were limited to three proposals, so they would prioritize, taking the time and effort to seriously ponder what was most needed and avoid a long list of unmanageable needs and ideas. The various supervisors were instructed to obtain input from their respective staff. Announcements and emails explaining the purpose of this goal-setting

---

[23] International Association of Chiefs of Police. (1999). *Police Leadership in the 21st Century: Achieving & Sustaining Executive Success.* Recommendations from the IACP President's First Leadership Conference, p. 31.

[24] Daniel Goleman, *Working with Emotional Intelligence*, p. 64.

session were provided to the division, and all members were encouraged to share and forward ideas through their chain of command.

At a scheduled supervisors meeting, all unit supervisors presented their three suggested goals, justifying their need, importance, and how the goals would improve organizational performance. Some supervisors prepared and presented their proposals using a PowerPoint presentation, while others used an outline or provided handouts for their researched recommendations. As the various supervisors presented their ideas, they were written on a board. At the beginning of this work session, it was evident that each supervisor brought three ideas that specifically benefitted their unique individual units. They were looking out for their personal interests and those of their direct reports more so than the division or department as a whole. However, after all the presentations were concluded, we began a group discussion on all the ideas, sharing input and opinions on each idea as we went through them individually. During this discussion, various supervisors began to concede and acknowledge that the proposals and ideas of others carried a higher priority than their suggested goal. The atmosphere went from looking out for their interests to considering each other and the organization as a whole. We began prioritizing the various suggestions and putting them in order of importance to the organization and successful future operations.

All the ideas had value. However, we determined that some had greater value than others, which were listed as high-priority goals. We shared this list with all staff as we concluded the work session. The list was then utilized as action items for the upcoming year. Some of the things we were able to implement almost immediately. Other items required long-term planning with incremental changes toward achieving the goal. For example, some easy purchases of equipment could be made promptly, and some required budgeting.

As we achieved the various goals throughout the year, we reported that to the staff. We explained the reason to the staff for those goals we could not achieve or equipment we could not obtain. This demonstrated that their input was critical and desired and that we cared about providing them with what they needed to be safe, well-trained, and effective on the job. This form of openness had the potential for a long-term impact on morale and work productivity, which is significant. In addition, this was also a great developmental tool for the supervisors. It allowed them to engage their direct reports, show support for them, work with their peers as a team, and gain experience conducting research, writing proposals, giving presentations, and engaging in persuasive discussion and debate. It was a win-win for the organization.

"Developing leaders occurs when organizational heads encourage their command staff to think on their own, to ask questions, and to challenge the boss in a constructive way. This kind of internal encouragement of managerial risk-taking and decision making strengthens a management team both individually and collectively."[25] One of the purposes of these goal-setting sessions was to get supervisors involved in organizational strategy and decision making to enhance their commitment to the organization by including them. Their involvement further benefits the organization by tapping into their ideas and the existing knowledge base, waiting to be used. In other words, to keep them communicating.

A previous police chief I knew utilized a Round Table Team to foster positive communications throughout the department. The Round Table Team is a small group of police department personnel selected from all divisions of the police department who meet with the police chief routinely, whether quarterly, semi-annually, or on an as-needed basis. The team's purpose is to improve morale and the organization's culture and keep the lines of communication open. The group is a device used to gain an understanding of the issues and needs facing the police department. This is obtained through a trusting environment where all participants are free to openly discuss, debate, and dissent in search of better solutions to the organization's challenges and problems. It is an informal group, not a decision making body, but a means of providing accurate and timely information to the chief of police, who maintains responsibility for final decisions. Every year new participants would be selected to represent their rank and division, giving as many department members an opportunity to participate as they desire. And yes, my friend bought a "round table" for their meetings. Why? The round table, he explained to me, "puts everyone who sits there on a level playing field. No one is sitting at the head of the table because there is no head of the table." This sends the message that everyone's ideas and input are equally important and desired as they should be. This multi-functional team of department members from all divisions and ranks is based on the premise that "most quality improvement opportunities lie outside the natural work group."[26]

If you want constant quality improvement in your organization, you need a system for collecting ideas and suggestions from your people. The police organization needs to be sincere in its desire to root out the answers to the problems and challenges they face by listening to the ideas and suggestions of their personnel.

I taught online criminal justice courses for a university for nine years. As is typical of online classes, a part of each course is a weekly discussion board, more commonly known as a "blog." Questions about class material would be

---

[25] Police Executive Research Forum. (2007). *Good to Great Policing: Application of Business Management Principles in the Public Sector.* Washington, D.C.: Police Executive Research Forum, p. 19.
[26] Peters, *Thriving on Chaos*, p. 76.

asked of the students, who were responsible for responding to each question. Furthermore, they were also required to respond to fellow students' posts. Finally, the instructor would facilitate and contribute to the discussion by asking follow-up questions and elaborating on the topic to add depth and keep the discussion going.

Businesses, too, utilize online platforms to create a discussion board of sorts where they invite others to provide suggestions and new ideas that would give them an advantage or improve operations. Likewise, law enforcement leaders can use technology and an online platform, be it via email or organizational discussion board, in a similar way; to ask questions, problem-solve, and solicit information from its personnel. Considering the higher rates of technically savvy employees today, the amount of communication and information the leader receives may increase, all of which may provide them with an advantage.

The examples above are just some examples and ideas for keeping your personnel talking and providing you with needed feedback. With some creativity and thought, I'm sure many additional ideas about how a leader can create listening opportunities can be found. For example, Michael A. Roberto's book *Why Great Leaders Don't Take Yes for an Answer* (2005) provides several suggestions on how an organization can foster healthy dissent leading to more effective problem solving and decisions. Regardless of the tactics used (e.g., surveys, goal-setting sessions, a Round Table Team, or an online platform), the law enforcement executive who keeps personnel talking by proactively seeking out avenues for ongoing communication gets more information, keeps their employees engaged, and ends up with improved performance.

I was fortunate to have several great supervisors, chiefs and deputy chiefs, and a sheriff who maintained an open door, allowing me to speak my mind regarding my opinions and thoughts on department matters. I know many other so-called leaders would not have had the patience these great leaders had with me. I have tried to do the same for those that worked for me, hence my self-control in not jumping across the roll call table and strangling anyone.

I was passionate about my job. Once I reached a leadership level, I was equally passionate about the people who worked for me. If I thought they were getting a raw deal or a newly made decision would have unexpected or long-term negative consequences for them, I was known for speaking up and discussing-debating the issues. In his book, *Turn the Ship Around*, David Marquet says, "Cherish the dissension. If everyone thinks like you, you don't need them." He further suggests leaders "encourage a questioning attitude over blind obedience" and asks, "Do you want obedience or effectiveness?

Have you built a culture that embraces a questioning attitude?"[27] Questioning the status quo is the first step in progress and can take us from where we are to where we want to be as a law enforcement organization. Questioning the status quo leads to new ideas, innovation, and problem solving. I was and still am a questioner.

There were many heated conversations with my supervisors behind closed doors. I cannot say I never raised my voice towards a supervisor in these discussions, nor can I say that there weren't ever times when I may have overreacted, gone too far, and had to later apologize for my behavior or overzealous speech. Now, I am not condoning anyone ever speaks to their supervisor disrespectfully. However, the point I want to make is that the freedom these supervisors gave me in hearing me out, allowing me to vent my frustrations, and sending the message that it was okay to disagree with them, played a significant role in developing me to get where I am.

We would have it out and passionately debate an issue, raising our voices periodically. Occasionally, I would persuade them to agree with me or change their decided-upon course of action. More frequently, however, their decision, which fired me up, would stand. But when that door was opened and I exited their office, I left committed to their suggested course of action. In other words, their respect for me and the value they put on my unique perspective and tolerance for respectful debate and dissension only increased my respect for them. When the discussion was over, it was over, and I returned to the field committed to them and the organization. I may have disagreed with the decision, but I was committed to it. My commitment wasn't necessarily due to anything I had done but because of the environment these leaders had created.

Furthermore, our discussions and debates gave me countless learning and development opportunities. It was never a "do it because I said so and don't ask questions" mentality. Instead, they challenged me and helped me to understand the "bigger picture," and I am sure it increased my confidence and desire to do more for the organization and the field of policing. I owe a lot to them and the "environment for success" they created (see Figure 8).

[27] Excerpt(s) from *Turn The Ship Around! A True Story Of Turning Followers Into Leaders* by L. David Marquet, copyright © 2012 by L. David Marquet, pp. 93, 200. Used by permission of Portfolio, an imprint of Penguin Publishing Group, a division of Penguin Random House LLC. All rights reserved.

Figure 8. Some of those leaders that supported me and created the environment that allowed me to thrive.

IT STARTS WITH THE LEADER

We started this chapter with a list defined as **Dynamics of Success and Effectiveness** as identified and created by the detectives of 2016. In addition to this list, an examination of the suggestions made in this chapter and other portions of this book to improve teamwork and commitment can create the kind of environment employees characterize as a "great place to work."

A first step towards creating that "great place to work," that environment for success, would be to heed the identified characteristics of success provided by the detectives of 2016. Additional steps are remembering to value your personnel, recognize their positive work, allow subordinates to learn from good faith mistakes, give everyone a voice, and by all means, keep your ego in check. After all, it's not about you!

The detectives of 2016 possessed the skills and character needed for success. It was up to me to create and maintain the right environment where they would commit and choose to voluntarily share those skills and the great results that came from them. I hope I was successful in doing so or played some small part. This chapter is dedicated to that great bunch of cops. Thank you, detectives of 2016!

Chapter 8

FIND YOUR JOHNNY P!

Who is "Johnny P"? Clint Eastwood, playing Detective Harry Callahan in his 1971 film *Dirty Harry* is requested to assist in handling a suicidal jumper. He handles the jumper successfully in a somewhat unorthodox manner. At the conclusion of the incident, after saving the man's life, Detective Callahan responds to his new partner, "Now you know why they call me 'Dirty Harry.' Every dirty job that comes along...." In many respects, that was my Johnny P. Not that he was frequently assigned undesirable or tasteless tasks or those not worthy of being handled by other officers. But Johnny P possessed considerable skills, strong endurance, and an even stronger "can do" attitude. He was tenacious, detailed, and thorough, committed to performing quality work and doing his best in all situations. In addition, he was empathetic and could sympathize and build rapport with anyone, so he would often be called upon to deliver death notifications or sit with a distraught family who had just learned their child was the victim of some serious crime. Likewise, he was called upon to deal with difficult arrestees who could not get along with anyone else.

If we believed a burglary suspect might be hiding on the roof of a local business, Johnny P would find a way to get himself on that roof, be it scaling the wall or climbing a nearby tree. His ability to withstand the elements of weather went well beyond most others. Whether we were searching for a suspect believed to be loose in the neighborhood or he was assigned to maintain surveillance from behind some bushes, bad weather would not deter him. The rest of us were ready to give up with the freezing conditions you frequently find during Chicago winters and find our way indoors, but not Johnny P. Obtaining the desired results and catching the bad guy superseded his comfort.

Johnny P was known for tracking suspects through the snow. If we responded to a burglary and found a footwear impression in the snow believed to belong to the suspect, expect a long, cold night in the great outdoors because Johnny P would follow those tracks until someone was arrested or the tracks disappeared. All he needed was a partial impression in the snow, some unique design no matter how small. Johnny P would tenaciously take his time, even down well-traveled sidewalks covered with multiple footwear impressions from various people. He would follow those tracks for hours across the city if needed. Ultimately, Johnny P was personally responsible for numerous arrests and the successful closing of over a hundred cases because of his willingness to set aside his comfort for the organization's benefit.

I remember the exact point in my career when I decided to climb high fences in pursuit of offenders no longer. "A man's got to know his limitations" is a quote from another Clint Eastwood *Dirty Harry* movie. I came to this same realization one cold winter night in 2007. I was the sergeant of the midnight shift. In the middle of the night, an officer on patrol of a residential area came across a suspiciously placed bicycle. In examining the bike, footprints in the snow were observed walking away from the bike and into the backyard of a residence. The officer followed these prints from yard to yard, determining we had a residential burglar working the area. The tracks would go through yards up to the back doors of homes and then lead away to the back door of another house. It was found that some of the doors were unlocked, and the offender had entered several homes removing purses and other valuable items he could quickly grab from a nearby counter or cabinets within the home. This occurred while the families, including young children, were asleep inside.

Officers responded and set up a perimeter around the area as the initial officer continued to follow the suspect's footprints in the snow. Suddenly there he was, the officer spotted the suspect, and the chase was on. But this suspect could run. He quickly outran the officer, and his whereabouts were again unknown. Now he knew the police were looking for him. So, we went from a covert blacked-out perimeter, where officers tried to hide their patrol vehicles, and presence in hopes of catching a glimpse of the suspect, to a highly visible lit-up perimeter with the lights of the various patrol cars illuminated. This tactic aimed to advertise the police presence in hopes that the suspect would hide within the perimeter, waiting for the police to leave rather than try to exit the perimeter and be spotted by responding officers. Once the suspect goes to the ground and hides, we would continue to follow his tracks or summon a K-9, if available, to help locate and apprehend the suspect. Unfortunately, this highly successful tactic in most situations wouldn't work so easily this time.

The suspect was having none of it. It became apparent that the suspect was bold and confident in his running ability. He would run from the perimeter, be spotted by officers, a foot pursuit would ensue, and the suspect would again outrun the officers who would lose him. We would readjust the perimeter based on the suspect's last known sighting and direction and start over, only to see the suspect break the perimeter again. Another foot pursuit would ensue, and he again would get away. This happened four different times. The final time, I was the one who spotted him.

I was positioned inside a local park. I heard some noise, looked up, and observed our suspect running down a nearby street toward me. The park and street were divided by railroad tracks and a small, wooded area. The suspect was not aware of my presence. My adrenaline increased as I became excited about the chance of being the one to finally catch this burglar who had been toying with us for the last hour. I started running from my position across the railroad tracks and through the woods towards the approaching suspect. Not wanting to alert the suspect to my presence, I didn't even call out over the radio that I had sight of him for fear that he would hear me and once again be off and out of sight.

As I ran through the woods, I was trying to adjust my speed to a pace that would have me exiting the woods and tackling the suspect as he passed by me before he recognized my presence. As I headed his way, it seemed as if it would work perfectly until, about twenty feet out, he heard some leaves rustling from my running through the woods. As soon as he spotted me, he put on the gas, increased his speed, and off he went. Another foot pursuit ensued. The suspect ran down the driveway of a home and then went over a five-foot wooden privacy fence like it wasn't even there. I prepared to climb over the fence as well, and it was then that it dawned on me. I was exhausted, breathless, and sucking air from the chase. I could get over the fence, but if the suspect was waiting on the other side, I didn't have much strength left to engage in any fight at that moment. The effort it would take to get over the fence was about all the power I had left. Yes, "a man's got to know his limitations." I chose not to go over the fence but instead called out the suspect's last known direction, hoping other officers already headed my way could cut him off.

The suspect smartened up and quit running down streets and sidewalks, changing his tactics to going down the middle of the block and hopping backyard fences, yard by yard, out of sight of responding officers. This might have worked, but the suspect was not counting on one thing: Johnny P was working that night.

Based on my radio traffic of the suspect's last known location, Johnny P got a hold of the suspect's footprints in the snow, and that was all it took. Johnny P, about a year older but in much better shape than me, was jumping those same fences just minutes behind the suspect. A few minutes later, Johnny P was on the radio. He came through a yard, turned a corner, and saw the suspect climbing through the window of a house, his upper body inside and his legs dangling out the window. We responded, kicked open the front door, evacuated the home, and took the suspect into custody. The suspect was a well-known eighteen-year-old soccer star from a nearby school. That explained his ability to outrun most of us and his confidence in his running skills. Fortunately for us, and unfortunately for him, those skills weren't enough to overcome the drive of Johnny P.

In April 2015, Johnny P received a well-deserved valor award for saving the life of an elderly man. The man was sitting in his vehicle at a local park and somehow got his car in gear, unintentionally causing it to move forward and into a pond in the middle of the park. Witnesses to the event called the police, and Johnny P was the first to arrive on the scene. At the time of his arrival, no vehicle was observed. The vehicle was completely submerged. As witnesses pointed to the area the occupied car went under the water, Johnny P could see the appearance of a shadow or a variance of color in the water near the center of the pond. Johnny P quickly removed his gun belt, vest, and shirt and swam into the pond in his remaining clothes, including his work boots. Although the air temperature was fifty-five degrees, you can bet the water temperature was colder than that, as the Chicago winter was barely over. Johnny P swam about ninety feet to a shadow, where he believed the car had rested. He swam beneath the surface and located the vehicle and the elderly man behind the wheel. Running out of air, Johnny P swam back to the surface, took a breath, and then returned underwater, hoping to save this man's life. Like something out of the movies, Johnny P made several trips from the car underwater to the surface for air until he eventually could free the man. Finally, Johnny P pulled the man through the driver's window and up to the surface. He then swam back to shore with the man in tow.

Johnny P wasn't the only person to enter the water that day. As additional police officers and fire personnel arrived, they entered the cold water to assist him. Johnny P was exhausted swimming back to shore with the unconscious man in his grips. Other officers waded out to take the man from him and help Johnny P back to shore. But only Johnny P took those dives back and forth below the water to wrestle the man from his car and back to the surface.

I might have been able to swim ninety feet to the area of the car, but again, "A man's got to know his limitations." That is probably all I would have had in me. I do not have enough confidence in my swimming ability to think I could have accomplished what Johnny P did, but I know him, and I bet there was never a doubt in his mind about what he knew he had to do.

When I arrived to work that day in April 2015 and heard the story for the first time, before anyone ever mentioned the name of the "hero" officer that saved that man's life, I was already thinking, "It's got to be Johnny P."

Other than honoring a good friend and a great cop, this chapter is not really about Johnny P. It's about what Johnny P represents. Johnny P had some great strengths. When he had the opportunity to use those strengths, great outcomes were achieved, and what a difference those strengths made to the organization. Knowing those strengths provided me with resources that could be used when needed. When chasing some bad guys through a residential neighborhood, having searched everywhere except the roof of a nearby school, we needed to check that roof. What was I to do? "Johnny P, find a way onto that roof!" Not everyone could do it, but I knew he could.

An armed, barricaded, drugged-up, and paranoid man was holding his boyfriend in his apartment against his will, threatening to hurt him if the police did not go away. I needed someone with competence and tactical strength to cover the balcony so the armed man couldn't escape or cause further threat or harm to the greater community. At the same time, we continued to negotiate with him. So, "Johnny P," who was a SWAT team member, "I need you across the street with an eyeball on the balcony!" He was the man for the job, as I knew he could withstand the elements and weather conditions.

Now that is just one person: Johnny P! Imagine a leader who knows all their personnel's strengths and skill sets and uses them accordingly. Wow! What might that leader be able to accomplish (see Figure 9)?

Figure 9. Officer John Pacewic after the awards ceremony where he received the Valor Award for risking his life to save a man inside a vehicle submerged under the water of a local pond.

In the last chapter, the detectives of 2016 identified how they had diverse talents and experiences and how they worked toward each other's strengths and compensated for each other's weaknesses. These were two of the factors they believed added to their success. In this chapter, we will explore this idea of a leader identifying and utilizing their subordinate's strengths to drive performance and move the organization forward.

When we used Johnny P for his strengths, quality work and success followed. Likewise, when the 2016 detectives got to use their strengths, quality work and success followed.

When the detectives were working on a sensitive and serious in nature case and needed an admission from the suspect, they turned to their team members who had more significant strengths in interrogation. It wasn't an "every man for himself" mentality. They positioned themselves for success by wisely using each other's strengths. If their case involved computers, requiring the need to data mine social media sites or conduct a forensic search of a seized computer, they knew which of their colleagues to turn to for that expertise. There was no shame in turning to another with a more significant strength if the difference was between success and failure. If there is a question concerning search and seizure laws, you don't just wing it and hope you don't violate someone's rights; you go to a person well-versed in case law for guidance.

When I wanted to enhance our community engagement to improve community relationships, prevent crime, and reduce the fear of crime, I did not introduce that initiative by arbitrarily assigning responsibility randomly or to those unqualified or unprepared. Instead, I gave the responsibility to two people with the drive, interest, and skill set for such a task. They led the way, paved the path, and created the success that demonstrated what can be accomplished. Then, with their leadership, influence, and the momentum they had created, we expanded the initiative outward to others in the organization.

In Jim Collins' book *Good to Great*, one of the critical components of going from a good company to a great company is "getting the right people on the bus, the wrong people off the bus, the right people in the right seats, and then figuring out where to drive the bus [what direction to take the company]."[1] Therefore, it makes sense that any organization, including a law enforcement organization, will benefit if they hire qualified, competent employees with the right attitude. Furthermore, it makes sense to remove those who do not possess the right attitude or cannot perform satisfactorily. Finally, when deciding where to take the organization, what direction to go, and what programs to initiate or enhance, it is equally important to assess the organization's capabilities, including its personnel, to determine if you can successfully go in the desired direction. For example, no police executive wants to create a plan or strategy to expend time, energy, and resources to

[1] Collins, Jim. (2001). *Good to Great* by Jim Collins, copyright © 2001 by James Collins, p. 57. Reprinted by permission of Curtis Brown, Ltd. All rights reserved.

find that they do not have the right personnel to carry out their strategy successfully.

I agree with Jim Collins on all accounts; these are all valid points. However, in this chapter, I want to focus on and take some liberty with the idea of "getting the right people in the right seats" on the bus. In other words, putting people in a seat that compliments their strengths and talents, where they can be successful.

Referring to one CEO of a large company Collins writes, "I spent a lot of time thinking and talking about who sits where on the bus. I called it 'putting square pegs in square holes and round pegs in round holes.'"[2] Do we have square pegs and round pegs inside the law enforcement organization? Are all police officers created identically? They all attended the same or similar basic training course, haven't they? Shouldn't they be equally skilled in all things law enforcement? Is that realistic? Of course not! We deal with people with different traits, talents, interests, and abilities. I will suggest that in law enforcement, we have not only square pegs and round pegs but also triangle pegs, rectangular pegs, and probably every other type of shaped peg. The point of this chapter is to demonstrate that this diversity should not be perceived as bad. Instead, we should recognize the differences between our personnel and use them to the organization's advantage. The ability to do this is a significant aspect of leadership and a key to driving performance.

General Dwight Eisenhower recognized that his soldiers had limitations. He recognized the uniqueness of the individual. He believed it was a leader's responsibility to know his people, to know their limitations, and manage those while at the same time utilizing their strengths to the benefit of the organization. Continuing with the words of the CEO of the large company, as shared by Jim Collins above, "Instead of firing honest and able people who are not performing well, it is important to try and move them once or even two or three times to other positions where they might blossom."[3] Moving employees to different positions can be challenging or downright impossible for many law enforcement organizations. A given police agency, especially small agencies which make up most of our nation's law enforcement organizations, may be very limited in the number of roles or positions to which they could move a person. Frequently an individual begins their law enforcement career attending and graduating from a police or training academy and is then expected to be assigned duties at the same entry level as all other new hires. In a police department, the new employee will typically begin as a patrol officer, expected to carry out all the duties of that position. The opportunities to move people from one place to another may not be there.

---

[2] Ibid., p. 57.
[3] Ibid., p. 57.

I am not at all suggesting that we create unnecessary positions for personnel. Further, I'm not suggesting that personnel should only be tasked with the duties that interest them or are considered a strength. For example, a police officer who struggles with or doesn't like writing reports still has to write reports. A deputy who may struggle with public speaking still, from time to time, must communicate with groups in the community as circumstances warrant. Every member of the law enforcement organization should be capable and required to competently fulfill all the basic expectations of the assigned position, which they are hired, transferred, or promoted to do. That is a given. But once the basic qualifications for a given position are met, utilizing personnel as often as possible for their strengths is "the icing on the cake." This is where giant leaps forward regarding good performance and positive results will be found. We might not be able to quickly move personnel from one position that doesn't fit their strengths to another that does. We can, however, identify and use personnel's strengths within their presently assigned role.

I knew the types of tasks Johnny P would excel at and those best reserved for someone else. There are officers whose strengths center around crime-fighting activities; they relish enforcement opportunities and making arrests. Others enjoy and excel at service-related tasks, serving and interacting with the productive members of society more so than criminals. Driving while intoxicated is a dangerous behavior and crime that takes numerous lives yearly. This crime is well deserving of attention from a law enforcement perspective. However, some enjoy and excel in DWI enforcement while others do not. Suppose you are holding a DWI campaign and putting out extra patrols over a holiday weekend or the night of the Super Bowl when alcohol consumption is high. Who do you want to participate in that campaign, officers who excel and are drawn towards that enforcement activity or those who are not?

Some officers enjoy speaking with community groups, while others prefer working with the youth. Some like and excel at conducting interrogations, while others do not. There are computer gurus, and there are those challenged by technology. Some enjoy dealing with physical evidence and assignments involving forensics. That wasn't me. I enjoyed, and still do, dealing with people. I liked interviews and interrogations, but lifting fingerprints and collecting blood did not get me excited. And, because it didn't excite me, I was neither drawn towards it nor excelled at it. I learned enough about forensics to perform my job competently, but if a case required more, I turned to those with expertise in that area. Likewise, those highly skilled in forensics have turned to me when a vital interrogation was required. Together, working towards each other's strengths, the job got done and got done well.

What might the alternative look like if we do not consider each other's strengths? For starters, we might end up with a weaker case that loses in court or gets pled down by prosecutors because of gaps in the case. For example, the crime scene is processed well, but no admission or information is obtained to help explain the evidence. Or perhaps a confession is obtained, but no physical evidence to corroborate the confession is gathered. Both of these scenarios are possible when officers, who excel in one area but not another, are required to perform both, even when more capable resources are available but not used.

William Bratton, previous Commissioner of the New York Police Department and Chief of the Los Angeles Police Department said it this way, "I came to see that a lot of cops in that district were not averse to meeting with community groups; they liked it. They listened to the complaints and went about the business of handling them. Other cops were perfectly happy to take their regular calls but said, 'Don't bother me with that other stuff, I don't want anything to do with it.' As a manager, I adjusted to the reality of my workforce. They're not all clones, they had different personalities and professional perspectives. I surveyed my cops and tried to match the assignment with temperament. I had to understand what turns cops on...if people are working jobs they want to work, it stands to reason they will do a better job."[4]

In an interview I participated in as a finalist for a chief of police position, I was asked, "If hired, who would be the department's PIO (Public Information Officer)? Would it be you, or would you assign that responsibility to someone else?" I thought it was a good question. My response was, "I don't know." I went on to explain that I believed some certain occasions or events are sensitive in nature, and the head of the department, the police chief, needs to be out in front of the community and thus should be the PIO during those events. I explained these events could be an officer-involved shooting, an unfortunate incident involving police misconduct, or another issue sensitive to the community.

I went on to explain that routine day-to-day events should be reported by the one most qualified for that position. Having yet to be a part of the organization and not knowing the strengths and weaknesses of department members, I could not make the call as to who specifically would be assigned the responsibility for PIO duties. Indeed, as the police chief, if no one else were better qualified, I would take responsibility for the role. However, if someone else, specifically a command team member who excelled in such a role, was interested and was more qualified than I, why would I not want to allow that person to use that strength? They will do the job better than I do, and who will benefit from that? I will, the organization will, the community will, and that person will, as they routinely do what they enjoy. Of General

[4] Bratton, William. (1998). *Turnaround: How America's Top Cop Reversed the Crime Epidemic.* Random House Inc., New York, NY, pp. 96-97.

Ulysses S. Grant, the general credited for winning the Civil War who later became president, it was said, "he studiously avoided performing any duty which someone else could do as well or as better than he."[5] How did General Grant know who could and who could not perform better than he? How did General Eisenhower get to know his people and their limitations and strengths? How does any law enforcement leader know what their personnel's strengths are and who their "square pegs" and "round pegs" are?

The most straightforward and obvious answer is that, as a supervisor and leaders, it is their responsibility to know their people. But do they? Sure, a leader or supervisor should be responsible for the performance of their subordinates daily and is usually responsible for completing an evaluation on the performance of their personnel at least on an annual basis. They are expected to know their people. They should accurately understand their subordinate's skill sets and abilities.

Do you believe this always to be the case? Do you think most supervisors know their people intimately enough to recognize their strengths and weaknesses to almost instinctually use them and assign them to their strengths? Is completing the annual evaluation sufficient to obtain and retain such detailed knowledge of one's subordinates?

Have you ever received an evaluation so general and vague that the same assessment could be copied and given to all unit members? Or your performance, good or bad, for the last month is covered in great detail, but all the excellent work done for the prior eleven months is missing. Or is the evaluation almost identical to the preceding years' evaluations? Or every mistake and error made in the previous year is covered in great detail. Still, none of the positive work and results made it into the evaluation, making you look like an incompetent buffoon? Like most suggestions in this book, knowing and understanding your personnel requires proactive effort. It is left to the true leader who consciously decides to proactively seek out the required information needed best to know their personnel from a unique individual standpoint.

In other chapters of this book, we have emphasized the importance of leaders creating opportunities to interact with and listen to their subordinates. I talked about my habit of wandering the halls looking for an opportunity for informal conversations with personnel. I kept my eyes and ears open, looking for a chance to recognize positive work being done. When I saw positive work, I often made a note of said performance, ensuring the note made it to the appropriate supervisor for future use on the annual evaluation when appropriate.

---

[5] Fuller, Major General J.F.C. (1957). *Grant & Lee.* MJF Books, New York, NY, p. 74.

Additional opportunities to interact with and listen to subordinates may include, attending roll call, watching and listening, or maybe engaging in discussions or debriefs about challenging calls officers responded to. Joining personnel in the field where you see and understand their challenges. How are they responding to those challenges? What are they talking about? What type of tasks do they run to, and what are those they are trying to avoid? What does an officer spend their uncommitted time on? What kind of self-initiated proactive activity do we find an individual routinely participating in? Who else in the department do they frequently associate or attach themselves to? People tend to navigate to and socialize with those most like them. If you are paying attention, you will begin to observe patterns of behavior. These patterns will signify a person's interests, strengths, and weaknesses. The more and harder you look, those attributes will make themselves apparent. You will begin recognizing the "square" and "round pegs."

One technique I used during my sit down with subordinates during the review of their annual employee evaluation was to ask them to list their strengths and weaknesses. I don't remember when I started using this practice or why, but I found it very beneficial in accurately understanding and getting to know my people. Then I follow up with, "Where do you think you add the greatest value (to the shift, unit, or department)?" Depending upon their response, we might discuss that for ten to thirty minutes or even longer.

The ensuing conversation served several purposes. First, I better understood them and their perceived strengths and weaknesses. Second, I learned whether their strengths matched their interests (which they always did). Third, I learned the work they enjoyed and what tasks they preferred to do (which I could then create opportunities for them to participate in those tasks in the future). Finally, when it came to the validity of the actual evaluation, I learned whether their perception of their strengths and weaknesses matched my opinion of their strengths and weaknesses. If the subordinate's identified strengths and weaknesses vastly differed from my observations and what had been recorded in the evaluation I completed, then there was a problem. One of us is either dishonest or has an inaccurate view of the person's abilities and strengths.

Fortunately, in almost all cases, after the subordinate explained their perception of their strengths and weaknesses, what they found written in the evaluation instrument matched their perception of themselves. That, in and of itself, has great power in sending a message to your personnel that you care enough about them to pay attention, not just at the end of the year when an evaluation is due, but all year long. You paid enough attention to get to know them as individuals and accurately record their performance on the annual review, even if some of the recorded performance is negative, whether reflecting weaknesses or areas needing improvement. Not to mention, it is much easier to gain cooperation in changing behavior, asking subordinates to make corrections, or assigning them additional tasks that complement their strengths when the acknowledgment of their strengths and weaknesses comes directly from their mouth before they even know what you had to say, or what was recorded on the evaluation instrument. Hard to later deny or take that back.

I began to receive positive feedback from my personnel once I started with what became this routine procedure when reviewing the annual evaluation. By having this conversation with subordinates before going over the evaluation, there were occasions when the subordinate might identify and explain one of their strengths and benefits to the organization, which I missed. I might say, "great point, you are very good at that, but I missed that." I would then add that point to the evaluation and include examples. So, this procedure also held me accountable for completing valid and accurate assessments of my people.

In all the years I followed this practice, only one person could not, or probably more accurately would not, identify a weakness. Interestingly, this is someone who had plenty of them. I would have probably considered this person part of my bottom "ten percenters," one of my lower performers. So, this practice may occasionally give you a glimpse into a subordinate's honesty and integrity. If you have a team member in a law enforcement agency who has a problem with integrity, do you think that is something important for a leader to know? Knowing your people is essential. It can help the leader excel and keep the leader out of trouble. But it takes proactive effort from the leader.

Jim Collins identifies Abraham Lincoln as a Level 5 leader. He further contends that Lincoln is one of only a few presidents of the United States that has ever reached Level 5 leader status.[6] Abraham Lincoln was able to "gain the trust and respect of his subordinates, building strong alliances with them. He wanted to know how his people would respond in a given situation: who would get the job done, and who was more likely to procrastinate and delay; who could be counted on in an emergency and who couldn't; who were the brighter, more able, more committed people; who shared his strong sense of ethics and values."[7]

Can you see how this knowledge of your subordinates could assist the law enforcement leader? In times of uncertainty and crisis that frequently arise in the world of policing, knowing who your "go-to" players are in any given situation is a tremendous advantage. Knowing who not to trust in a lifesaving, urgent, or matter of great importance and sensitivity is just as important.

---

6 Collins, *Good to Great*, pp. 22-23.

7 From *Lincoln on Leadership* by Donald T. Phillips, copyright © 1991, p. 27. Reprinted by permission of Grand Central Publishing, an imprint of Hachette Book Group, Inc.

Putting the wrong person in the wrong bus seat at the wrong time can have devastating consequences that a law enforcement executive might not be able to come back from.

Getting to know your personnel is also a two-way street. Another advantage of taking time to interact with and know your people is that they get to know you too. Abraham Lincoln wanted his people to know him, "how he would respond in a given situation, what he wanted, demanded, and needed."[8]

I was a corrections officer in one of Illinois's worst, most violent prisons. Full of murderers, rapists, notorious Chicago gang leaders, and other nationally recognized criminals. When I was employed there in the early 1990s, it was an extremely dangerous time and place that has since been improved upon. However, at the time, gangs and gang leaders had much influence. The gang leaders could move pretty freely throughout the institution, meeting with other gang members, conducting gang business, and just hanging out enjoying their day, not in their cells, but in the yard, the tunnels (hallways), or the galleries of the cell house. In this environment, the officers were frequently the target of threats, intimidation, and assaults.

For this reason, officers had to stand together and watch each other's back, sometimes using unorthodox methods to maintain discipline and control that may not be deemed acceptable by today's standards. In some respects, some officers resembled their own street gang more closely than a group of professional officers. This, however, was done to protect each other so that we could go home safely to our families. The inmates had shanks (homemade knives) they could attack us with, and sometimes did. Some of us had our own stash of shanks hidden within the prison walls that we would arm ourselves with upon arrival at the institution. Being unarmed in most cases, we wanted to protect ourselves, so we carried shanks unbeknownst to the administration.

How does this relate to Abraham Lincoln's desire for his personnel to know him, what he wanted, and how he would respond to a given situation? I had a good friend I worked with in the prison named Stephen. We hung out and spent time together, on and off duty. We got to know each other well. We learned how each other thought. What difference did knowing each other as intimately as we did make inside the prison?

When things went "bad" inside the prison walls, Stephen and I instinctually knew how each other would respond. There were multiple things that could go "bad" inside the prison, such as a large gang fight or riot; a murder, stabbing, or serious assault on an officer; or a bad count where the number of inmates we counted as being present in the cell house was not the same number of inmates that we were accountable for or were supposed to have. I knew what Stephen would think and do in each situation so I could respond promptly

[8] Ibid., p. 27.

and accordingly. I did not have to tie up the radio or waste valuable time by asking him for detailed instructions on what he needed.

Depending on the situation, I may have responded directly to Stephen's location to back him up or responded to a different location of the cell house to secure that area, as I knew what he would be doing at the other end of the cell house gallery and what he needed me to do. As an incident unfolded, the radio lit up with urgent messages, warnings, and calls for help, or the roar of inmates throughout the cell house alerted us to a problem, Stephen and I would respond, taking necessary action without the need to speak to each other. Knowing Stephen was located near the front of the cell house and would begin securing the front gallery gates, I would respond to the back gallery gates or secure the door from the cell house to the yard to isolate the problem. Doing so would prevent the problem from reaching other areas of the cell house and prison. Of course, these gates and doors would be routinely secured in today's prison environment, where a prisoner's movements are greatly restricted. However, during my time in the prison system, inmates were allowed significant freedom and movement within the facility. Supervisors allowed these gates to remain unsecured to accommodate the inmates and eliminate the need for officers to make multiple trips to open secured cells and gates simply to escort inmates.

Under stressful circumstances, I didn't need detailed instructions from Stephen. I knew him well enough to know how he would react, and he knew how I would. By the tone of his voice, what he'd say on the radio, and, as importantly, what he didn't say, I knew what he needed, and I responded accordingly. If Stephen was working on the catwalk armed with the shotgun and I was walking the gallery below, I did not have to call or look for him, as I knew he was watching and protecting me, ready to intercede on my behalf. With him there, I could maintain my focus on the inmates in my presence. I knew he would control the radio traffic and get me help if an incident occurred. If deadly force was needed, I knew he wouldn't hesitate. His presence enabled me to perform my job better and with more confidence.

Our relationship and knowledge of each other saved valuable time responding to emergencies. It led to successful outcomes while reducing the risk of harm to us and others. The leader or supervisor can obtain the same benefits Stephen and I did. Taking the time to know your people genuinely and for them to know you can be a game changer in driving performance to new heights.

The time spent getting to know your personnel, and learning their strengths and weaknesses, gives the leader the opportunity to reinforce the mission and lay out expectations. This, in turn, puts personnel on notice of what is expected and important to the leader and organization, and provides personnel the information needed to make rapid decisions in the field, eliminating any delay caused by constantly seeking out direction from the supervisor as to which way to go. Decision-making and performance are then enhanced, and everyone is better off.

Your subordinates are already watching you; make no mistake about it. They scrutinize your every move. It comes with the territory. Remember, it can be lonely on top. But this should not be perceived as a bad thing or something negative. On the contrary, you can work towards eliminating this void in leadership and use it to your advantage. You get to show them what is expected, what you would do in a given situation. If you are a competent leader, spending time interacting with personnel provides them with training and growth opportunities.

Navy Seal Jocko Willink "watched his platoon leadership, watched them make their tactical decisions and tried to understand why they made the choices they made."[9] I was fortunate to have good relationships with many of my superiors. I was able to question their thought processes and learned much from the rich discussions that came from them. Watching them, questioning them, and sometimes even debating them helped me grow and understand the big picture in many cases. And I know they benefited from those discussions. They learned my strengths, what made me tick, and what motivated me and allowed me to use them. And who benefited? They did, I did, and the organization did. That's sound leadership.

People are more satisfied and motivated when they get to do work they love doing. These internal emotional motivators can be stronger than external motivators, such as financial benefits. And a person's strengths are usually directly correlated to those tasks they enjoy doing. As a result, they are naturally drawn to the work they are interested in and good at. So, find your Johnny P. Know who your "go-to" people are for any given challenge or task.

Some command-level personnel excel in the field, functioning well in a stressful environment. They are quick on their feet and can make split-second decisions under extreme and unpredictable conditions. You've seen these guys. The more severe and dangerous the crisis, the brighter they shine and the more fun they seem to have. You wouldn't necessarily want to advertise to the public that this person is having fun during a public crisis when someone's life is at stake. But watch these masters of the field at work, and they light up under stress, get that boost of energy, and take off making tough decisions in seconds as if they have not given it any thought. It is more of an instinct; it comes to them naturally. This can make a chief executive who may not possess that same level of strength nervous. Still, time and time again, if you have correctly identified this person as one of your "Johnny Ps," positive and successful (not perfect) outcomes become the norm.

---

[9] Willink, Jocko. (2020). *Leadership Strategy and Tactics Field Manual.* St. Martin's Publishing Group, New York, NY, p. 15.

Then there are other command-level personnel who may not possess the strength to deal with these same types of crises in a natural and apparently at-ease manner. But their strength may be in the handling of administrative matters. They may be very detailed, taking in vast amounts of information and, after pondering it, can see the big picture and understand the good and bad long-term effects. This commander may excel at planning significant community events, budgeting, creating policy, or long-term organizational strategy that would put the field commander to shame.

Are both personalities important in the law enforcement agency? Absolutely! Could assigning the wrong commander to the wrong position cause significant problems? Absolutely! Under stressful circumstances, the commander who excelled in administrative tasks might have difficulty making split-second decisions in the field. If they freeze up under stress, hesitate, or make no decision, bad things can happen; lives can be lost.

On the other hand, the commander that excels in the field and can make split-second decisions may suffer in the ability to forecast the long-term effects of a series of strategic decisions that need to be made today. This could waste time and resources, bring about arbitrary and ill-advised policies and procedures, or have devastating effects on the morale of department members. Therefore, knowing your personnel's strengths and weaknesses is necessary to drive performance to the highest level.

When I was a patrol sergeant and later commander, I was fortunate to have several members of my team that excelled in the area of tactics. I would use these officers to train the rest of the shift. They would provide scheduled roll call training, lead a discussion or debriefing on a previous response to a high-risk call, or may have an impromptu training event as circumstances allowed. For example, suppose an open door was located at a business after responding to a burglar alarm. In that case, once the building was deemed secure, the tactically minded officer might take advantage of that opportunity to work with a less experienced officer in clearing buildings, searching staircases, making tactical entries, etc. Those tactically sound officers were responsible for increasing the depth and performance level of the entire shift.

When an actual event requiring tactical intervention occurred, these same officers naturally took the lead and began making decisions to resolve whatever crisis was before us. They did not wait for me to make all the decisions. Because I spent time interacting with them routinely, I already knew their strengths and abilities and whom I could trust. Because they spent time with me, they knew how I thought, what I would expect, what my "rules of engagement were," how hard they could push and what limitations they had, and when they needed to seek additional guidance.

So, even in those situations where my performance during a high-risk call was not optimal, like the field commander introduced in the paragraph above,

I usually had several people on the shift that possessed the required strength to make the right decisions and get the job done. In other words, I had my Johnny Ps. Of course, they went by many different names. But there were countless calls, armed subjects, people being shot, domestic partners being held against their will, barricaded subjects suffering from delusions, and more. Yet, they would show up, start making decisions, put a plan together, and get the job done. Theodore Roosevelt once said, "The best executive is the one who has sense enough to pick good men to do what he wants done, and the self-restraint to keep from meddling with them while they do it." I find this to be true. The professionals I worked with consistently made me look good again and again. It came down to knowing their strengths, developing and reinforcing them, and then getting out of their way so they could use them. That's a win-win for everyone, except maybe the bad guy who would frequently lose when my personnel got to do what they do best.

A significant study on great managers found that you can't tell a great manager by appearance. Great managers might have little in common regarding personality or one right way of doing things. However, a reoccurring theme among great managers which they do share is understanding and appreciating the uniqueness of the individual. "This is the one insight echoed by tens of thousands of great managers; people don't change that much. Don't waste time trying to put in what was left out; try to draw out what was left in."[10]

Do you want to drive performance? As a leader, get to know your people, identify their strengths, and put those strengths to use for your organization. As a result, the subordinate will be happier, and the organization will benefit from a more satisfied, motivated, and productive employee. "Focus on each person's strengths and manage around their weaknesses."[11]

In his book, *How Good Do You Want to Be?*, Nick Saban, arguably the greatest coach in college football, tells a story of being the quarterback during a game in his sophomore year in high school. They were down by six points, it was fourth and 12, and there were only twenty-five seconds left in the game. Saban asked his coach what play he should call. The coach responded that he did not care so much about what play was called as much as getting the ball to one of the two team playmakers. Saban did just that, and they went on to win the game. The coach would later tell Saban, "In critical situations don't think of plays, think of players."[12] This same principle applies well to law

---

[10] Used with permission of Gallup, Inc., from *First, break all the Rules: what the world's greatest managers do differently* by Gallup, copyright © 1999/2016. pp. 55-56. Permission conveyed through Copyright Clearance Center, Inc.

[11] Ibid., p. 153.

[12] Saban, Nick & Curtis, Brian. (2005). How Good Do You Want to Be?. Ballantine Books, New York, p. 82.

enforcement and probably every other business. Know your people, know their strengths, and put them to use. Then, when you most need the ball in their hands, get it in their hands. Find your Johnny P! I was blessed to find mine and had many of them.

Chapter 9

RELATIONSHIPS, IT'S ALL ABOUT RELATIONSHIPS

In the last chapter and other areas throughout the book, I emphasized the need to foster and enhance positive internal relationships with all personnel within the law enforcement organization. A leader or supervisor must be concerned with their assigned personnel and spend time interacting positively with them. They must be equally concerned and engaged with their peers and superiors alike. As mentioned, some hoard power or possess dysfunctional egos where they feel sharing information somehow puts them at a disadvantage. To get ahead and be successful within the law enforcement environment, they feel the need to manipulate or withhold information to serve their personal needs better. This can affect their behaviors regarding whom they talk to, cooperate with, or work well with and whom they tend to distrust or avoid. Traditionally, our organizations end up with information silos and work groups at odds with each other, e.g., sworn employees vs. non-sworn, patrol vs. detectives, SWAT officers vs. negotiators, etc.

For an organization to drive performance to an optimal level, these information silos must be dismantled and torn down. Instead, all aspects and functions of the agency must stay focused on the organization's mission and goals. The desired success can be obtained only by all functions working together towards the common goal of achieving the mission, regardless of their status (sworn or non-sworn, or as supervisory or non-supervisory). These are the ever-important and required relationships where nurturing inside the law enforcement organization must be accomplished. But what about external relationships between the law enforcement agency and outside individuals, groups, and agencies? It is these outside relationships that this chapter turns to.

When it comes to external relationships, we often create and maintain the same dysfunctional silos and behaviors that we find inside the organization, which are counterproductive and hinder positive results. In his and Zachary

Tumin's book, *Collaborate or Perish*, William Bratton put it this way, "the reality is that most organizations are still locked into the old silo overconfidence. 'We don't need to change. We'll continue to do more of the same thing.' It might be a matter of arrogance – 'nobody does it better,' or pessimism – 'it doesn't get any better than this.' These attitudes ensure that an organization stands still while the world moves forward around it. The Los Angeles Police Department was operating on a structure of exclusiveness, resenting anybody, whether outside or inside the organization, who questioned what they were doing."[1]

Early in my career, I would resent any outsider who wanted to tell me how best to perform my job. After all, I'm a trained professional, have been through a ten-week police academy, and have two years of police experience, right? So, "No, thank you, Mr. Citizen. I will tell you what your community problems are and how they should best be addressed." With this mindset, it's no wonder police often respond to the same calls over and over, reacting merely to the symptoms of the problem without ever really recognizing what the actual problem is and how it might be resolved. The police often don't see the real problems. The police don't see the world the same way others in the community do. Who should better know the problems and concerns of the community? How about community members who must live with the conditions of the problem every day? Why would we, the police, not desire their input?

For police officers, typically, the more serious the crime, the more excited they get about addressing it and catching the bad guys. However, the average citizen is often not concerned about the so-called serious crime but spends more time, thought, and concern on other issues. These issues could include speeding cars; a house with college students that have loud parties every weekend late into the night; homeless people sleeping in the park; a barking dog; or a neighbor who refuses to clean up their property. What may be perceived by the average police officer as a nuisance call may cause significant stress and concern to the community member.

Fortunately, as the role of policing has changed and become more complex in today's world, we are starting to realize that police services go well beyond the traditional role of "crime fighter." We also recognize that we can't solve the many social problems that become police problems without help and partnerships with other agencies and the community. When considering significant community problems, such as mental illness, the opioid epidemic, or the response to homelessness, it is only through partnerships that there

---

[1] Excerpt(s) from COLLABORATE OR PERISH!: REACHING ACROSS BOUNDARIES IN A NETWORKED WORLD by William Bratton, 2012 by William Bratton and Zachary Tumin, pp. 258-259. Used by permission of Crown Business, an imprint of Random House, a division of Penguin Random House LLC. All rights reserved.

is any chance for success. Success for tomorrow begins with building relationships today. Community members and public health and safety each possess a piece of the puzzle regarding these pressing societal problems. As partners with well-built positive relationships, the complete puzzle of our communities' many critical issues becomes visible. A more accurate picture of the problem increases the likelihood that an appropriate response can be determined and implemented to make our communities safer and healthier.

Imagine if the law enforcement agency got in the habit of routinely asking community members for their input. And not only their input but how about their help? We might be surprised by the information received just by asking. Just as I encourage leaders to create practices to increase their interactions with subordinates, the police must get in the habit of building community engagement opportunities. Not only will we more accurately identify the real problems, but more innovative ideas and support for combating the problems will likely follow.

The response to the problematic bar introduced in Chapter 6, "An Outdated Leadership Model," was partly successful because of the input and cooperation of various people. Ideas and input were certainly requested internally from officers responsible for handling the numerous calls to the bar. But the bar managers, employees, taxicab companies, the city's Public Works Department, and residents of the nearby condominium building were also included and leveraged to reduce the area's problematic behavior.

A previous relationship with local business owners became a valued asset in addressing a local drug house. It was known that this specific home involved multiple young people using and selling drugs from the house. Prior attempts to investigate and make a substantial case against the house's occupants failed with minimal results. The house sat on a busy main street, making a covert approach and surveillance difficult. We suspected that the occupants possessed a police scanner, as they seemed to immediately disappear upon the police department receiving and assigning a 911 call to that address. And there were many calls for suspicious people, drug activity in progress, fights, etc., around that house, but upon our arrival, we found nothing.

The police department determined that the residence behind this drug house belonged to a couple who owned a local business. A positive relationship with this couple had already been built from prior interactions, which made it comfortable for me to request their assistance. They granted the department the use of their home. Every night, for two weeks, we sat in their living room conducting surveillance of the drug house. They allowed us to use their home and tried to feed us, ordering pizza as we sat together. I'd be staring out their back window watching the drug house with binoculars, and they would be sitting together on the couch thirty feet away, drinking wine and watching a movie. It was a little unorthodox, but through the use of their home, we were able to make some firsthand observations that led to the arrests of the drug house suspects. The couple benefited from improvement in their neighborhood and an increase in their quality of life, at least for a little while. Because of a previously built positive relationship and our willingness to ask community members for assistance in solving a community problem, we solved this problem successfully. It was a win-win for the department and the community we serve.

Leveraging relationships to work for law enforcement's advantage requires a change in mindset away from the traditional way of policing, the "No thank you, Mr. Citizen, I'm the professional here and don't need your help" mindset. In referring to the business world, author Tom Peters wrote in *Thriving on Chaos*, "we'd be much better off if we could pretend that our customers are foreigners who do not speak our language; because they don't...we know and probably cherish our product as we live with it day in and day out...Our customers see the product through an entirely different set of lenses."[2] I think Peters' comments speak directly to the law enforcement profession. Do law enforcement members see the world as it is? Or do they see the world as they are? They see the world through the law enforcement lens. Those outside the agency, unless they have close attachments or associations with members of law enforcement, see the world through a different set of lenses, and this can cause conflict if not recognized and acknowledged.

Consider the contrasting views of Republicans and Democrats and the polarized views of the events involving police use of force in recent years. How can observations of the same event be perceived so differently? The answer? Reality lies in "the eye of the beholder." The cop sees the world as a cop – the fireman as a fireman. The doctor considers the world as a doctor. The teacher or school principal as an educator. The counselor as a mental health professional. They all see things differently based on their world, what they deem important, and the priority in their life.

I have seen these differences cause significant problems in delivering competent and professional services to the community. For example, when I started my policing career, our relationship with the local fire department was poor. On death investigations, where the decedent was obviously dead, there would frequently be struggles with the responding EMT/fire personnel who wanted to check on the body to ensure it was deceased. The responding police officers, convinced that the person was dead with no chance of returning, would refuse the fire personnel entry to where the body lay. At this point, it was considered a crime scene, and the police were trying to limit access by unnecessary personnel to maintain the scene's integrity. This led to frequent

[2] Peters, Tom. (1987). *Thriving on Chaos*. Alfred A. Knopf Inc., New York, p. 154.

arguments and complaints, which the mourning family on the scene should not witness.

A local drunk was found deceased and floating in the river. He had long been dead, with the skin slipping off his face and maggots inside his facial cavities. After the scene's initial response and processing, the fire department was summoned. The purpose of requesting the fire department was for the use of their boat to retrieve the body from the water. Upon arrival, some fire personnel were incensed when they were not allowed immediate access to the body. They started yelling "lifesaving measures, lifesaving measures," trying to convince me to allow them free passage so they could save this man's life. When told there was no life to be saved in this incident, I was told I should retrieve the body myself without their help or boat. It got tense, and I thought a physical fight might break out over this.

After several of these incidents, the Deputy Chief of the police department entered roll call one day, telling officers present to arrest any fire department member who entered a crime scene after being told not to. Arrest a member of the fire department from the same city? Wow! Under some circumstances, that type of drastic action may become necessary. Still, in most situations, that is probably not going to help us be successful and accomplish our mission in the future. Imagine the news headlines and the type of cooperation we could expect from the fire department the next time we called them for their help.

During the same general time in history, the police would always try to arrive at any accident involving a school bus before paramedics because the police knew what would happen if they didn't. Whether or not the accident was minor in nature, resulting in a small scratch, dent, or no damage whatsoever, and even with no reported injuries, the paramedics were going to speak to every child on that bus and contact every parent to ascertain whether the parent wanted their child transported to the hospital. The idea was that the juvenile was too young to decide for themselves, and, for liability purposes, none of the paramedics wanted to determine that medical attention was not required. Thus, depending on how many students were present on a school bus involved in a minor accident and whether their parents could be reached, the bus could remain parked in the roadway for hours, obstructing traffic, regardless that no student had sustained any injury. So, police officers would race to the accident scene, quickly determine if the accident was minor, and speak to all the kids via a quick announcement, "Is anyone hurt?" If there were no injuries, the police would block the bus door and not let the paramedics on upon arrival. We refused the paramedics access to the bus, told them there were no injuries, and informed them they could return to the firehouse. We instructed the bus driver to leave or relocate to another area where an accident report was taken out of the roadway. Do you think blocking the door and denying paramedics access generated cooperation and goodwill with our fellow first responders?

Early in my career, the relationship with local sexual assault advocates was also poor. Again, when a call was received from the local hospital regarding a sexual assault victim being at the hospital, I would race there to beat the sexual assault advocate. I was thinking like a cop and wanted to gather the information required to help us collect evidence and identify and arrest the alleged perpetrator. But, thinking like an advocate whose primary concern was the victim's well-being, the advocate wasn't always so cooperative in helping me achieve my objective. The advocate would be sure to tell the victim various things that could hinder my investigation. For example, the advocate would tell the victim she did not have to talk with me if she didn't want to; that I could come back at a later time when the victim was feeling better and felt like talking; or if she chose, the victim didn't have to make a report or submit to a sexual assault evidence kit. I'd think, "Yea, and lose all our evidence or let the perpetrator assault other victims in the meantime." The interactions between police and the advocates in the hospital's emergency room were often hostile, and complaints would often be made through the chain of command of both groups.

At the time, I thought I was right; the firefighters were arrogant and incompetent, and the advocates were anti-police and could not be trusted. However, with some added wisdom and experience, I learned that it did not have to be this way, and I was equally at fault for the uncooperative environment we encouraged. Yes, I'm a cop and think like one. They are firemen or sexual assault advocates, and that's how they think. But what if we took the time to build relationships? Time to communicate and try to understand each other's perspectives? How about showing each other respect for our individual and unique perspectives, and maybe, just maybe, we can work together?

Fortunately, that is precisely what happened. The sexual assault advocates became allies. Yes, I became more conscientious of the trauma the victim was going through and the harmful effects my drive for immediate answers, and results could cause. I was educated on the trauma-informed approach to investigating these types of incidents. I became more patient in my immediate need for information. And I began to trust and work with the advocates instead of against them. I would explain to the advocates what I needed and was looking for, and they would share their concerns with me. As communication and respect for each other increased, the advocates began to help me obtain the information I needed, but in a manner that respected the well-being and needs of the victim. Another win-win!

I went from not wanting or allowing the advocate to sit in on the interview with the victim to having the advocate assist. I realized the advocates often had a better rapport with the victim, had gained their trust, and thus could obtain more detailed and accurate information than I could. I leveraged that trust, and my cases were better because of it. It was, again, a win-win for me, the advocate, and the victims. We were all better off, as we accomplished more together than as adversaries. What was the secret? What changed? It was simple, just a change in mindset, a realization that we do not see the world as it is but see the world as we are.

Although I was not involved in any significant way in the change and transition from a poor relation to a positive relationship between the police and fire departments, I sure saw the difference it made. I guess the new leadership of both agencies decided it was time to change the mindset of how the two groups interacted with each other. So, we ended up with a great working relationship with the fire department. And isn't that how it should be? Both are city agencies whose mission is to serve the same community. Why should the success of one take away from the success of the other?

We compromised and worked together when we understood each other's concerns regarding the response to death investigation cases. If there was any chance medical attention could save an individual, as it had always been, EMT/fire personnel had complete access to the patient and scene for life-saving purposes. If the police were convinced the victim was deceased, and it was now a crime scene, we arranged it so just one paramedic, escorted by a police officer, would get a chance to view the body. If they then chose to check the victim's vital signs, they were allowed to, but if it were an apparent death, such as a decapitation, they wouldn't. This way, only one member of the fire department entered the scene where minimal disturbance to the scene occurred. We had an orderly process that maintained the integrity of the scene. The police officer would escort the fire department member, tell them where to stand, what not to touch, point out evidence in the area, etc. The paramedics were more comfortable and confident, knowing no life-saving measures would have made a difference in the case. This procedure prevented multiple people from stomping over our crime scene, where evidence might be destroyed, and required the police to identify all the people present for the investigative report.

Regarding traffic accidents involving school buses, we also compromised. When the police arrived on the accident scene first, assessed the accident, and determined there were no injuries, the police officer was allowed to sign one form acknowledging that no injuries had been sustained. The bus driver and school would then be required to ensure all parents of the children were notified of the accident. This expedited clearing the roadway and opened the road to regular traffic while simultaneously relieving the paramedics of their liability concerns regarding contacting the parent of every juvenile occupant on the bus. And that was just the beginning. The fire department became one of the greatest allies and supporters of the police department. I considered them brothers of the badge.

The fire department became a supplemental force regarding service delivery by the police department. We would frequently call on them for assistance or use some of their fancy equipment. For example, they possessed large vehicles with substantial lighting. We would use these lights to search for evidence after a significant crime, such as a shooting that occurred at night. The city owned a mobile command post, and it got to the point that a fire department member would deliver the command post to the scene of any significant law enforcement-related incident. Not only did a fire department member transport the mobile command post, but they would remain on location as a liaison to the police department. As part of this liaison, they would run the command post during a law enforcement incident, such as an armed barricaded suspect or an elderly person who was missing for a substantial period or under suspicious circumstances. The fire department liaison ensured that the command post had the necessary equipment and supplies, such as radios and cameras, and that they functioned correctly. They didn't wait around for police command to make a request; they were there taking the initiative to minimize any need for requests. If there were a need, the fire department would handle it rather than putting it on law enforcement, as they were already busy attempting to resolve the incident. The liaison would make coffee, ensuring food and drinks were available. They remained present and available to support and help the police department in any way they could. From a command standpoint, it was outstanding to know the logistics of food and water and basic needs were taken care of and not something else the commander of the incident had to do.

During a major fire incident, the police department would reciprocate. We would assign a member of the police department to join the fire command at the command post as a liaison to assist them in any way possible. Likewise, we ensured the fire personnel had refreshments, food, and water as needed. The police liaison was also on hand to take immediate action if assistance was required, such as traffic and crowd control, making a necessary notification, or sometimes an unruly person "popped up" and needed to be addressed. Having a police liaison on hand and present saved significant time requesting additional resources and putting things in motion from the law enforcement standpoint. Our goal during these fire-related incidents was to remove as many ancillary details and tasks as possible so that fire personnel could focus on their primary mission.

I'm not sure this is common practice for most communities nationwide. From time to time, I still hear about poor relationships between police and fire departments, similar to the negative relationship we had many years ago. For us, however, this support for each other became the usual routine way of doing business with law enforcement assisting fire personnel with any considerable fire call and fire personnel supporting the police department on any significant law enforcement response. In essence, each department had an instant increase in its workforce and equipment resources because of the excellent working relationship we maintained. And unique individuals interacting and spending time getting to know and valuing each other is critical for driving performance forward, as has been stated multiple times thus far in this book.

When a crisis comes, and we know it will, relationships are the glue that keeps people together side by side, working until the end, until the problem is over, and success is the result. But these relationships must be built before the crisis comes. And it does not matter what leadership level you hold in the law enforcement agency. Every leader needs to be surrounded by positive relationships. The chief or sheriff must build relationships with others. They must take the time to build relationships with other department heads, as well as with business and local church leaders, special community groups, media outlets, and even local politicians who make decisions that directly affect the law enforcement agency's mission and budget.

The agency's first-line supervisor, the patrol sergeant, is at the other end of the organization's leadership hierarchy. They need to have strong relationships with the street supervisors from nearby law enforcement agencies, who they may need to call in the middle of the night when there is an emergency and mutual aid is required. Will it make a difference when the on-duty supervisor gets a call for help from someone he knows, respects, and trusts?

The patrol sergeant should consider building relationships with local businesses. How about the bar managers they must deal with when the bar goes up for grabs at 2:00 A.M.? Can that relationship make a difference? They should work towards positive relationships with their counterparts at the fire department, the paramedics, the campus police at the local college, or the security officers at the local hospital. How about the hospital staff working in the emergency room? Can you think of any other non-law enforcement group as important? Stop in the emergency room occasionally with a box of bagels and coffee with a note that reads, "To the E.R. staff from the P.D. midnight shift." Then see the improvement in how you are received and helped when you require their assistance on a case or when a member of your patrol shift requires medical attention. You get to know them personally by name and face, and they recognize you as an ally. This is a much easier and more comfortable place when you must call on someone for help.

This type of relationship requires action on your part. Like much of this book, I encourage leaders to be proactive, not reactive. When you are reactive, you wait for things to happen to you; and they will, but not all of these things will be positive. However, when you are proactive, you are taking action to make good things happen. You are investing in the future. You are creating positive relationships today that ensure your success and that you will have the resources you need for that success in the future.

I was fortunate enough to be an Illinois Crisis Negotiators Association board member. An outstanding group that I believe provided some of the country's best training regarding crisis negotiations. My work with this group introduced me to several negotiators from the FBI. These were good people I formed strong relationships with. But I did not stop with just a positive and friendly relationship. The FBI would schedule and teach the forty-hour Basic Crisis Negotiators course several times yearly. I offered and coordinated this training at my local police department even when no member from my department would be attending the class. It was an excellent place to host a class with a robust downtown area, numerous restaurants and bars within walking distance, and hotels nearby. Not only did I offer and arrange for them to teach their course at our station house, but I was there on day one to assist with set up, welcome everyone (FBI and students), introduce the FBI instructors, and even make coffee for the class. I pumped up the FBI instructors, introduced them with flair, and made everyone's stay as comfortable as possible. With this treatment, the instructors kept requesting that their future courses be taught at our station house. Why all the effort? Why was the commander making coffee for the class?

These were good people whom I genuinely liked and appreciated, but there was more to it. When the FBI thought about my department, I wanted them to think, "great people, very supportive of us." When my name was mentioned among people at the FBI, I wanted the same thing. I wanted them to picture me and say, "great guy; we'll do anything to help him." Let's face it, the FBI has many resources, both in people and equipment. If my agency was in a crisis and could use the help of the FBI, I wanted to be in the best position to get the assistance we needed when we called for help. Therefore, investing early in those relationships made it that much more likely to get their cooperation in the future. And it did.

I readily called on the FBI for help on numerous occasions. In one instance, soon after opening an investigation on a businessman allegedly involved in sexual crimes with children, the suspect disappeared, "just up and moved away." Through social media mining, we learned he had relocated to Florida. Over time, we received information that he had made several trips back to Illinois to visit family or friends. This information was always stale; by the time we realized he had visited Illinois, he was already back in Florida. I contacted a friend with the FBI, and it was arranged so this suspect's name would be monitored through the FBI's resources, contacts, and relationships with the airline industry. I would be alerted of any scheduled flight with the major airlines under his name.

Would I have received this type of help and information had I just made a cold call to the local FBI office without any prior relationship? No chance! It was because of previous relationships that I could obtain this assistance and information. Then, I got the call. We learned when and where he would be coming into Illinois. We were able to locate and arrest him and subsequently obtained a needed statement from him.

There is an ongoing debate about how long an officer should be assigned as a detective. Should the detective position be permanent, or should there be time limits, such as three or five years, after which they return to patrol, and another officer is allowed to be a detective? There are pros and cons to both sides of the argument that will not be addressed here at any length except to say that your best detectives have networks of people they call on for assistance and information. These networks and relationships take time to create and nurture to heed the desired results. Any good detective knows that relationships are vital to being successful. For instance, building positive relationships with bank professionals, especially in the security field, can ultimately save significant time and energy. Because of these relationships, people in these networks may provide preemptive or insightful information. This information could be "a heads-up" about what would be found if a court order for a specific bank account was obtained or, to the contrary, what wouldn't be found. This can give your investigation direction and save precious investigative hours. All because of a prior built relationship. Any good detective already understands this. A leader within any police organization needs to understand this concept just as well.

I occasionally contacted my counterparts in other law enforcement agencies to say hello, check up on them, and learn how business had been for them lately. I would meet supervising agents from the FBI or DEA (Drug Enforcement Administration) for breakfast or lunch to stay connected and ensure the relationships were maintained and healthy. I also learned a lot from those meetings, staying current on the trends these professionals saw in their businesses. I could bring information to my department to keep my work group updated and prepared. And, of course, when a need arose, "I got a guy," an immediate contact and resource to help fill that need.

One of my responsibilities was liaising with campus security at a four-year private university within our jurisdiction. Even when there was no present need or related incident requiring contact, I made it a practice to be seen and heard and to build relationships. For example, I might stop by the campus to say hello, drop by for a cup of coffee with the security director, or make an unsolicited phone call to the director just to catch up, see how he was doing, and whether there were any concerns worth discussing. Investing in these relationships built the Emotional Bank Account that I could take a withdrawal from when needed without burning down the relationship.

When detectives were investigating a sexual assault alleged to have occurred on the college campus, I denied the security director access to the victim, refusing to allow him to sit in on the victim's interview. He wasn't a detective, and he wasn't a cop; he was the director of campus security, and I was concerned that the filter he was looking through at that time, how he was seeing his world, was not beneficial to our investigation. The director was not happy. He was upset with my decision. However, because of the already-built relationship, he got over it; we moved on, and the relationship stayed intact. Without the prior relationship, an incident like that could have done significant harm and created additional problems with future encounters and investigations. Fortunately, that wasn't the case here.

Two months after arriving in North Carolina as the head of the sheriff's office Criminal Investigation Division, I got to oversee a case of significance that made national news. What started as an assist to a sheriff's office in another county turned into a kidnapping and homicide investigation where our sheriff's office was the lead agency! The nearby sheriff's office had attempted a traffic stop on an individual who fled first by vehicle and then on foot into the Pisgah National Forest. Shortly after, the suspect kidnapped a camper holding him in the forest at gunpoint before releasing him later. A manhunt for this offender ensued, which involved multiple agencies and SWAT teams. Over the next four days, as the manhunt continued, the offender went through the forest into our county. Exiting the forest, he accosted an older man getting into his vehicle. He forced this victim to drive him from the area, still overwhelmed by law enforcement personnel searching for him. The victim was reported missing by family, and a much more extensive multi-state manhunt began. Finally, the offender would be located in possession of the victim's vehicle later that night. The victim, still missing for several days, would be found executed inside a cornfield.

As news of the missing victim spread, I began receiving calls from multiple agencies offering their assistance; the North Carolina State Bureau of Investigation, the ATF (Bureau of Alcohol, Tobacco, and Firearms), the U.S. Marshals' Service, and various nearby local sheriff and police departments among them. Having only been in North Carolina for two months, I had not yet established any significant relationships with these outside agencies. I had no deposits in the Emotional Bank Account with any of these groups. All I had was the reputation of my department. As a result, I was nervous and hesitant about accepting help from these groups. I knew myself and the capabilities of those working in CID but knew nothing of the performance of these outside agencies.

Furthermore, I'd had prior experiences in the Chicago area during significant events when what some call the "alphabet soup" (ISP, FBI, DEA, ATF) got involved. Unfortunately, the organization and cooperation during some of these events were poor. It usually wasn't the individual contributors on the front line that was problematic. Still, supervisors and administrators would often jockey for positions, and conflict would occur regarding what was to be done, who was to do it, who was in charge, and which agency was the lead agency.

As these calls offering assistance came in, I tried to refuse some. When I didn't see an immediate need for their expertise, I said we would get back to them if we needed their assistance, but many of them self-deployed and arrived at the command post to help anyway. Others were welcome to help, but even then, I tried to maintain some control by assigning representatives from my agency to partner with members from the outside agency so we could ensure some level of quality control over the case. I just did not know these people or anything about their normal performance levels. The relationships weren't there, and I wanted to ensure the investigation was handled appropriately and competently.

The fact is that this case was too big for me and my agency alone. There was just too much to do. I had to relinquish control to get the results we needed. And the point is? It is much easier to trust others, relinquish that control, have confidence, and set your Johnny P's free to perform when positive relationships have been invested in beforehand. Unfortunately, I did not have that luxury in this case.

This case was the beginning of many relationships that I would treasure and use again in the future. All those responding agencies were professional and helped us accomplish in a short period what we could not have done alone. We were able to track the offender's whereabouts and movements in two states, including through the Great Smoky Mountain National Park and back to North Carolina, where he was taken into custody. Surveillance videos were recovered along the way; witnesses were identified and interviewed, and the suspect's family members, social media accounts, and phone records were monitored. The resources of federal agencies promptly connected physical evidence to that of the offender and victim. Valuable evidence was recovered because of the overwhelming assistance provided by outside agencies. The leadership and experience provided by the North Carolina State Bureau of Investigation members cannot be overestimated. Their presence was a blessing in this case, as it also came to be in future cases.

As we conclude this chapter, I want to provide a word of caution. This chapter encourages leaders to build relationships with others who can help them be successful. I am not encouraging people to "use" other people. This is not about using or manipulating others for your selfish purpose. People will quickly catch on if they are being used and manipulated, which will not sustain any positive relationship. That behavior will lead to an overdrawn

Emotional Bank Account that can't survive. You will find yourself alone without the resources you need to be successful.

A relationship is a two-way street where there is give and take, and both sides benefit. If I expect others to give when I am in need, they should be able to rely on me to reciprocate and give back. This could be covering a shift for a peer who needs the day off, a call requesting you prepare and provide a last-minute unpaid presentation at the local college, or presenting some training for a community group. On the other hand, it may require you to rearrange your schedule to fit in time to meet with others to provide a law enforcement perspective on a newfound problem. Or maybe making the time to check on a friend experiencing some difficulty in their personal life.

There should be a benefit to all parties of the relationship. Suppose we can demonstrate that benefit so others see our vision that things can indeed be better with the relationship than they are without. In that case, we just might be able to tear down those underperforming silos and change the still-present law enforcement mindset that "knowledge is power and I'm not sharing it." Successful people "use relationships to build a foundation for success... They understand that strong relationships create loyalty and are the basis of partnerships and teamwork."[3] The relationships invested in today will drive performance and lead to tomorrow's successes. So, don't wait!

[3] From *The Fred Factor* by Mark Sanborn, copyright © 2004, p. 43. Used by permission of Waterbrook Press, a division of Random House Inc.

Chapter 10

WHAT GETS MEASURED (OR MONITORED) GETS DONE!

What gets measured, monitored, and rewarded gets done! This is a fact all leaders should come to grips with. "We don't get the behavior we hope for. We don't get the behavior we beg for. We don't get the behavior we demand. We get the behavior we reward."[1] So the key and the challenge are to measure, monitor, and reward the right stuff. Measuring the right stuff gets you the right results. Measuring the wrong stuff will get you the wrong results.

One of the first memories I can recall of this concept of driving performance in the workplace was in the early 90s. I was a young rookie police officer working in one of Chicago's more progressive and professional suburbs. The neighboring communities surrounding us were plagued with a significant street gang presence and problems. However, for the most part, our community did not have as big a problem as other nearby areas. In the early '90s, there was an increase in local street gang membership and the gang-related activity that goes along with it (drugs, assaults, burglary, vandalism, runaway juveniles, etc.). The gang problem continued to manifest itself and grow until it culminated with the gang-related shooting of the nephew of former heavyweight boxing champions Leon and Michael Spinks. The shooting paralyzed the victim from the neck down, landing him in a wheelchair permanently.

The police chief entered roll call one day and committed to fixing the problem. He provided officers with a mission, a call for action if you will; zero tolerance when it comes to the illegal activities of gang members. It did not matter how minor the offense might be. If they commit a crime, enforcement action should be taken. So, we began surveillance on these groups and took action when we could, an example of George Kelling and James Wilson's *Broken Windows* Policing. We were going to monitor and address minor offenses, nuisance behavior, and quality of life issues to take

[1] LeBoeuf, Michael. (1985). *The Greatest Management Principle in the World.* Putnam Publishing Group, New York, NY.

back our community from the gangs and prevent more serious crimes and offenses so we didn't have more shootings and assaultive behavior targeting our youth.

In recent years "zero tolerance policing" has come under attack and for a valid reason. Community and people problems are not "black and white." We need law enforcement professionals to use wisdom and sound discretion in determining what actions they should take in responding to calls for service and community problems. The "black and white," bright-line approach to arresting any and every violation of the law can create as many problems as it may solve. But the zero-tolerance encouraged by the police chief was focused solely on those identified as criminal gang members, causing consistent issues in the community. Following the 20/80 rule, that 20% of habitual criminals cause 80% of the problem, if we could make a difference in those 20% problem-people, we could improve the community significantly. This was an example of offender-focused deterrence before the term became popular.

We knew who the players and problem people were, so officers were provided bulletins with the names of gang members, their photographs if available, what gang they belonged to, and their addresses if known. With this information in hand, upon seeing a gang member in the community, officers could check for warrants before ever making contact with them. Initially, an officer might not have a legal justification for stopping the gang member, but by checking the system, the officer could confirm if there was an outstanding warrant. If there was, the officer could take enforcement action. If the gang member was driving a car with an equipment failure, such as only one headlight or a defective windshield, or with no front license plate, which Illinois law required, they got stopped. And they did not get a warning, something the average community member might get for such a violation. If they were known gang members, they received tickets. Let them be inconvenienced to come to court and pay a fine. It was a token of our appreciation for the destruction they caused in our community.

A law on the books prohibited anyone under eighteen from possessing tobacco. At the time, a juvenile could be placed under custodial arrest for possession of cigarettes. At first, I was pretty leery of enforcing such an offense. It didn't seem right to me as I smoked cigarettes in high school. "We are going to arrest kids for smoking cigarettes?" However, I realized it was a tremendous tool in this battle to rid the community of the gang problem. If we found the juvenile gang members possessing tobacco, they were taken into custody and transported to the police station, where their parents would be called and would have to come to pick them up. They would then receive a court date that often brought a fine. It also inconvenienced the parents, hoping to get their attention in managing their child.

Do you think this made things uncomfortable for the gang members? What do gangs like to do? Hang out in their group, loiter in public areas, act out, be loud, and smoke cigarettes. We could crimp their style by not allowing them to smoke their cigarettes openly. And, what else did we get with a custodial arrest, a custodial search? So, they were arrested for possessing cigarettes, and now we were finding their drugs and weapons too.

I did not know what was happening at the time. I knew nothing of the Broken Windows Theory, community policing, or data-driven policing (as the data showed us who our problem people were, and we allocated our resources towards them). I was just a young officer having fun chasing bad guys and enforcing the law. But the police chief had a mission; we knew what he desired, what he and his supervisors were paying attention to, and where the rewards were. Recognition came from putting a dent in the gang problem, so that is where we spent our proactive time, looking for and taking action against the known gang members. And it worked!

Gang members don't want that kind of oversight and pressure. They want to be able to hang out, drink beer and smoke cigarettes and weed. They didn't want to get arrested or cited every time they turned around, ending up with another court date, in jail, or paying more fines. So, they eventually moved on, left town, and found somewhere else to call home. Occasionally, another group would show up and rear their head, trying to set up shop in the city, but we knew what worked. We provided them the unwanted attention, and they tended to disappear just as fast as they showed up. And not only did that tactic work, but I found that making a real difference and solving a known community problem was fun and rewarding.

This type of response and progress can be made with various community problems. If we ask the right questions, collect and measure the correct information, and use appropriate measurements to direct the organization's priorities and resources, there are no limits to achievable success. But do we sometimes put our focus and law enforcement resources on the wrong stuff and then find ourselves surprised and exasperated when the results aren't exactly what we hoped for? You bet!

Simon Guilfoyle, in his book *Intelligent Policing,* recognizes the importance of measures when it comes to identifying priorities and managing performance for the organization. The selected measures and priorities should directly relate to the organization's mission. However, he argues that numerical targets as performance indicators change behaviors and often bring negative consequences. The focus of agency performance under numerical targets changes from "quality to quantity."[2] I do not believe any law enforcement

[2] Used with permission of Triarchy Press Limited, from Intelligent Policing: *How Systems Thinking Methods Eclipse Conventional Management Practice* by Simon Guilfoyle, copyright © 2013, pp. 136-162. Reproduced with permission of the Licensor through PLSclear.

leader would argue against the idea that the desire and intention are to provide quality law enforcement or policing services to the community. With that in mind, I believe any agency or leader asking what they should be measuring would do well to consider Guilfoyle's view and research as provided in *Intelligent Policing*. He makes a strong argument against numerical targets as appropriate measures of performance. Below is just one example of law enforcement organizations measuring the wrong stuff.

As a patrol officer, my organization did not have quotas. No specific number of tickets or arrests was required during any given period. Supervisors kept track of an officer's self-initiated activity every month, and if there was a lack of activity, I'm sure a supervisor would bring that to the officer's attention by saying something along the lines of, "What are you doing out there with your free time to help forward the agency's mission?" There were various self-initiated tasks an officer could participate in, both enforcement and service-oriented, to demonstrate appropriate use of their patrol time. But, no demand that a set amount of traffic tickets, parking tickets, arrests, etc., be made monthly or otherwise. If, after receiving a traffic ticket, an angry traffic violator commented that I must be trying to reach my monthly quota, I was always proud to advise them of the truth. "No, I don't have a quota. I'm writing you this ticket because I want to," I might tell them. Or maybe I'd let them know, "I'm writing you this ticket because of your poor driving habits."

But then, the leadership of the police department decided to implement performance standards. They weren't called quotas, we were told they weren't, but they sure looked and smelled like quotas. These performance standards dictated that a specific amount of traffic tickets, parking tickets, DWI arrests, bar checks, community contacts, and suspicious person contacts be conducted annually. Whether an officer met the required performance standards would be noted on the officer's annual evaluation and discipline would be served upon those that did not meet the criteria.

The leadership team who decided to create these performance standards, and discipline those who did not meet the appropriate performance level, were not bad people. On the contrary, these were good men, supervisors, and leaders I respected greatly and who always treated me well. They were responsible for mentoring me and my development, allowing me to do what I have been blessed to do with my career. I owe a lot to these people. Furthermore, their intentions were good. They came through the ranks of a professional police organization where most employees performed admirably. However, as they rose through the ranks, they observed that a small element of the organization was not carrying its weight. They were not using their time on the job to benefit the community. They tried to avoid work and do as little as possible while the good people of the organization picked up their slack and worked and served the community around them. They were making the same amount of money and receiving the same benefits as other employees but were doing very little regarding performance. So, when these leaders rose to the top of the organization, it was this small unmotivated group, often with a negative attitude, that they intended to hold accountable by introducing required performance standards. Their heart was in the right place.

Indeed, this group of leaders is not alone in this thinking. These types of performance standards or quotas have been debated for years and are still used in many places today. When these standards were introduced to the organization I worked for, most other departments had been using quotas for years. These numerical targets were typical and the way of doing business at many police departments. So, one could argue that my department was only catching up to the times, finally doing what everybody else had already been doing. What was the result? Remember, good or bad, what gets measured gets done!

At first, I didn't think much of the introduced performance standards. I was the sergeant of a patrol shift at the time, and there had been no mention yet of discipline. We already recorded monthly activity that looked at how individual officers and varying patrol shifts were doing regarding their self-initiated activity. I considered these standards like recommendations officers should strive for, guides that demonstrated where they stood compared to the average officer (the standards were created by taking an average of all officer's current activity). But then, progressive discipline was introduced by the department, which bothered me as I feared a predicted behavioral change like that described by Simon Guilfoyle in *Intelligent Policing.*

The goal was to affect behavior change in the bottom "ten-percenters," those not carrying their weight, but I feared it would also hurt our good officers, our best assets. I brought these fears to the attention of management. As always, they heard me out, treated me with respect, and gave me a voice. But this time, I was unable to persuade them otherwise. They were moving forward with the performance standards. The wheels were already in motion.

The result: the focus went from quality to quantity of work. Officers focused on getting their numbers (outputs) to avoid discipline instead of improving the quality of services (outcomes) provided to the community. This introduction of performance standards affected all officers, not just the bottom "ten-percenters." These included good officers – people who cared about the community and the type of service they provided. Self-preservation is a powerful motivator. When discipline, suspension, and loss of money were on the table, they adjusted their behavior accordingly to reach the numbers at all costs.

Emphasis on specific rating numbers or policing tasks de-emphasized others. For example, there were eight categories in the annual evaluation. Yet, the self-initiated activity category was the only category where discipline was meted out for not meeting requirements. What did this do? Obtaining a rating number that successfully met the self-initiated activity category became the priority. All seven other categories, including verbal communication, written communication, teamwork, work habits, etc., received less attention. They were less important.

Officers began making more traffic stops, which these performance standards hoped to achieve. But now wisdom and discretion were set aside, and officers, desperate to reach their numbers, started writing cheap or weak tickets. Minor traffic offenses where the violator may have previously received a warning or not even been stopped were now getting stopped and receiving tickets and a fine. It didn't take long before we started hearing complaints and negative chatter from citizens in the community. I never observed this personally but was told that some officers had been telling citizens they didn't want to write them a ticket but had to because management demanded it. I certainly would never have said something like this and was disappointed to hear that any officer in my department would, but these are just some of the adverse side effects measuring the wrong stuff can bring. The relationship between the police and the community began to erode.

The morale of officers also fell. Teamwork suffered, as taking care of yourself and getting your numbers trumped it. Officers with special assignments, such as Evidence Technician and K-9, spent significant amounts of their patrol time assisting other officers with their calls for service and attending additional required monthly training specific to those assignments. However, they were still expected to achieve the same numerical targets. Did the quality of work on some of these other responsibilities suffer? I do not know, but I suspect shortcuts occurred if they stressed over issuing a few tickets before their shift ended. And the performance standards did nothing to consider officers' strengths and weaknesses.

The previous chapter, "Find Your Johnny P," emphasized how important it was to utilize people to their strengths to increase performance. These performance standards created everyone equal and expected them to achieve the same self-initiated numbers. But at what cost? The officer with a natural ability for drunk driving enforcement, who frequently made DWI arrests and removed dangerous people from the street, now had to curb his DWI enforcement to set aside time "to go hunting" for parking tickets, all to ensure he did not fall short in that category. Meanwhile, the older officer, who was still active and contributing by monitoring public places and issuing more parking tickets than most, had to refrain from what he was good at to look for DWI opportunities, which rarely came without help from others. So, to ensure this older officer met his DWI quota, the officer with the natural ability for drunk driving enforcement would find a drunk driver and have the older officer assist, enabling the older officer to claim the arrest statistic. This enforcement activity now involved two officers instead of one, resulting in inefficiency.

The department got what they measured; self-initiated numbers went up. But where was the quality and benefit to the community? I have had hindsight conversations with the Chief of Police, who approved introducing these performance standards. Again, a good man and one for whom I have much respect. I am confident that he would tell you to be careful what you measure because you might get what you ask for.

UNEXPECTED RESULTS AND A LESSON LEARNED

I was a patrol sergeant when the "What gets measured or monitored gets done" concept hit home. For most of my career, the annual evaluations I received from my supervisors were borderline worthless. The evaluations I completed on subordinates early in my supervisory years were no better. Having an updated performance evaluation on file was a city requirement. Still, the content was rarely more than a sentence or two paraphrasing the category definition to be rated. For instance, the category of Relationships with Citizens may have a SUPERIOR rating definition of: "Is very much at ease with citizen contacts. Quickly establishes rapport and leaves people feeling that the officer was interested in serving them. Excellent non-verbal skills."

My supervisor might rate me as superior in this category and then leave the comment:

"Very easy-going demeanor with the public. Easily establishes rapport. Already possesses good interview skills."

This really has not told me anything specific about my performance. Yes, I appreciate your favorable opinion of my work, but what exactly can I do with this evaluation for future growth? What are my strengths and weaknesses?

I decided I wanted to do better for my personnel. They deserved a proper and accurate evaluation that gave them specifics on their strengths (what behavior they excelled at and were expected to continue with), and those areas where there was room for growth, and how they might achieve that growth. They deserved to know this information. Therefore, I committed to paying attention to my subordinates' performance and taking note of it routinely. As part of this new commitment to making myself accountable to my personnel for accurately assessing their performance, I created a spreadsheet to track subordinates' report writing to assist me with that portion of the evaluation instrument.

Up to this point, I had minimal to no data to evaluate, only my faulty memory. I would sit there with limited information and think to myself, "well, I do send back some reports to this officer for correction but not too many" or I might only be able to recall the last month of reports, good or bad. Therefore, I assessed subordinates primarily on the previous month's results. But utilizing my new report writing spreadsheet, I began to make notations during the entire evaluation period. After this, I possessed a significant amount of yearlong data to evaluate their report writing and written communication performance more accurately.

More details referencing this spreadsheet will be presented in the next chapter, "Execution." But the point of introducing it in this chapter is that once personnel learned I was collecting data and measuring their performance related to report writing, their reports improved without my intervention. I didn't have to say or do anything. My new spreadsheet wasn't a secret, but I didn't publicly announce it. I just went about monitoring their report-writing skills. It took a while before my practice of logging the report writing data came to light, but when it did, along came improvement. Reports started getting turned in with more detail. Officers quit taking shortcuts and started following proper protocol when it came to investigative or report-writing procedures. There was a significant decrease in the number of reports I had to send back for correction. Personnel knew their reports were being measured, and it changed behaviors.

Supervisors had always reviewed their subordinate's reports. Still, once completed satisfactorily, even if it took three attempts and returns for corrections, the reports were forwarded to the records division, not to be seen again in most cases. Now, detailed information was being collected and measured that could be used for future decision-making involving personnel evaluations, promotions, or specialty assignments. This is important stuff. So, like the required numerical performance standards discussed above, self-preservation kicked in. But this time, it led to improved response and documentation of calls for service. This was a win-win for everyone.

Reports got processed and forwarded quicker, meaning they landed on the detective's desk and received follow-up investigation sooner. It was more efficient with less work and follow-up for the officers and me. And it returned the officer to the field where they were needed rather than them having to leave their assignment in the community to follow up on a deficient report. This meant they were in the field patrolling and handling their calls instead of another officer picking up their slack because they had to work on a report that was not done right the first time. This positive change occurred just because they found out I was monitoring their performance related to report writing. It took no special program. It took no significant effort on my part.

It took no additional training. It was a simple spreadsheet I created to hold myself accountable to the officers and their performance evaluations.

The unintended results of creating the report writing spreadsheet led me to search for other leverage opportunities to achieve similar performance improvement results. I made a second spreadsheet that monitored officers' In-car camera use. All patrol officers had cameras in their patrol vehicles. As a sergeant, I would randomly review two videos from each officer under my command a month. Any observed behavior of interest, good and bad, would be logged in the spreadsheet. Later as a commander, I expected the sergeants that worked for me to follow the same procedures in utilizing the report writing and In-car camera spreadsheet.

What performance-related behaviors could you find on an officer's In-car camera video? Officer safety, how they communicated and interacted with community members, decision-making skills, a proper understanding of search and seizure laws, and compliance with department policy and procedures, to name a few.

What I found was like that of the report writing spreadsheet. When officers knew supervisors were reviewing samples of their In-car camera videos, it changed behaviors, specifically officers' demeanor. It changed how they talked with citizens, and their compliance with procedures, as the proper use of the camera system increased, with officers being sure to record all required police actions. But, again, these improvements came automatically without intervention from supervisors. This alone improved the organization's performance, reduced citizen complaints, and provided more quality evidence for the prosecution of recorded offenses. And I did nothing but take a few minutes monthly to monitor and measure officers' performance using the available tools and technology.

Of course, for measurement to work and improve performance, there must be some level of accountability when personnel don't perform as expected. We will explore accountability in greater detail in the next chapter on execution. But, for now, the idea is that creating measures and consistently monitoring those measures provide a foundation from which personnel are motivated to perform based upon the measures the organization determines appropriate. But what are appropriate measures?

WHAT SHOULD WE MEASURE?

Tom Peters says, "Measurement is the heart of any improvement process. If something cannot be measured, it cannot be improved."[3] William Bratton

[3] Peters, Tom. (1987). *Thriving on Chaos.* Alfred A. Knopf, Inc., New York, p. 74.

said, "you can't fix what you can't measure, but you can expect what you inspect."[4] But what should the law enforcement agency be measuring?

The typical police organization will have mass amounts of data and information coming in and being processed daily. There will be multiple requests from constituents and community groups, each with their concerns and agendas, occasional crises erupting, fires to put out, and the routine problems and decisions that must be made daily. Where do we begin?

We need to begin with clarity of focus. We start by examining the organization's mission. What is the purpose of the organization? What are we in business for? What are the priorities? Where do we want to take our agency? If you do not know your mission, vision, purpose, or priorities, you must find that out first. Without focus, we end up ineffective and inefficient in using our resources. As a result, we waste time, energy, resources, and maybe our credibility too.

Eliminate processes that don't add value to the mission. They suck up resources providing minimal, if any, benefits. The chief, who instituted the above performance standards, expected officers to increase their proactive self-initiated activities. More performance sounded like a good thing. But the negative ramifications and de-emphasizing of other essential services worked against the organization's mission and ultimate goals.

In a previous chapter, I mentioned how my organization collected data on the number of bar checks being conducted by patrol officers. Officers were required to fill out a "Bar Sheet" after walking through one of the local bars and checking for law violations. This sheet was sent to front desk personnel responsible for collecting the data from multiple sheets and creating one "Master Bar Sheet" with all the data combined. Then, they took the same information and entered it again into a computer database. No one was looking at this database or doing anything with the data, wasting time and resources that could have been spent furthering the organization's mission.

IDENTIFY YOUR PRIORITIES

Japan's attack on Pearl Harbor brought America into World War II. But what did General Eisenhower do in response? What was his first course of action? America was fired up; they wanted vengeance on Japan. This was an understandable emotional response and expectation, but that was determined not to be the first priority. General Eisenhower had clarity of focus. He

[4] Excerpt(s) from *Collaborate or Perish! Reaching Across Boundaries In A Networked World* by William Bratton, 2012 by William Bratton and Zachary Tumin, p. 16. Used by permission of Crown Business, an imprint of Random House, a division of Penguin Random House LLC. All rights reserved.

prioritized "securing England, retaining Russia as an ally, and defending the Middle East."[5] Eisenhower stayed true to his priorities, and action against Japan would have to wait.

What are your organization's priorities? Every community is unique. In the same way, every law enforcement agency is unique. Yes, there are often similarities in the services provided but look closely at the mission statement of various departments, and you will find different ideas, outlooks, and priorities. Some will emphasize the law enforcement function, and others stress service, some community policing and partnerships with the community, and others crime reduction. Then there is a focus on problem-solving, fear of crime, constitutional policing, transparency, legitimacy, treating people with respect and dignity, personnel development, etc. Most organizations probably embrace several of these concepts but place different levels of emphasis on them. The fact is that every community is diverse and has particular problems and expectations of its police agency. It is this uniqueness that the leader must identify as they determine the organization's priorities. Once the priorities and mission are known and understood, a strategy can be created to get the organization moving.

I once read a quote from an unknown author. It said, "the man who is committed to everything is committed to nothing." There is always busy work to be done. There are always people in the community and otherwise who want the attention of their local law enforcement officers. Requests are coming into the organization daily. If we had all the money and personnel we wanted, we could maybe serve and commit to everything. Even then, in policing, when one citizen wins and gets what they desire from their police department, another citizen often loses and doesn't get the result they hoped for. And law enforcement is financed by tax dollars, and we know there is a limit to those dollars. So, we must use them wisely and cautiously. We must ask, where can we get the most "bang for our buck?" What are our priorities? The man committed to everything is committed to nothing! He tries to please everyone, do everything, and solve all problems, wearing himself and the agency too thin and only providing mediocre service in the process.

We must start by identifying our mission, purpose, and priorities. That may require significant data gathering and measurement efforts to determine where we want to go, the problems worth addressing, and what the community desires or needs. Once completed, with our mission and priorities in hand, we can gather and analyze the data required to demonstrate the organization's present status as it relates to where we want to be. For example, suppose a priority is improving the police-community relationship. In that case, we

[5] Used with permission of John Wiley & Sons Books, from *Eisenhower on Leadership: Ike's Enduring Lessons in Total Victory Management* by Alan Axelrod, copyright © 2006, p. 28. Permission conveyed through Copyright Clearance Center, Inc.

may hold town hall meetings with residents, speak with business owners, and survey members of the community to determine what the current relationship between the police and the community looks like. We cannot improve it if we don't know what it is presently.

The difference between where we want to be and where we stand presently is the gap that strategy is to help the organization close. What is needed to close the gap: the right performance measures. What gets measured gets done, but we must measure the right stuff.

Commissioner William Bratton explains how he found the borough commanders at the New York Police Department deficient in that they had no detailed understanding of the incidents of crime occurring in their respective boroughs. How can they make decisions that will positively affect crime if they do not understand or have the appropriate awareness of the crime in their area? This behavior was not consistent with his priorities. Bratton committed to changing this, and one measure he took was to be informed of every shooting and homicide in the city. What was this going to accomplish? "This meant the borough commanders would have to have the same awareness as Bratton did before he came asking about it. The same would be true for precinct commanders and lieutenants. It would all trickle down. To stay ahead of Bratton, the commanders would need news of shootings or homicides to start its way up the chain of command even before the smoke had cleared or the body went cold."[6] A well-informed borough commander, captain, lieutenant, sergeant, detective, patrol officer, and any other personnel of the law enforcement organization will benefit by having the information available to make the best decisions required of them at their level and expectation of performance. The leader is responsible for creating the systems and processes to measure the right stuff so personnel have the resources to perform optimally. By insisting he be notified of every shooting and homicide (the process or strategy), Bratton motivated his personnel to ensure they had up-to-date information that helped them make better, more informed decisions (improved performance; the measurement).

The data Bratton gathered told him where the gaps were. His commanders did not possess the situational awareness needed to achieve the mission. So, Bratton created processes and measurements to reduce that gap – his decisions and chosen measurements directly connected to the organization's priorities and mission.

When we recognize the importance of measurements, collecting and analyzing data, the answers we seek may be staring us in the face. With the correct information, solutions will become more apparent. The gaps between where the organization is and where we want it to be will manifest themselves.

[6] From Bratton, *Collaborate or Perish! Reaching Across Boundaries in A Networked World*, p. 17.

Problem-solving efforts will be enhanced, and making the right decisions will become easier. The correct measurements should drive decisions.

Some questions that appropriate data gathering and measurements may help us answer and drive our performance forward, to name a few, are:

- What are the community's concerns? Are they concerned about serious crime in their neighborhood or more about nuisance, quality of life type behaviors?
- What crimes are occurring and where?
- Where are the reoccurring problem locations?
- Who are the problem people? The 20% percent rule tells us that 20% of criminals or problem people cause 80% of the problems; do we know who they are? Do we know where to find them?
- Who are the victims? What are the characteristics that make them more susceptible to victimization?
- What's the level of fear of crime in the community? Is it consistent with actual crime rates, or might education reduce some of the fear?
- What are the clearance rates in the detective division? How about conviction rates? Are there any processes, improvements, technology, or training that will increase clearance and conviction rates?
- Is the community satisfied with its police organization? What might increase their satisfaction?
- What kind of complaints is the organization getting from citizens?
- How about the use of force? Are there any training deficiencies that might enhance officer safety and reduce the use-of-force events?
- What kind of lawsuits has the organization been involved in? What action might reduce or eliminate them?

When the data is inconsistent with the organizational priorities, it allows you to make adjustments and decisions more aligned with the mission.

THE STRATEGIC PLAN

I attended an out-of-town weeklong management class. In this class, I first saw and heard of the strategic plan I would later work under at the sheriff's office. As the instructor – a high-ranking member of the same sheriff's office I would later work for – presented the plan, I was amazed by what I heard. I came from a professional organization. Traditionally our performance levels were high. We were a respected police agency. We had a mission statement and set priorities; at least these were discussed at the top levels of the organization. But we did not have a strategic plan like what I saw in this class. This sheriff's office had a strategic plan that set priorities and gave direction to the entire agency. The plan made expectations clear. And the sheriff didn't just hide the strategic plan in a binder somewhere in his office. Everyone knew what was being measured and what members of the organization should be working towards. This plan was talked about throughout the organization. It was the topic of ongoing and numerous command staff meetings. And it was posted on the sheriff's website for all to see, including the community. This sheriff had a vision and was holding himself accountable for obtaining the results of his strategic plan. He also held town hall meetings where he shared his strategic plan with the community, again a means of keeping himself accountable to the plan.

One of his goals was to *"reduce agency-targeted crime."* An objective under that goal was to *"Reduce Part 1 Crimes in high crime areas by 10%."* So, the sheriff was putting the community on notice that he was going to reduce crime. But what if he didn't, I thought? What if he failed? Wasn't he taking a huge risk? He was an elected official. If crime went up instead of down, the sheriff was setting himself up to be raked over the coals. What would the community think and say about him and his strategic plan then? It was bold. I was unfamiliar with other law enforcement agencies doing this, even those I perceived as the most progressive and professional. I had read about NYPD's COMPSTAT program, a process created to ensure agency accountability for reducing crime in New York. But that was New York, the largest city in America with its many resources. I read about strategic planning and the importance of setting goals and creating measurements to achieve them. Still, I had never personally seen them like this in a local law enforcement agency, so transparent.

On a break, I asked the instructor if he would email me a copy of the organization's strategic plan. Having seen how appropriate measures can lead to increased and improved performance, I wanted to study this strategic plan further. It was something I might be able to use in my department. The instructor emailed me a copy, and I returned to my home agency in Illinois, intrigued by what I had seen.

About a year later, I noticed a job announcement. This same sheriff's office sought a Captain to run the Criminal Investigation Division. Again, the strategic plan inspired me. Not necessarily the contents of the plan, the specifics as to what was being measured and what wasn't, but more so the vision, boldness, and leadership to create such a plan, a roadmap by which to guide the agency and hold himself and the agency accountable to the community they swore to serve. Many law enforcement executives may prefer to create and discuss their goals and priorities in closed-door meetings where plans are documented using an erasable pencil, thus minimizing future pain from not reaching their goals or meeting their targets. But is that what true leaders do? So, intrigued by the strategic plan and vision of this particular sheriff, off to North Carolina I went. I wanted to be a part of this. I wanted to help.

The purpose of this section is not to go into any depth on the technical aspects of creating a strategic plan. There are multiple resources out there to help one go through that process. One such publication is Community Oriented Policing Services (COPS) *Law Enforcement Tech Guide for Creating Performance Measures that Work.* I have also included the sheriff's office's strategic plan and a plan from the North Carolina's Association of Chiefs of Police. These can be found in Appendix C. These are two basic plans that provide an example demonstrating the process of identifying priorities, the agency's goals, objectives for meeting the goals, and the strategies to be used to meet those objectives.

An organization should identify a few goals that directly support its mission. These goals become the organization's priorities and guide the organization toward high performance and results. Goals should be few, as an organization has limited resources and cannot be all things to all people. Taking on too many goals can lead to failure or mediocre results when resources must be disbursed across numerous goals instead of being appropriately invested for success on a few identified priorities.

The sheriff's office's goals, as shown in Appendix C, were:

- Goal #1: We will use our financial and human resources fairly, efficiently, and effectively.
- Goal #2: We will reduce agency-targeted crime in the county.
- Goal #3: We will provide high-quality service to the citizens of the county.

After an organization identifies its mission, purpose, and priorities (goals) – in other words, "the what" – they now know where they want to go, and it is then time to create measurements to get them there. The strategic plan presents "the how" – those measurements are the roadmap to get them there. The organization's goals should rightly be identified and determined by the chief executive office, the police chief, or the sheriff. Goals should remain consistent and not be readily changed over time. However, objectives and strategies should be flexible and subject to change, as the environment, based upon the measurements and collected data, dictates.

For instance, under Goal #2, *reduce agency-targeted crime*, an objective was to *reduce Part 1 Crimes in high crime areas by 10%.* One strategy to reach this objective was to identify the four highest crime areas in the county. Extra patrols were assigned to those four areas. After three years, there was a 16% decrease in part 1 Crimes in those areas combined. However, the data revealed that the crime occurrences in one of the four identified high-crime areas were significantly lower than in the other three. In such a case, deciding to take the extra resources and patrols from the area with significantly lower crime rates and assign them to the three areas with more crime may be a sounder approach to reducing even more crime. This would require changing the strategy as the agency would target three high-crime areas instead of the original plan to target four. The data didn't justify maintaining four high-crime areas. The organization's goal of reducing agency-targeted crime remained the same; however, the strategy changed.

Another objective for *reducing agency-targeted crime* was to *reduce domestic violence recidivism rates within the county by 15%.* When I was a captain at the sheriff's office, almost one in five (18%) reports taken by patrol involved a domestic situation. Eighteen percent of reported crimes, including all other crimes – larceny, breaking and entering, robbery, damage to property, financial crimes, etc. – were domestic-related. We were seeing the same offenders over and over committing domestic violence offenses. The data told us and my experience and observations confirmed that we had a problem – indeed, one worth addressing. So, addressing domestic violence recidivism became an objective, and rightly so. However, after several years, the data reflected no significant change in attacking the domestic violence problem. Over time we made several adjustments to the strategies set to reach this objective but found that the critical pieces required for success were missing.

Accomplishing this objective required assistance from outside stakeholders, i.e., judges, the district attorney's office, other local police departments', women's shelters, domestic violence advocates, counselors, etc. This was known upfront and planned for, including these stakeholders in the agency's plan. But while we had excellent cooperation from some stakeholders, we couldn't garner cooperation from others. Over time deputies faced challenges trying to carry out their required roles, referencing the agency's Domestic Violence Initiative when collaboration was not being received by other stakeholders needed for success. Deputies became frustrated, and their efforts began to wane as they saw the extra effort being for naught. Eventually, the objective of reducing Domestic Violence recidivism rates was discontinued. Again, the goal of reducing agency-targeted crime remained consistent and didn't change, although the objective or strategy did. Resources were removed from this unproductive domestic initiative and reallocated to other strategies for reducing targeted crime.

Having a strategic plan as a roadmap helps all personnel see the big picture and understand how they fit into that picture and how their personal investment and performance make a difference in the organization's success. This can be motivating, especially considering the Type A personalities often found in law enforcement. People want to feel good about themselves, feel like they are participating in something of value, and that they are genuinely making a difference, improving both the community and the organization. However, understanding the "big picture" presented by the agency's administration means little if personnel don't accept or buy into that picture. For example, we want the patrol officer working the beat alone and unsupervised at three o'clock in the morning to understand and support the organization's mission. When this beat officer responds to a call for service or decides what he will spend his self-initiated activity on in the middle of the night, we want him to know and accept the big picture and his role in it. Would it make a difference in the officer's performance if his input and suggestions were sought as part of the strategic planning process?

Although it remains the right of the police chief or sheriff to determine the goals and mission of the agency, the input of those on the front line, should be sought, considered, and utilized when deciding upon the objectives and strategies used to reach the agency's goals. Personnel on the front line know what's happening in the community. They live it. They are closer to the action and the problems and have a pretty good idea of what works and what doesn't when they respond to them. This knowledge must be sought and included in building the strategic plan. Strategies should also be built with some flexibility to allow unit managers and individual contributors to innovate and be creative in accomplishing goals. Allowing all personnel to contribute to the agency's strategy can foster employee commitment and increase the likelihood that the unsupervised officer on patrol at 3:00 in the morning will support the organization's mission.

Through the strategic plan, the organization should conduct various trial runs and experiments, with feedback from front-line personnel, to learn what works and what doesn't, and adjust accordingly. Did we learn anything from the lack of success in the above-described Domestic Violence Initiative? Absolutely! The importance of building strong relationships with others before they are needed, as presented in the last chapter, might be one such lesson. Many of the profound social ills that law enforcement is called to intervene in, such as domestic violence, drug addiction, and homelessness, cannot be addressed with any level of success without the help of non-law enforcement partners. Building relationships is vital.

Secondly, too much time and resources were spent trying to salvage the initiative when data told us it would not work. Our hearts were invested, wanting so badly for the initiative to work that we dragged it out too long; we dragged it to a slow and painful death. We could have discontinued it earlier and utilized our resources better. Is that a failure? I don't think so. Lessons learned that can make us better, more effective, and more efficient in the future are not failures. So, give your people clear guidance with transparent goals and strategies, but ensure they have opportunities to try new things and innovate in reaching those goals, and you may be surprised at the positive results you get.

NO STRATEGIC PLAN, NO PROBLEM!

What if you are not the sheriff or police chief and your organization has no strategic plan? Most law enforcement agencies today do not yet have a formal strategic plan. At least, as I search various law enforcement organization websites, it is rare to find one. There may be discussions within the organization about strategy, but having a formal plan or document prepared and presented as a roadmap for the entire agency to see and follow seems to be lacking. Strategic plans are more common in the business world than in government. The good news is that you do not have to have an official strategic plan to use measuring and monitoring to your advantage. Just like the report writing and in-car camera spreadsheet that I created that improved performance, there are measurements that any leader in the organization can make to drive performance.

If you are a group supervisor within your respective agency, ask yourself, "What are the chief's priorities? What are my supervisor's priorities, goals, or expectations?" You may already know this information, thus providing a starting point. If you aren't sure, ask. Or look at the agency's mission statement. You are probably on safe ground if you can improve performance within your work group, which helps achieve or make improvements to the organization's mission.

For example, take a mission statement that says*: The XYZ Police Department is going to increase public safety by partnering with the community, providing quality services based upon progressive police practices, and empowering the department's human resources to perform at their highest capacity.* There are three distinct goals within this mission statement that processes and measurements can be created to improve upon.

1. Partnering with the community
2. Providing quality services based upon progressive police practices
3. Empowering the department's human resources to perform at their highest capacity

As a unit or division leader, you can take the initiative to improve your work group's performance and ensure it is consistent with the three identified aspects of the mission. There is no need to wait for an official strategic plan or even specific direction from the organization's chief executive officer for that matter. As a supervisor, nothing excites me more than seeing a subordinate take the initiative to improve department operations by being creative and coming up with new and innovative ideas. That is the type of commitment we need from leaders in policing. The mission statement provides goals and priorities; you can now create strategies and measurements for your work group to accomplish the stated goals. For example:

Partnering with the Community

- Historical crime data told us we could predict an increase in robberies during the holiday season (Thanksgiving and Christmas). Therefore, we created a crime prevention pamphlet specifically highlighting robbery prevention and how to be a good witness when a robbery occurs. This pamphlet is disbursed to local businesses that are open late and are typical robbery targets (gas stations, convenience stores, hotels, etc.). Members of patrol or detectives are assigned to meet personally with employees at establishments where the pamphlet is provided and initiate discussions. The police department, in essence, is educating would-be victims and asking them for help in preventing, investigating, and prosecuting robbery offenders.
- Similarly, data tells us there is an increase in crimes against the elderly, particularly financial-type scams. We meet with social service agencies, those providing services to the elderly–the police department partners with these service providers. We begin holding classes at various group homes and facilities that concentrate on the elderly residents of the community. We explain the present trends related to financial scams and how to recognize, respond to, and report them. Additional services and resources are provided for them and their family as needed.
- Create opportunities to interact and engage with the community. The police department cannot help if they don't understand; any given geographic area within the greater community will likely have different perspectives and problems. Thus, be willing to host and attend community meetings where the police department can get to know residents and better understand their unique needs, concerns, and problems. Get the word out to the community of your desire to help by advertising everywhere–through the media, newspaper, social media (such as FaceBook), the agency's website, and word of mouth during officers' daily calls for service.

Providing Quality Services Based Upon Progressive Police Practices

- I requested that crime data be sent to me from the department's crime analyst every week. The crime data was broken down into police beats. It further identified the location, day, and time of the offense. I could reallocate staff based on the need and any identified problem locations with this information. Traditionally, staff would be allocated evenly across the various police beats. However, when one beat or section of our jurisdiction demonstrated a higher crime incident, I would reallocate patrol assignments, putting more officers in the areas requiring attention. In addition, I would reassign officers to respond to various identified problems. For example, when the data demonstrated an increase in graffiti as being restricted to one area of the city and occurring on weekends, I assigned bicycle officers to that area where they could monitor specific areas conducive to the graffiti, such as schools and parks. Likewise, when data showed increased property damage throughout the downtown area, we looked at the times and locations of said damage. We determined the damage was likely random and occurred while offenders were probably walking home from a bar or leaving one downtown bar and walking to another. With this information, I increased patrol visibility during those times. I also assigned officers to foot and bicycle patrol, which resulted in numerous arrests for drunk and disorder-type behaviors in the downtown area **and decreased** damage to property-type cases. Rather than maintain the traditional standard of having patrol assignments evenly across all geographic areas, I used timely data on crime, disorder, and complaints to allocate personnel to improve the quality of service provided.

Empowering The Department's Human Resources to Perform At Their Highest Capacity

Assessing training needs and providing appropriate training would certainly fit this category, but developing personnel doesn't stop there. Create other opportunities to enhance your personnel's skills, experiences, and abilities to perform at higher levels.

- Remember the goal-setting sessions I conducted in Chapter 7? I would meet with the supervisors of the division, and together we would determine our priorities for the upcoming year. This allowed supervisors to engage and seek input from their direct reports, ensure their personnel's opinions were heard, and obtain experience developing proposals, presentations, and debating priorities among their supervisor peers. In addition, these supervisors from different units collaborated, increasing teamwork and building consensus.
- As a patrol sergeant, I would identify those among the patrol shift I believed had the potential for future promotion into leadership positions within the agency. I would then create opportunities to develop their skills by assigning them as the shift supervisor for a day while I tended to other tasks, such as attending a meeting, working on an employee's evaluation, or researching needed equipment. In addition, of course,

I was still on duty, present, and monitoring the radio for any urgent matters that required my immediate attention. Still, for the most part, the officer was in charge of the shift that day, and all patrol officers were expected to report to them as such. This provided invaluable experience and boosted employee morale when they recognized my trust and faith in their ability to perform at a supervisory level. I was always amazed at how they willingly stepped up and exceeded my expectations when given this opportunity.

- In Chapter 8, I highlighted the importance of investing time into getting to know your personnel to recognize their strengths and weaknesses. Once you know their strengths, look for some stretch goals and opportunities for them. For example, if they excel at community engagement activities, ask them to develop new ideas for engaging the community. Then put them in charge of making it happen. If their strengths lie in tactical operations, get them involved in training others in the unit on tactical operations to further increase your group's ability to respond to crimes in progress and active shooter-type incidents.

The examples above are actual practices I participated in, along with other professionals with the drive and desire to make a difference in the community. The point is not to suggest that you must do these exact things. Instead, these examples demonstrate what can be done with or without a strategic plan with some initiative and creativity. Once you know what is essential to your agency, you can begin to leverage your own processes to improve performance. Any improvement in performance, no matter how small or incremental, is still an improvement, and your work group or organization is a little better because of it. In fact, small incremental improvements are often the best way to proceed. Asking for too much of your personnel too quickly may lead to resistance or outright failure. So, identify the process that will get you the desired results. Then, create measures to ensure employees follow the process and consistently monitor performance, rewarding personnel that adhere to the process and deliver the intended results.

It should go without saying, but for measures to work, they must be transparent and known by all subordinates to which the standards apply. I suggest creating a feedback process to keep personnel informed on goals and any progress toward achieving said goals. Consistent feedback and two-way communication will keep employees engaged, as the following and final example of the "what gets measured gets done" concept demonstrates.

I decided to create monthly reports for the police chief. This had not been done before, but I initiated these reports to hold myself accountable for the appropriate use and allocation of the personnel assigned to me. In addition, I knew that if I submitted monthly reports on my work group's performance to the chief, I needed to pay attention to what was occurring in the community. What did the crime picture look like? What were the trends, problem locations, community complaints, etc.? And, just as important, what were we doing about it? Although this report was to be created as an initiative to hold myself accountable for my performance, like the report writing and In-car camera spreadsheets previously discussed, unintended consequences occurred.

The report highlighted significant events occurring during the month, including the following: spikes in crime, locations where repeated incidents occurred, changes in officer allocation based upon present or predicted increases of crime, special operations, community engagement efforts, significant community complaints and concerns, as well as to recognize positive work by members of the department. A sample of a similar report can be found in Appendix D.

At first, the report was a document solely to be forwarded through the chain of command to the chief's office. At some point, however, I thought it might be interesting to subordinate officers to see the report as well, and that is where the unexpected consequences came from. Although I did not plan for it, I received way more benefits from the officers receiving this report than I ever did from the command. Once officers saw the data, the issues, and what was important to the department and community, they began to self-deploy. They did not wait for directions or an assignment to the problem area. Instead, they would add extra patrol to areas that warranted it. They would increase enforcement activities where appropriate. They would leave their patrol cars and go on foot patrol if that were best. They began approaching me with suggestions for resolving the present issues. "If you want to put me in a crime car (a two-man car, often in an undercover capacity, with the primary purpose of enforcement) Friday night, we'll get in there and make some arrests," one officer told me. "How about we assign a couple of bicycle officers to that area for a week?" was another suggestion. And still, others approached me and asked, "What do you think about initiating a crime prevention campaign targeting our victim group?"

Once officers saw the issues, what was essential to the organization, and what we were measuring and monitoring, they changed their behavior, stepped up, and increased their performance. And when great things happened because of their improved performance, they would get recognized (rewarded) in the next month's report for their efforts and performance in solving a problem or advancing the organization's mission.

FINAL THOUGHTS ON MEASURES, MONITORING, AND REWARDS

It is worth repeating the caution provided to us by Simon Guilfoyle in his book *Intelligent Policing*. When it comes to measurements, we should be careful when identifying numerical targets. Numerical targets can be manipulated and lead to quantity over quality, such as the number of arrests made, tickets written, suspicious persons stopped, business checks completed, and crime reduction percentages ("reduce robberies by 10%"). These types of results can prove detrimental to the law enforcement organization and do little to nothing for the community.

As part of their regular patrol duty, officers were expected to monitor the liquor establishments in their assigned patrol beat. Monitoring included bar checks, which required the officer to leave their patrol vehicle and enter the liquor establishments looking for violations. They were also required to monitor the businesses to ensure they were closed on time. The previously mentioned bar sheet was then turned in, and the officer received credit for said bar check or closing (a numerical target). A quota, in theory, could then be established, requiring each officer to complete a set number of bar checks, such as twenty a month. But what will it tell us if an officer obtains the twenty-a-month requirement? What if they conducted thirty or forty bar checks a month? What do we know about the quality of these bar checks? Are we settling for quantity over quality?

Suppose monitoring local liquor establishments is important to the community to limit disorder conditions and maintain an appropriate quality of life. In that case, there is nothing wrong with expecting officers to complete these tasks. A professional officer committed to his duty, the community, and the organization's mission will know and understand that he is responsible for monitoring the liquor establishments in his assigned area. The good, committed officer will make time during a patrol to get out of the car and check on the bars. At closing, he may park his car, get out, ensure the business doors are locked, and look in the windows to confirm that patrons are no longer present. Or, finding an unlocked door, the officer will enter to ascertain if it is merely employees cleaning up after hours or patrons actively drinking. How about the less active, less committed, or downright lazy officer, our bottom "ten-percenters"? They may slowly (or not so slowly) drive by the liquor establishment and, from the seat of their patrol car, glance over at the business and through a window, not see patrons drinking, thus concluding that the bar is closed. Both these officers then complete their bar sheets, getting the same credit, though the quality of work is vastly different.

Rather than insist upon these types of numerical targets that I often refer to as "the lazy man's game" (as long as the numbers are up, we must be doing ok), I believe leaders would be wise to adhere to the concepts laid out in Chapter 8, "Find your Johnny P." If leaders take the effort and time to get to know their personnel, their strengths, weaknesses, and their business, their personnel's performance levels and abilities will become evident. You will know who your superstars are, your middle 70 percent, and bottom "ten-percenters." Then, instead of creating arbitrary numbers everyone is expected to equally adhere to, you, as the leader, can deal with your personnel as individuals, providing them the unique support and development they need to meet expectations and take their performance to a higher level.

As a sergeant or even a commander, when an officer was identified as lacking in any notable self-initiated activity during their uncommitted patrol time, I gave them an encouraging word or a request to increase their activity. If that didn't work, it wasn't uncommon for me to jump in the patrol vehicle and go out into the field with them. "Show me what you do while you patrol," I'd say to the officer. If they didn't use their time wisely or find self-initiated activities to participate in, I would take over and direct our patrol activities (as far as I recall, I never had to do so, they always found something to do, and we usually ended up having a great time). This tended to get everyone's attention. Besides a few exceptions, most people did not want the boss riding with them because it brought relentless ribbing from their peers. So once again, "what gets measured gets done." "If you don't want the boss jumping in your car; you better give him what he wants," peers would tell each other. The point is that I addressed the lack of self-initiated activity with the deficient person. I did not create an arbitrary number forcing everyone, good or bad, to obtain it.

Another example of a numerical target that I suggest cautiously considering is the crime reduction percentage or similar type of measurement. Indeed, reducing crime, fear of crime, and disorder is an appropriate goal worth working for and measuring. However, when arbitrary numbers are attached that employees are accountable for achieving, sometimes the behavior change and results the organization receives differ from what the measurement was meant to achieve.

After obtaining a 40% reduction in breaking and entering offenses over five years, as part of the goal of reducing crime, an objective of the sheriff's office strategic plan was to maintain the reduction of breaking and entering offenses at a minimum of 15% from the previous levels five years earlier. The goal of this objective was to keep the breaking and entering offenses from returning to the high rate of violations, as seen previously. Keeping breaking and entering crimes down is a good and valid measurement. However, too much focus and insistence on the arbitrary number of 15% could lead to harmful and counterproductive behaviors if personnel felt that reaching their numbers must be made at all costs. Similar to the previously mentioned introduction of performance standards that led some officers to sacrifice the quality of tickets and arrests to avoid discipline for not reaching quotas, the same could occur at a leadership level. For example, suppose a commander, who is accountable for crime reduction, is going to potentially face harsh discipline, demotion, or embarrassment for not reaching set goals. In that case, self-survival might lead to an adverse change in behaviors.

I cannot say that I ever witnessed this. But, still, the allegation has been heard, that offense classifications have been changed to present a more pleasant picture for an agency or at least for the personnel who are going to suffer if the numerical targets aren't met.

For instance, in this example, might a breaking and entering where a front door to a residence is kicked open and entry made, but nothing of value stolen, be classified as damage to property instead of a breaking and entering? Might they classify an attached garage differently from a detached garage though the actual offense and intent of the perpetrator be the same? These small but significant misrepresentations can make the numbers appear as if the organization is achieving its desired goal. Yet, the intention of the desired goal is not met, the quality of performance remains the same, or worse, quality and service suffer. Again, I never personally observed this. However, even if a sheriff or police chief would never condone or participate in this kind of number manipulation, if it did occur at lower levels in the organization or even if it never actually occurred, but personnel perceived it did, the credibility of the measurement and hence the commitment and support of the individual contributors expected to carry out the mission will be lost.

We began this chapter with a quote from Michael LeBoeuf's book, *The Greatest Management Principle in the World*: "We don't get the behavior we hope for. We don't get the behavior we beg for. We don't get the behavior we demand. We get the behavior we reward."[7] Rewards, like the behaviors we consistently measure and monitor, let everyone in the organization know what is important; what behaviors and types of performance are valued. It lets everyone know what the agency's leaders are paying attention to and measuring. Due to the power of self-interest and preservation, your personnel will adjust their behavior to align with agency measures and rewards if that serves their interests. People want to be successful. They want to feel good about themselves and valued as a contributor to the organization and the greater community. And, on some occasions, such as the instituted performance standards and required quotas discussed earlier in the chapter, they will change their behavior to avoid trouble, negative feedback, and discipline. The key is to measure and reward the right behaviors.

---

[7] LeBoeuf, *The Greatest Management Principle in the World.*

So, returning to the previous question, "What should we be measuring?" Again, I'll refer to the words of Tom Peters in his book *Thriving on Chaos.* "I have become a fanatic about quantifying, but a new sort of quantifying. I insist upon quantifying the "soft stuff;" quality, flexibility, service, innovation, people involvement, and even how much time is spent breaking down inappropriate inter-functional barriers."[8] Likewise, Larry Bossidy and Ram Charan explain, "You should reward not just strong achievement on numbers [high levels of performance], but also the desirable behaviors that people actually adopt."[9] What are you measuring and rewarding?

- Are you measuring and rewarding collaboration and teamwork, or does the "lone wolf glory hound" that excels at conducting criminal investigations, identifying, and apprehending offenders but does so at the cost of alienating and belittling others get your attention and commendations?
- In Chapter 5, I told a story of a burglar trapped inside a home. As other officers were preparing to make entry to locate and arrest the burglar, I provided cover and security from behind a tree at the front of the home to ensure the burglar could not escape. I was playing a crucial support role to those officers entering the house. Do you recognize and reward your support personnel and bench players, including civilian employees, or are your words of appreciation reserved solely for your superstars who play prominent roles?
- Do you reward the person willing to take appropriate risks to carry out the mission yet sometimes errs, or does the person that never errs because they play it safe and take no risk get complimented?
- Do you reward the officers who take a little extra time to speak in depth with a victim, identify additional witnesses, or ensure their investigation is thorough, or do you publicly applaud the officer who completes their assignment promptly and returns to patrol, while the quality of their work is lacking?
- Do you reward the person who frequently generates new ideas even though most are not adopted, or does your demeanor tell this person you are too busy and your time too valuable to be bothered with their ideas and input?
- Do you reward the supervisor with high-performance levels, but who obtains that performance by micromanaging his subordinates and destroying their morale?

---

8 Peters, *Thriving on Chaos*, p. 40.

9 Excerpt(s) from *Execution: The Discipline of Getting Things Done* by Larry Bossidy and Ram Charan with Charles Burck, copyright © 2002 by Larry Bossidy and Ram Charan, p. 94. Used by permission of Crown Business, an imprint of Random House, a division of Penguin Random House LLC. All rights reserved.

- Are your employee evaluations and promotions consistent with the agency's priorities, values, and decided-upon measurements, or do you preach one publicly but promote and evaluate with different criteria?

"When the wrong people get rewarded, the whole organization loses. Problems don't get fixed, non-performers get ahead, and the good performers start looking for jobs at places their contributions will be recognized."[10]

The fact is that what the organization and its leaders measure, monitor, and reward will get done. The critical and challenging question is, are we measuring, monitoring, and rewarding the right stuff? Our ability to drive performance higher depends on it.

---

[10] Bossidy, *Execution: The Discipline of Getting Things Done*, p. 133.

Chapter 11

EXECUTION

"Judging from our observations, a high proportion of those who actually rise to the top of a business organization have made their mark as high-level thinkers. They are the kind of people who get caught up in the intellectual excitement of each new big idea that comes out and adopt it with enthusiasm. They are articulate conceptualizers, very good at grasping strategies and explaining them. This, they know, is what it takes to get ahead. They aren't interested in the "how" of getting things done...They don't necessarily understand how to execute. Many don't realize what needs to be done to convert a vision into specific tasks because their high-level thinking is too broad. They don't follow through and get things done."[1]

The above quote is from Larry Bossidy and Ram Charan's book *Execution: The Discipline of Getting Things Done.* The basis of their book and this chapter of the same name is ensuring things in your organization get done and done right. Too often, the leader, whether the agency head, or a patrol division sergeant, provides personnel with instructions, creates a new procedure, or otherwise directs the work that subordinates are to complete going forward. Then, after making the pronouncement, this leader in charge walks away without a plan or thought regarding any follow-up or measure of accountability to ensure the work that is supposed to be done by their personnel actually gets done. I know I'm not the only one who has ever sat through a staff meeting where decisions were made, and everyone appeared to agree or at least understand what was to be done. Still, nothing changes, the problem isn't resolved, and you find yourself sitting in another staff meeting six months later having the same discussion.

How about the boss who jumps on every new fad or idea that they find in their most recent policing publication or conference they attend? They

---

[1] Excerpt(s) from *Execution: The Discipline of Getting Things Done* by Larry Bossidy and Ram Charan with Charles Burck, copyright © 2002 by Larry Bossidy and Ram Charan, pp. 35-36. Used by permission of Crown Business, an imprint of Random House, a division of Penguin Random House LLC. All rights reserved.

eagerly put the latest initiative in motion on top of all the other initiatives they have established that went nowhere. Their personnel think, "Just wait them out; this too will go away in time." Cost, time, and leadership credibility are wasted, and the organization's performance does not benefit from the leader's inability to execute.

The inability to execute undermines all other positive characteristics of leadership you may have. It will not matter how nice you are, trustworthy, hardworking, approachable, or visionary. If you can't influence your personnel to get the job done, you are holding the organization back from reaching its optimal level of performance. "Too often, leaders at the top concern themselves exclusively with plans and policy, with "doctrine or methods," to the exclusion of monitoring the execution of orders, principles, plans, and policies. Plans and policies mean nothing until they are implemented and implemented adequately."[2] "Brilliant execution is more important than brilliant strategy."[3]

How do we execute and ensure the right things are getting done? I am certainly not perfect in any respect when it comes to execution. There were times when the work groups I led excelled in execution and getting the right things done, and then there were times when I ultimately failed to execute as I should have, and problems or performance deficiencies lingered. But there are some consistent practices that I will share in this chapter that served me well and made a significant difference in the ability of my work groups to achieve high levels of performance, along with maintaining positive attitudes and high levels of morale.

This chapter is included as the last chapter of this section on "Driving Performance" because it brings the previous four chapters, "An Environment for Success," "Find Your Johnny P," "Relationships, it's all about Relationships," and "What Gets Measured Gets Done" together. If you prescribe and diligently practice the concepts described in the last four chapters, you will be well on your way as a leader who knows how to get things done and execute.

An Environment for Success

You are well on your way if you can create such as environment as we saw in Chapter 7, where the Emotional Bank Account of all personnel, regardless of rank, is high; an environment where all parties are heavily invested; where genuine commitment beats out mere compliance; where open communication and candor is the norm; and the truth gets told, and problems get solved.

---

[2] Used with permission of John Wiley & Sons Books, from *Eisenhower on Leadership: Ike's Enduring Lessons in Total Victory Management* by Alan Axelrod, copyright © 2006, p. 97. Permission conveyed through Copyright Clearance Center, Inc.

[3] Peters, Tom. (1987). *Thriving on Chaos.* Alfred A. Knopf Inc., New York, p. 142.

I have sat through command meetings where the agency head was preaching the mission, giving direction for the organization, and imposing their will and ideas on how to solve a given problem or move the agency forward. As I looked around the room full of supervisors and high-level command personnel, I observed almost everyone nod in agreement, yet I, and probably many of them, knew what the agency head was saying would not work in the real world. But they said nothing. Instead, they returned to their respective divisions, and very little agreed-upon gets done. This is not how a culture operates that knows how to execute. When you create a team-centered atmosphere where everyone is valued and the leader provides opportunities for ongoing communication in a trusting environment, people are more comfortable speaking out, disagreeing with others, and sharing their thoughts and ideas. With the minds of many working towards creative ideas and solutions, more effective decisions are made, and progress is the result.

Find Your Johnny P

When the leader takes time to interact with and get to know their personnel, they understand and appreciate the individual uniqueness of every member of their work group. When you know your subordinates' strengths and weaknesses, you can more accurately utilize and assign persons to their strengths. You know their talents and what they excel at and can therefore use them in those areas to benefit the agency. You put your round pegs into round holes and square pegs into square holes. When people sit in the right seat on the bus, there is momentum. You have identified your "go-to" people, who, in various situations, make things happen and get things done. There were times when I was called upon by my superiors to accomplish tasks they knew I could excel at. Then there were those occasions when I wasn't the man for the job, and someone else was more appropriate, as they had the ability to best accomplish the task.

Getting to know subordinates' weaknesses also serves the leader well, as they can customize training and developmental opportunities specific to an individual's needs. Such training can enhance the person's competence and increase their capabilities and abilities to be successful, which in turn creates a more substantial asset, thus improving the organization's ability to execute in the future.

Relationships, it's all about Relationships

Leaders need to develop partnerships with the community and outside groups or organizations, whether law enforcement or not, that possess needed resources or are willing to share responsibility for improving the quality of life in our communities. Instead of viewing outsiders skeptically as adversaries, today's complex policing environment calls for identifying stakeholders who can provide perspective and add depth and unique resources to complement our desire for improvements. When we break down the secretive silos of the past and welcome input and participation from others, we may finally be able to tackle and resolve some of the social ills and problems facing our communities instead of merely responding to the symptoms of the problem without having any real long-term effect. This concept should not be reserved solely for those at the organization's top. Personnel at every level should seek community engagement opportunities and invest in relationship building. You never know when a relationship built today will pay dividends in the future. The key is to form these relationships and make friends early before they are needed and a crisis occurs. When you have a trusted "go-to" person or group, the problems and crises do not have to be paralyzing. You'll possess the tools needed to tackle the problem, to execute, and get back on track. You have the resources to be successful and get things done.

What Gets Measured (or Monitored) Gets Done

There is no guesswork when an organization has clearly identified its mission and priorities. If you do not know your mission, you can't execute it. At all levels, every organization member needs to see the big picture, understand where they fit in, what is expected of them, and the type of performance that gets rewarded. When the proper controls and measurement systems are in place, accountability to the agency's priorities is reinforced. Those who execute and get the job done right are rewarded. Others are developed, counseled, corrected, and given opportunities to improve their performance. Ultimately, if they aren't competent enough to perform or choose not to, they should be removed. Larry Bossidy states, "When I see companies that don't execute, the chances are they don't measure, don't reward, and don't promote people who know how to get things done." "Execution has to be a part of an organization's strategy and goals."[4] However, when expectations aren't clear; when measurements aren't in place to ensure expected work is being completed; when employee evaluations are not filled with honesty and candor, the risk is high that accountability within that agency is lacking.

NO ACCOUNTABILITY, NO EXECUTION

This entire book centers on the idea of accountability. Great leaders are accountable. They are accountable for their actions and decisions; they are

[4] Bossidy, *Execution: The Discipline of Getting Things Done*, pp. 73, 19.

accountable to the organization; to their superiors; to their direct reports; to the community; to the constitution; to current law; to their families; and so on. Great leaders step up. They are proactive. They make things happen. There are too many in leadership positions that are reactive. They just get by, waiting for something to happen, and then respond. And things do happen. These reactive leaders seem to go from crisis to crisis, just surviving. They seem to be busier than others but never achieve any substantive progress. They may fight fires daily, always seemingly in the midst of some crisis, often leading the charge of some sizeable disciplinary investigation involving a member of the agency. But in the end, they show little progress toward a greater tomorrow; they don't know how to execute and get positive things done long-term for the organization.

Great leaders, on the other hand, are accountable for results. They are thinking and preparing ahead of time. They are proactive, looking down range to the future, making moves and decisions that improve their position, set them up for success, and may divert or prevent an impending crisis.

Show me a leader or a law enforcement organization that is not accountable, and I'll show you a leader or organization that doesn't execute. But on the other hand, an agency with a culture of accountability or execution is proactive. They put systems and controls in place to ensure proper performance by their personnel. For example:

- They create policy that gives clear guidance on what behaviors are appropriate and expected in given situations. When procedures aren't followed, proper action and correction are taken. They don't ignore inappropriate behaviors until an adverse event occurs and receives widespread media attention, forcing the agency into reactive back-peddling and face-saving actions.
- They stay current on best practices by providing appropriate training, such as the use of force, pursuit driving, excited delirium, crisis intervention, sexual harassment, etc., to prevent catastrophes, instead of waiting until forced to provide relative training after a catastrophe, and the impending consequences have already occurred.
- They ensure the organization is staffed with competent supervisors who are also held accountable for ensuring the quality of work of their subordinates is on par with the agency's priorities and expectations.
- When an employee's performance is not up to standards, corrective action is taken to improve it. Continued violation of agency expectations is met with appropriate discipline. In addition, honest feedback is provided to personnel during their evaluations. As a result, they do not sugarcoat poor performance.

Law enforcement organizations that often are not accountable ignore personnel performance deficiencies to the organization's detriment. They put their head in the sand until they can't hide anymore. The result is often much more severe than had they been upfront and accountable for their errors, misjudgments, or deficiencies in the first place. They ignore reality until reality bites them. The behavior of an unaccountable organization often results in one or more of the following: lawsuits, arrests of police officers for misconduct, injury or death to a citizen or member of the agency, preventable termination of an employee, or significant damage to the relationship between the community and the law enforcement agency.

In the last chapter, I explained how I conducted random checks of the patrol officers' in-car camera videos every month and then expected sergeants working for me to do the same. I've heard officers at other agencies say no one, including supervisors, was allowed to review their recordings unless there was a reason, a reported incident that required investigation. This is reactive; conducting a review post-incident after the damage is done. That is not a sign of an organization that is accountable and executes. I consider that negligent supervision. A supervisor's job is to ensure that their personnel are performing acceptably. A vast amount of information is available in a quick review of an officer's recording that can help that cause. For example:

- If an officer is not activating their in-car camera microphone during traffic stops, I would like to correct that behavior before a minority traffic violator complains that the officer was using racial slurs towards them. In such a case, if the officer's improper use of the recording equipment was ignored, a situation could arise that negatively impacts the community. Community members could, and most likely would, argue that we were not being transparent and were covering up the incident because we had no recording. However, in reality, we had both the equipment and policy in place, which implied such a recording should have been made and been available. This is not a position I want to be in.
- If we have a deputy whose officer safety skills are deficient, I'd like to see that corrected before the deputy is injured or killed.
- Suppose an officer's communication skills are lacking and the officer is demeaning towards citizens they meet. In that case, I'd like to fix that problem before it leads to a significant use-of-force incident. Such an incident could cost the officer their job and require the agency head to stand before the media, embarrassed and stressed, as the community targets them and their organization.
- Suppose a deputy frequently violates policy regarding vehicle pursuits. In that case, I'd like to remedy that behavior before vehicles, which cost thousands of taxpayer dollars, get significantly damaged in a crash, or

> innocent people get hurt. The pain of facing the family of an officer or an innocent civilian killed because pursuit violations and reckless behavior were ignored will be much greater than being accountable today to the policies already in place to enhance professionalism and protect lives.

The point of randomly reviewing officers' in-car camera videos is not to catch someone doing something wrong or get someone in trouble. We all know some supervisors act like they can't be happy unless they do just that. But I think an honest look at my perspective within this book will demonstrate that differently – I'm not that guy. I'm not looking to get officers in trouble. I am looking to keep them out of trouble. A typical in-car camera review might go like this:

I review a video of an officer's traffic stop. I notice the video is on, but the audio is not functioning. That is a deficiency and a policy violation. That prompts me to pick out a couple more traffic stop videos from this officer. Now, suppose I see that both the video and audio are being utilized appropriately in the extra videos I choose to review. In that case, I would go no further, as there could be numerous legitimate reasons that the audio was not functioning on that one particular video. For example, there was equipment failure, such as the batteries died. The officer may have removed the microphone to place the battery in the car charger and forgot to reattach it to his person before responding to a call for service or conducting a traffic stop. But if I review extra videos from different days and see that the audio was still not being used, a conversation with the officer becomes warranted. Again, there may be a reasonable explanation for the microphone not working. Perhaps it was broken and reported to another supervisor, who failed to either document it or inform me. In that case, we can still demonstrate our accountability and ability to get things done. We can now follow up and ensure the equipment failure is documented and fixed promptly. This itself will send a message of accountability and execution to personnel. We act and get things done.

Suppose we determine the officer failed to properly activate their microphone. In that case, we now have the opportunity to train them on the applicable policy, ensuring they know how the equipment works, the expectations of using the equipment, and how having an accurate and complete recording provides better evidence. The situation becomes a great training tool and protects them from false accusations, should any be made (when the community learned that all patrol cars were outfitted with cameras, citizen complaints dropped significantly). This is usually all it took, and the officers' performance improved. If an officer chose to disregard or ignore what was expected, it was then that more formal discipline was considered. But formal discipline wasn't what I was after.

I wanted personnel to practice self-discipline and personal accountability. Those are the best measures of discipline and accountability, which I found naturally occur when leaders demand accountability from their people. Certainly, personnel who are accountable and practice self-discipline are a more significant asset to the agency and benefit personally. For example, being accountable and practicing self-discipline enhances job satisfaction, as officers know they are adding value to the organization and community; it provides officers with more significant opportunities to become involved in decisions and activities that affect their job, as their leaders have confidence in their performance and decision-making abilities; and it reduces unsafe practices and risks that can lead to trouble, including physical harm.

Law enforcement is a complex and high-risk profession that only gets more challenging. There are a lot of harmful and bad things that can go wrong. Suppose I can keep officers from getting hurt, losing their job, getting sued, or a variety of other negative consequences that occur when things go wrong in law enforcement by being an accountable leader. In that case, that is what I want to do. That is in everybody's best interest.

For the same reason, I used to conduct random audits of the evidence room monthly or quarterly. See Appendix E for a report of one such audit. I did not wait until a big court case was lost because we learned evidence went missing, was tampered with, or was not collected, packaged, or processed correctly. By conducting audits of the evidence room, reporting deficiencies, and holding those responsible for defects accountable, the level of performance regarding evidence collection and storage improved. In other words, the agency was able to execute when it came to evidence-collection procedures. And, if it was later found that there was a discrepancy or problem with a case's evidence, we could at least show our diligence in trying to prevent such a discrepancy through frequent audits. Compare that to the alternative of being embarrassed and losing credibility with the community when an outside law enforcement agency must come into your department to investigate because drugs or money went missing. People, including police executives, then lose jobs and employees get indicted. How will that type of publicity fare for your agency?

When I arrived at the sheriff's office, I did not find a culture of execution. As a visionary, the sheriff was undoubtedly working hard to create such a culture of accountability and execution. He updated the agency's policy and procedures to reflect best practices. He hired several experienced professionals from outside to assist in managing this culture change. He created a Professional Standards Unit responsible for training, internal investigations, hiring, and promotions. He made processes for both hiring and promotions to ensure the best candidates received the positions rather than relying on old fashion nepotism. He held daily meetings with his command team and encouraged open discussion and debate on matters about the sheriff's office. The sheriff also created and instituted a strategic plan, a roadmap identifying priorities to get the agency moving consistently and uniformly. He took his vision and strategic plan into the community holding Town Hall Meetings and making himself available to county residents. This vision, the sheriff's desire for accountability and professionalism, inspired me to retire from my previous department and travel several states away to join him in his efforts. However, after adjusting to the new culture after my arrival, I discovered an agency still lacking execution and accountability.

Too many supervisors and people in leadership positions throughout the rank structure suffered from various leadership voids. For sure, some supported the sheriff and his vision and desired to help the sheriff accomplish his mission; however, they didn't possess the expertise or competence to carry out the complex tasks required of them for success. Therefore, in Chapter 4, "Control without Competence is Chaos," I asked how important competence is in law enforcement leadership. What are you willing to accept in your organization, a 95% competence level among your leaders? How about 75% or 50%?

Others suffered from the first leadership void covered in Chapter 1, "The Number One Rule of Leadership – It's Not about You." They placed more effort into maintaining the status quo, staying in their comfort zone, and protecting their personal interests and positions rather than putting forth the effort to improve performance and bring about the required change. These leaders sat quietly in command meetings, saying nothing, although they had a different perspective or disagreed with the decisions. They left the meetings working to maintain the status quo instead of implementing what was discussed and agreed upon. They took the information received from command, filtered it, and put their spin on it, delivering that which served their own agenda instead of the organization. In other words, there was no follow-up and no execution. Instead, they took the path of least resistance.

Others yet did not want to be the bad guy. Instead of holding members of their work group accountable for results and complying with the desires of the sheriff, they protected them, covered for them, and further reinforced the status quo and inappropriate behaviors. As a result, they fell victim to the "It's Lonely at the Top" leadership void.

These were not bad people. Most likely, they were ingrained in a culture that had been in place for years. This is what they knew. This is how it was always done as far as they were concerned. And, it's further possible, that in the sheriff's drive to move towards a culture of execution, he moved too fast in his attempt to go from the previous culture of dysfunction to that of professionalism. Too much change too quickly can scare and paralyze people. It is uncomfortable. People often fear the unknown future more so than present conditions of comfort, even if they recognize that the current conditions are not the best. So, people resist. Again, these were not bad people, but they weren't the leaders they could have been. But they are not alone. I believe most of us in leadership positions can relate to struggling with the various voids in leadership discussed in this book and the inability to execute from time to time throughout our careers. I know I sure can.

So how do we create a culture of execution?

FOLLOW UP

"Strategies most often fail because they aren't executed well. Things that are supposed to happen don't happen."[5] When a strategy, goal, plan, or decision is made, specific steps of accountability must be put in place to actually ensure the things that are supposed to happen get done. How does the leader ensure things are getting done correctly? Like my random audits of the evidence room or checks of officers' in-car video recordings discussed above, they create systems or a means of follow-up. A means of ensuring work is first being done, and, secondly, being done right, in a quality fashion. "Follow through is the cornerstone of execution, and every leader who's good at executing follows through religiously."[6]

I expect a first-line supervisor, often a corporal or sergeant, to be responsible for reviewing and approving incident reports submitted by the individual contributors and officers under their command. For example, suppose the reports demonstrate an improper investigative technique or lack of completeness or quality. In that case, I expect the supervisors to return the reports to the original officer for correction or additional investigation. But how do we know if our first-line supervisors are doing this?

Their supervisor, a lieutenant, or another command person is responsible for conducting the necessary follow-up to ensure the sergeant performs their job as required. For example, suppose the sergeant must review and approve all subordinate reports. In that case, the lieutenant can create a system of follow-up where the lieutenant randomly chooses several reports a month from different officers in the sergeant's command to ensure the final reports are ultimately completed and meet appropriate standards. If the lieutenant determines the sergeant is approving reports lacking in quality, the lieutenant is expected to resolve that with the sergeant. The sergeant's work performance is managing the quality of their subordinates' work and maintaining accountability of their personnel, which they record for future

[5] Ibid., p. 15.
[6] Ibid., p. 127.

follow-up and evaluation purposes. Again, going back to the principle of "What Gets Measured (or Monitored) Gets Done," the sergeant will be more inclined to do the job right the first time, knowing there will be follow-up and accountability by their supervisor.

And what about the lieutenant; how do we ensure they are doing what they are supposed to when holding their sergeants accountable for proper investigations and report writing? There isn't any reason their supervisor – a captain or commander – shouldn't also make it a point to pull out random reports to review routinely. The sergeant is expected to review and approve every submitted report from their direct reports. The lieutenant maybe, on average, pulls and reviews ten reports a month that the sergeant approved. The captain pulls two or three a month for review. Over time, if the captain is routinely finding deficient reports and investigations, it can be inferred that both the sergeant and lieutenant are not doing their job; they are not holding their personnel accountable and thus are lacking in execution. But, if this is the process used and it is done right, with a competent sergeant and lieutenant, I think you will find a group of officers with high levels of performance because accountability for proper performance has been reinforced from the captain on down.

Every month the lieutenant would meet with the sergeant of the drug unit to audit and balance the books pertaining to drug funds, which consisted of both funds held in a bank account for future use and cash on hand for immediate use in undercover drug investigations. Knowing this meeting would occur monthly encouraged the sergeant to ensure proper protocols and policies were adhered to by his personnel. His proactiveness helped to ensure the finances and related paperwork would be accurate and complete for these meetings. As the captain, I would occasionally join the lieutenant or decide on conducting the monthly audit in the lieutenant's absence. This kept me apprised of the operations and accountability of the drug unit. Were they doing what they were supposed to? Likewise, on occasion, a random sampling of the confidential informant files could be conducted to ensure the safe practices put in place to protect the organization from this high-risk activity were also being followed.

These are just a couple of examples of conducting follow-ups to promote accountability and improve the capability to execute. Systems can and should be created and used to ensure execution in all pertinent operations within the agency. These may involve the use of money. Are employees with the authority to make purchases on behalf of the organization doing so appropriately? How about equipment-related issues; do we have the right equipment to do the job most effectively and efficiently? Do we know to whom the equipment is assigned and whether it is being cared for properly?

Shortly after beginning a new command position, I was approached by a subordinate about the need to purchase new digital cameras for use by detectives at crime scenes. As I attempted to follow up on the request, I was informed by the command that there had just recently been a purchase of new cameras for the detective division. I began an inquiry about where these recently purchased cameras were, but no one knew to whom they were assigned or where they were. As a result, accountability was absent, and the agency spent more money on new cameras that may or may not have been needed. We subsequently created a process to record what equipment was issued, to whom, and when.

How about training? Are we assigning personnel to suitable types of training? Are there gaps or training needs that need to be filled? Are some employees receiving significant training while others get little to none? How about the agency's interaction and relationship with the community? Can it be improved upon? How about the organization's problem-solving efforts and initiatives? Are officers taking a proactive approach to identifying and resolving ongoing problems in the community, specifically in their area of assignment? How do we know? Follow-up ensures the right things are happening as they should.

William Bratton's strategy for reducing crime in New York City, which became the basis for the introduction of COMPSTAT, was based upon having accurate and timely information, rapidly deploying resources, and using effective, proven tactics. And the final component and linchpin to the success of COMPSTAT were conducting follow-up and assessments to ensure the police were obtaining the desired results and making appropriate adjustments when needed.[7] Consistent follow-up changes behavior. It obviously changed behavior at the NYPD, significantly decreasing crime and creating a safer community.

You might be reading this and thinking, "I'm already busy and overworked with my present duties. I don't have time to take on additional tasks and create new systems and behaviors for follow-up." Or "How can I get anything done if I'm running around conducting follow-up on the work rightly assigned to others to do?"

First, any systems or controls put in place should directly connect to the agency's identified mission and priorities. Otherwise, you might wear yourself too thin trying to do everything. As I previously quoted, "the one who is committed to everything is committed to nothing." Remove busy work inconsistent with the organization's mission doesn't put the organization that doesn't in a better position to win. Conducting follow-up activities not supporting the mission would waste time and effort better served elsewhere.

[7] Bratton, William. (1998). *Turnaround: How America's Top Cop Reversed the Crime Epidemic.* Random House Inc., New York, NY, pp. 224-225.

Secondly, and most importantly, in my experience, the opposite occurs when you have a culture of accountability and execution. If your organization is not used to such a culture, it will take time and effort on the front end. But once you get there, the work gets easier. Your people will rise or fall to your level of expectation. I desire to consistently raise the bar on performance, even if only slightly. When people know what is expected of them, are given the training and tools needed for success, are encouraged and supported, and then held accountable to those expectations, they will rise to meet them. As a result, their confidence will grow, they will make better decisions, and there will be less turmoil and problems in your work group. It is at this point that the group's performance can really take off. With better-made decisions and fewer problems to follow up on, you now find yourself with more time for other tasks, projects, and initiatives, having confidence in the abilities of your personnel to perform admirably.

I previously mentioned how my subordinates made me look good over and over. I often received a "job well done" from my superiors when I did very little all along but stayed out of the way and let my guys execute as they knew how. Even during high-risk operations and significant crimes in progress, I had confidence in the abilities of my work group to get the job done right. The need for me to respond to such a significant event was often more to show support to them than it was because they needed my presence. So, in the end, I did less, and my job was easier because a culture of execution was present. But I still made follow-up part of my routine. As the saying goes, "Trust but verify." You can never completely abandon the need for follow-up, as it is needed to reinforce and maintain a culture of execution. Still, you can get to a place in a culture of execution where follow-up is not so time-consuming because employees are executing as expected.

THE FOLLOW-UP PROCESS

A decision made is just the starting point. Once made, action of some sort is required. In other words, execution of the decision is needed. Have you ever attended a meeting where a decision specific to an identified problem was made; however, six months later, people who participated in the meeting not only had a slightly different, or in some cases significantly different, perspective or memory of not only what had been said, but also what the final decision and required action were? These different perspectives lead various leaders to hold different expectations for their personnel based on their own memory and perspective of what the decision was or should have been. Have you ever heard a statement such as: "Shift A doesn't have to do that," "The detective sergeant doesn't make the detectives do this," or "Why do we have to do this? No one else is doing it"? What happened?

Sometimes it is an intentional act. For example, a person suffering from a void in leadership clearly knows the expectations but chooses to do their own thing, often for selfish reasons. But it doesn't have to be an intentional act where one consciously subverts the desires of the organization's top leadership. Sometimes we subconsciously take in information and filter it based on our values, perspectives, and priorities, what we think is essential. This can lead to slight variations in how decisions made are interpreted and put into action by different people. It is done without ill intent. In these unintentional instances, a system of recording information can help minimize this occurrence.

Eventually, I learned to use a process to record decisions and then a means of follow-up to ensure I didn't forget what was decided and what action was required. I began using journals easily found at your local department or office store. I had a journal for command meetings and individual journals for meetings held with subordinate supervisors, full division meetings, and daily decisions and conversations related to the division.

At formal meetings, I would take notes on the items discussed, decisions made, and any action required of me. After a meeting, or as soon as possible, I would review those notes and add any relevant details that would help me remember the specifics of the discussion and final decision even months and years into the future. These notes could always be referred to if there was confusion, indecisiveness, or inconsistency, as it related to the topic of discussion. These notes also documented the details and assumptions made during the discussion that led to the final decision. If a future change in the internal or external environment occurred and the previous assumptions were no longer valid, a brief review of the discussion points may quickly identify the need to alter the decision or change the course of action. Thus, rather than starting over from scratch with countless new meetings and redundant discussions about ground already covered, these notes can expedite necessary modifications to previously made decisions.

I used a journal to document daily discussions and decisions about the shift, division, or department I supervised. The primary purpose was to ensure the accountability of those for which additional action was required, including me. For example, a journal entry might involve a corrective conference regarding a subordinate's performance, including future expectations. Or regarding a hallway discussion where personnel asked about a specific agency program or process for which I did not immediately have an answer. Or it may have been a discussion about a new piece of equipment that a direct report introduced me to, and I requested they conduct some additional research and get back to me. By memorializing it in these journals, I could circle back around and ensure appropriate follow-up occurred, and the right things got done.

Regardless of which journal I used (i.e., command team meetings, supervisor meetings, daily activities), I created a system where I placed a star (*) next to any item requiring additional action. This allowed me to quickly scan my documentation and locate those tasks that still needed my follow-up. Then, about once a week, when I set time aside for planning for the days ahead, I would pull out my journals and briefly look over the items that still needed my attention. Once the action item was completed and no additional follow-up was required, I would put a checkmark (√) next to the star indicating I had completed the necessary follow-up. This process kept me on track, kept items requiring my attention from being forgotten, and helped me plan my daily tasks, accomplish more, and make the most of my time.

Below are several examples from one such journal:

- *February 1st*
  *√ * Gave Officer Smith his evaluation. At the conclusion and based upon his expertise in this area, I requested he reviews policies 303 and 304 on evidence processing and procedures and provides any input or recommended changes in policy to me via email. Received Smith's recommendations on 2/16.*

- *March 6th*
  Sgt. Smith (crime control unit) requested that Officer Jones' patrol vehicle be changed from a marked car to an unmarked car. I responded that I wanted to put that on hold for now. I agree that an unmarked vehicle would be more productive in many situations. However, it is the only marked car in the unit, and there may be times when a more visible police presence is necessary or beneficial.

- *April 11th*
  I met with Deputy Smith, welcoming him to the shift. I talked about my expectations, the required attitude needed, teamwork, decision-making models, his getting out of his comfort zone, and not being afraid to make good-faith mistakes.

- *May 16th*
  **Forwarded warrant service and operation planning policy to Sgt. Smith and the Lt. for their review on when utilizing SWAT in serving search warrants is appropriate. Future discussion to be held.*

- *June 21st*
  I met with District Attorney-asked for assistance in scrutinizing financial crimes against elderly cases forwarded from the Dept. of Social Services. He would like to investigate more of these if appropriate.

*√ *Reference case 21-12374 will not be able to prove drug trafficking without more. They wanted me to check if the offender's fingerprints might be on the packaging. Assigned to Evidence Technician Smith and forwarded to lab June 28th. Lab results returned negative.*

- *July 24th*
  I spoke with Sgt. Smith about wearing his body armor during operations. I also referred to policy for such. He said he understood and would wear it accordingly. Emphasis was on his safety.

- *August 27th*
  **Spoke with the chief reference case 21-12520. A complaint was received, and the case was possibly mishandled. Review the case and speak with Lt. Smith when he returns from vacation.*

A glance would identify those areas with stars where follow-up was required of me, such as May 16th and August 27th. Those with a check mark (√) next to them could be skipped over as previously handled and closed out. As days turned into weeks and months, and the daily issues and problems arose, I could be sure not to forget my prior commitments and tasks requiring my attention. I also used this system to ensure accountability for the obligations and tasks expected of direct reports. For instance, referring to the August 27th entry, I might make another entry to the journal after Lt. Smith returns from vacation.

- *September 2nd*
  **See Aug. 27th entry. Reviewed case finding a couple of potential deficiencies. Why was the scene not processed for evidence? Why was the listed suspect not interviewed? I spoke with Lt. He is to follow up with Sgt. and officers on scene and report back.*

There is a star next to the September 2nd entry. If I didn't hear back from the lieutenant in a timely fashion, I would follow up with them on the status of the case. This ensured accountability. When this type of follow-up becomes the norm, it motivates people into action. If they know without a doubt that the boss will follow up, they want to get the job done right before the boss asks about it. This then becomes the culture.

What about the boss that is responsive to their subordinates? When personnel have questions that the boss doesn't immediately have the answer for but replies, "Let me look into it and get back to you," how is the boss perceived when they follow up with an answer every time? People will take note of a supervisor who cares about their questions and concerns and is accountable to them. This system of keeping journals keeps tasks from being overlooked or forgotten. It also provides a means for genuinely listening to direct reports, providing feedback, and expediting follow-up action when appropriate. It says, "I care," "I am accountable," and "The organization and my personnel are important." It puts the supervisors' words into action, demonstrating their commitment to "walk the talk," and can go a long way towards building respectful relationships and improving the work group's morale.

I tried to set out a time at the end of each business day to review the day's activities and plan for the upcoming day. It usually took no more than fifteen minutes. This daily practice didn't always occur, as new challenges and crises occasionally popped up, but I would get back to it as soon as possible. At a minimum, I would pull out and review my journals every week. Planning, which included using these journals, enhanced my ability to execute. The hours spent at work were more productive with a purpose and direction. These journals helped keep required tasks on the radar screen and at the forefront of my mind. I used them to plan my daily activities, in determining my priorities. They helped to answer the questions: "What was of the utmost importance?" and "What tasks were no longer pertinent, and what could be put off or delegated to others?"

Not only would I maintain documentation on decisions and discussions during meetings with personnel, but I would frequently follow up with an email highlighting what was discussed, what the final decisions were, and who was responsible for follow-up activity. These emails put everyone involved on notice as to what the expectations were. There could be no future argument that someone did not know their role, what they were supposed to do, and how they were to do it. If they were confused or needed clarification, the email I sent summarizing the meeting results was their opportunity to ask for such. I would then often begin future meetings by going over the decisions made in the previous meeting and asking those present for a status report on what they had accomplished since we last met or how well decisions were being implemented or received. This was another means of follow-up. Knowing I would publicly ask about the actions taken since we last met would create an environment where personnel came prepared for the discussion. Better preparation meant more would be accomplished in a shorter period.

When a leader communicates with personnel, they must be clear about their expectations of what tasks are to be done. But the leader cannot stop there and assume the work will be done and done right. Follow-up is essential to being a good leader and crucial to an organization that knows how to execute. So, create a system for follow-up. Then, when your organization reaches the pivotal point where everyone expects follow-up, less follow-up will be needed because the agency will be well on its way to maintaining a culture of execution and getting things done.

THE LEARNING ORGANIZATION - NEVER STOP

A commitment to constant learning and improvement is necessary for a culture of execution. Law enforcement is a complex operation that seems ever evolving into an even more complicated venture. There is constant change. Laws change, trends in criminal behavior change, technology changes, best practices change, and the expectations of the community change. What was once expected and acceptable behavior of the police in many cases is not acceptable today. Our law enforcement professionals are expected to be attorneys, social workers, paramedics, teachers, and, oh yes, an expert in military tactics when violence comes to town. More is expected from law enforcement today than ever before. How can we stay current and keep up with the array of expectations when most organizations are on tight budgets funded by tax dollars?

Indeed, formal training is a benefit and a necessary part of the equation, and many great training programs are available for law enforcement personnel. But is it enough? I suggest that formal training programs alone are not sufficient. Often formal training is one of the first items cut out of the budget during hard fiscal times. Also, more and more training mandated by politicians, often with minimal experience or knowledge of what training is needed by local agencies, leaves little time and resources available for substantive training. To stay on top of the learning curve so we can remain competent in our abilities to serve our communities requires more.

We miss so many learning opportunities within our organizations in the form of questioning, debriefing, and analyzing what is happening in the field on a day-to-day basis. General Ulysses S. Grant "learned something of importance from each operation he undertook...and every engagement was a lesson, not merely a victory or defeat."[8] This should be the purpose of questioning and debriefing incidents and operations, not merely did we do a good or bad job. But how can we improve? What worked and what didn't? Improvement increases competence, which increases the chance for success.

I believe law enforcement does better in recognizing and pointing out when things go wrong. We quickly point fingers and identify and correct mistakes made during operations. Taking advantage of learning opportunities brought on by errors is important if handled correctly and used to drive improvement and not to make excuses, belittle or embarrass. But I don't think we do as well in debriefing and dissecting operations that go well. We assume that since it went well and we got positive results, all must be good, and we move on. Unfortunately, I don't believe this to be the case. I think there is a fine

[8] Fuller, Major General J.F.C. (1957). *Grant & Lee*. MJF Books, New York, NY, p. 82.

line between a good job and good luck, and we often confuse the two, as the following story emphasizes.

It was nearing shift change, and the shift was making its way toward the police station to go home. I was new with only a short time on the job. I received a call about a suspicious vehicle. The caller saw a truck drive into a warehouse under construction within the industrial park area. From this point forward, I made numerous "rookie" type mistakes. The first mistake was calling off my backup. When the call went out, I checked the time. Seeing that it was about 7:00 am, I thought, "It's about time for the workers to be showing up for work. I'm sure it's just an employee." So, I called off my backup. What didn't come to my mind was that it was Sunday. There were not any workers coming in at 7:00 a.m. on a Sunday. This first and false assumption I made led to several other errors.

The building was under construction, with about 90% complete. However, the large truck bay doors still needed to be completed, so nothing kept you from walking or driving into the warehouse area. As I entered the building alone, numerous pieces of equipment and gang boxes were scattered about the large warehouse floor. From a distance, I could see one lone person sawing something. I observed sparks flying everywhere from his saw. Still believing my false assumption about this person being an employee, I made my second mistake. I did not use any cover as I approached this man. Instead of walking along the wall, moving from corner to corner, or using the various large items of construction equipment for cover, I walked right down the middle of the warehouse towards the man without any cover.

Walking towards this man, I noticed a pickup work truck about twenty feet behind him. I could see numerous unknown items in the bed of the truck. Still sawing away with sparks flying as I continued towards him, he finally observed me when I was about 100 feet away. With a gasp or a growl, the man threw his saw about twenty feet and it crashed into the truck bed. But, instead of this being a "red flag" or what we might call a clue, my rookie mind thought, "Wow, that guy doesn't take very good care of his tools."

Then the man began walking directly towards me. He was moving fast and looked angry. His body language clearly said he wasn't happy with my presence. And what did the rookie think? "Great, this guy is one of those people who doesn't like the police. He will be a pain in the butt and start complaining that I'm harassing him and that he's just doing his job. Why don't I catch some real criminals, or maybe how he pays my salary."

Still coming directly towards me front and center, the man got to about ten feet in front of me and quickly diverted, making a sharp angle away from me as he tried to walk past me. Still clueless to the reality of the situation, I thought to myself, "How rude! Clearly, I'm standing here wanting to talk with this guy, and he has the nerve to walk past me."

I reached out and grabbed his arm. Now I was angry. I started yelling at him for being rude and demanded his identification. As he fumbled for his identification, he finally announced, "Okay, I'm breaking into the place." Finally, the rookie got the picture. I wrestled for my gun like Barney Fife, which was still in its holster. I got the man on the ground at gunpoint and took him into custody. The man had been using the saw to cut open various gang boxes where he stole tools from within. The multiple items in the bed of his truck were tools he had already removed from other gang boxes before I arrived.

So, what is the point of this story? I was the star of the day. Back at the station, I was getting high fives and pats on the back for the great job I did. I single-handedly captured a burglar. The bosses and my peers alike were telling me what a great job I did. But, of course, at the moment, I took the glory and didn't tell them what really happened, about how bad of a job I actually did. Had the man been a desperate drug addict or an armed gangbanger, the result might have turned out quite differently, with serious harm or death coming to me. So, was it a good job or just good luck? Let's not confuse the two. By breaking down our successes, we can determine more precisely what works and can be considered good tactics and what can't. Then, together we can learn from each other's experiences.

Are you routinely debriefing significant calls for service or police response? Or, when a significant incident occurs nationally, do we take the time to dissect that and learn from it?

In 2014, a man was killed at the hands of police in one of our country's largest cities. The man resisted arrest and was taken to the ground by an officer using a headlock. I do not argue with using the headlock to bring him to the ground and get control of him. However, the first time I saw the video of them on the ground, I said to myself, "Get off his neck." When they were on the ground, this obese man was on his stomach, and several other officers were maintaining control of his arms and legs. At this point, the man was not much of a threat to the officers, yet the officer continued to retain the headlock on him, which was reported to have subsequently suppressed his air and killed him. I do not believe for a second these officers intended to cause the harm they did. I don't think they were bad people. As I see it, this death represented a training issue.

I bring up this event as an example because I do not believe this would have occurred at the agency I worked for at that time. Why? Because we talked about these types of events over and over, to include an open discussion about that particular incident; what they could have or should have done to change the outcome. We routinely reviewed policy related to excited delirium, making it a part of the roll call discussion. I am unable to count the times that someone spoke up immediately following a similar takedown and arrest to remind us to sit the person up, if possible, but at a minimum, to get them off their stomach. This was routine, and a person's rank did not matter. Most officers would be comfortable reminding the supervisor to get the offender off their stomach, sit them up, roll them on their side, etc. This was how we did business. Yet, the country has experienced unrest again due to another police officer contributing to the death of a man by kneeling on him and suppressing his airway as other officers stood by.

That could have been me. Early in my career, I responded to an officer-involved shooting. A person significantly impaired by drugs attacked an officer, trying to kill him as he responded to a domestic call at the offender's home. In defense of his life, the officer shot the man, striking him in the legs. Unfortunately, this did not stop the man, who was feeling no pain and continued to attack the officer. Upon the arrival of backup officers, the drugged-out offender attempted to cut responding officers with the glass broken from a coffee table.

Officers used their batons to knock the glass from the man's hands. Additionally, the man was sprayed with OC spray and wrestled to the ground. As the man was being wrestled to the ground by several officers, I placed my foot on the side of the man's neck, attempting to hold him down while others secured him in handcuffs. A more experienced officer to my right hit me in the leg, telling me to get off the man's neck. At the moment, I was surprised and didn't necessarily understand. My immediate thought was, "This man is violent and trying to kill officers. Who cares that I'm holding him down by the side of his neck? He tried to kill a police officer, and deadly force had been justifiable seconds before, and now I'm being chastised for putting my foot on the side of this man's neck."

Note that I said the deadly force "had" been justified. The moment I placed my foot on this man's neck, he was on the ground, being held by multiple officers. In reality, I used my foot to hold him down because there was no other space for me because of the crowded condition of multiple officers involved in securing the offender. The fact is, I probably did nothing to help the matter. Under stress, angry about the severe injury to a fellow officer, and wanting to help led me to the impulsive decision of putting my foot on his neck. The subsequent discussions and training about such incidents opened my eyes and improved my performance and everyone in the agency.

We discussed recognizing and managing the adrenaline rush that often accompanies stressful high-risk police responses. After a high-speed, high-risk pursuit, how often have we seen responding officers converge on the driver of the fleeing vehicle and use physical force, be it punches, kicks, or batons? Sometimes, this response may be justifiable to get a resisting offender under control and in custody. But in other cases, the chase was over and the offender was compliant, but the beating continued, even when officers knew the incident was being recorded by a helicopter above. These officers made decisions based not on reason but on impulse and stress. The adrenaline hijacked them. Again, these are good officers. They want to go home to their loved ones. Their lives were put at risk because of an individual with no respect for the lives of others. Most people couldn't do their job or handle the pressure. The job is left to our police heroes, who run on adrenaline. An agency's leadership must bring these topics to the surface, educating personnel on what to expect and how to cope. Ultimately, better decisions are made, and because of it, personnel become safer.

Most law enforcement officers will never become involved in an on-duty shooting, but we still take the time to prepare them for such an incident if it were to occur. We recognize the seriousness of such an event, so we invest in training and discussion on the topic to better prepare officers to be successful if such an event occurs. The same concept can and should be used in all areas of policing to improve performance.

If the first time an officer ever thinks about what he will do on a traffic stop if a person pulls a gun on them is when it happens, this officer has set himself up for failure. Officers must ask themselves that question at every traffic stop they are involved in. How should I approach the vehicle? Where is cover, if needed? If the driver pulls a gun, where will I move to? Where is the best place to stop the car for my advantage? By having these conversations, you are providing your mind with alternatives that can be called up and used in the future under real and stressful situations. Over a career, officers can prepare themselves thousands of times to be ready if and when such a deadly force encounter truly happens. Suppose we do not think and talk about these situations, options, and alternatives. Then, under stressful conditions, when the mind needs to make a decision, it may find nothing, leading to delay in action or to the wrong decision, and ultimately leading to failure. This is widely understood in law enforcement today regarding serious or violent incidents or potentially deadly force encounters. For example, as a trainee, when driving past a 24-hour convenience store, my training officer would ask, "Ok, you drive by this store and see it being robbed. What do you do?" We then discussed the various alternatives and the pros and cons of each option. Then, sitting around the table for our monthly command staff meeting, the chief walked into the room, and with no advanced notice or preparation, he announced, "A plane just crashed at 3rd and Elm. What do we do?" And suddenly, we jumped right into a tabletop exercise for the next hour.

These discussions and mental exercises prepared us to think for ourselves under stress, providing alternatives where the pros and cons had been vetted and dissected in non-stress environments that could now be used under actual stressful conditions. The information consumed during these developmental opportunities was recalled throughout my career and used to handle real problems.

But we don't have to reserve these debriefings and discussions solely for the most severe cases. Every day the organization's personnel are routinely carrying out tasks successfully. We need to make recognizing and understanding the dynamics of successful operations a part of the agency's culture. Why did the suspect confess to his crime? What tactics worked during that interrogation? How did the officer successfully de-escalate a situation with a mentally ill person? What challenges were present and overcame while collecting evidence at a crime scene? What might have happened if a different alternative had been chosen for those challenges? There are lessons to be learned in each type of routine and non-routine law enforcement operation.

The law enforcement agency needs to make open discussion and debriefing police operations part of their daily routine. And everyone in the agency needs to be a part of the dialogue, learning from each other. Referring to other chapters of this book, the leader must create an environment where personnel are comfortable opening up and sharing their thoughts and opinions. This does not come by accident. Dealing with the typical control-oriented Type-A personality is challenging regarding candor, sharing ideas, and personal feelings on a topic. Cops hate talking about feelings. Personnel often feel unsafe providing input in front of others if it may highlight a weakness or demonstrate they are wrong. Instead, they keep their thoughts to themselves to everyone's detriment. A potential lesson learned was lost because members of the agency refused to speak up and share.

A way to break down the barriers and engage personnel in ongoing discussion is to work towards building the "Environment for Success," as discussed in Chapter 7. Also, the organization's leaders or work group leaders should set an example by sharing their weaknesses or thoughts on what might have worked or not worked in a given situation. For instance, I would share the false assumptions that led me to make a faulty decision, or I might credit an individual contributor with a better idea than mine. I might say, "I was going to ________, but then Officer Smith came up with the idea to ________, and it worked great. Thanks, Officer Smith for your input; a much better idea than mine." When the boss admits weaknesses and mistakes in front of subordinates, it lets them know it is a safe environment for such discussions. We all have flaws, so admit them for the sake of building up your organization or work group's capacity to learn and improve performance.

These debriefings and discussions must be something other than leader lectures. Instead, the leader becomes a facilitator, initiating the discussion, allowing the group to engage in ongoing dialogue and work through their own assumptions and choices made during an event; the leader has already demonstrated a willingness to share mistakes and weaknesses. The discussion is not about finding consensus, finding the one right or wrong way, or having everyone agree on the appropriate course of action. Instead, the discussion may end with several opinions on how an incident could or should have been handled. The magic is in the process. Various participants will likely have different perspectives depending on their values and the role played in an event. It is the hearing of different perspectives and the proposed alternatives that go along with those perspectives, and the willingness of others, specifically the leaders, to validate those perspectives and give them genuine thought that provides this exercise with the power to break down the barriers that encourage silence, and thus open the door for continuous learning.

By using these opportunities to enhance learning within the organization, what led to success in various circumstances can be reinforced and more likely to be repeated in future instances. The confidence levels of personnel increase and better decisions are made with less need to seek supervisors' input for direction constantly. If individual contributors are confident and competent to make decisions independently, more is getting done faster, which means improved service to the community. In all, it demonstrates that people are executing.

DON'T IGNORE POOR PERFORMANCE

Ultimately, the leader's primary goal is to ensure their personnel perform quality work as expected by their position. If the supervisor tolerates poor performance, then poor performance will inevitably continue. As a result, the law enforcement agency does not execute and achieve its mission by performing poorly or providing mediocre service. Instead, it is the reoccurrence of exceptional service and performance that takes an organization to the next level and gets it recognized as an organization that executes.

I'm not suggesting that a supervisor nitpick every decision made by a subordinate nor intervene in addressing every potential deficiency observed. This would lead to an immediate charge of micromanagement, an accusation dreaded by most leaders. This behavior would also paralyze the workforce and halt creative decision making by those on the front line. Instead, subordinates would become programmable robots carrying out the very tasks specifically directed and spelled out by supervisors but doing nothing else for fear of making a mistake and being judged for such. Have you worked for this person? I have. Everything you do seems wrong, and you can't do anything right. Carrying around this feeling is not a motivator. Instead, it leads to the prevailing attitude; "If we don't do anything, we can't get in trouble." Just the opposite of what an agency that executes desires of its people.

Suppose the leader intervenes in every mistake others make or intervenes too quickly. In that case, they may also eliminate a learning opportunity for their personnel or deter them from taking risks, risks that can open doors to a better future for the law enforcement agency or the community they serve. Often the best teacher is the mistakes we make. Chief Robert Olson, in *Leadership Matters: Police Chiefs Talk about their Careers,* said, "because you have a lot of experience, you've seen all the mistakes, so there's a temptation to intervene too much. But bite your tongue and let them go at it. Let them make mistakes and don't punish them for it."[9]

I will also not suggest that all incidents of poor performance be handled the same. There are errors made in good faith and those made from laziness, a poor attitude, or, worse yet, intentional misconduct. There are mistakes made by new employees with minimal experience and those made by veterans that should know better. Some slip up for the first time, and there are those who step in it quite often. Then there are minor rule violations, deficiencies, oversights, and serious infractions that demand a quick and severe response.

Take, for example, one of your superstars, a consistently high performer. In my experience, often, the leader can get away with saying very little regarding an honest mistake made by such an individual. They usually recognize the error of their way and beat themselves up, taking any needed corrective action without input from the supervisor. For instance, I may ask a high-performing employee in passing, "What happened on that call yesterday with that angry citizen?" The subordinate then explains in detail what they did, their decision, their intention for making such a decision, and what ended up happening. They may say something like, "In hindsight, I shouldn't have done that. It backfired and made the situation worse. What I should have done was _____. That would have worked better and resolved the issue." They admit their mistakes, take accountability, and learn from them. In most cases, there might not be much else required of the supervisor. They have already learned from their mistake, and they don't need their nose rubbed in it.

On the other hand, I have seen employees who fight tooth and nail not to admit a mistake. Instead, they make excuses and blame others for their deficiencies; they are perfect in their own eyes. The leader will need to be very direct and clear with this individual about the expectations, how they failed to meet them, and the consequences for such failures.

The point is not that the supervisor needs to be heavy-handed in dealing out formal discipline in every known example of a performance that needs to be improved. On the contrary, the leader must be ever cognizant of their ultimate role in promoting and improving performance. Rather than succumb to the various leadership voids depicted in section one of this book,

---

[9] Police Executive Research Forum. (2009). *Leadership Matters: Police Chiefs Talk About Their Careers.* Washington, D.C.: Police Executive Research Forum, p. 24.

true leaders abhor the status quo. Their desire for continuous improvement remains at the center of their mind. Once at the center of their mind, the leader can choose appropriately what response, if any, is required to respond to an identified deficiency.

Maybe no response, other than a mental note, from the supervisor is best. Are open-ended questions, without judgment, to help the employee process the situation most beneficial? Or is a delayed response, where the supervisor allows the subordinate to work through their problem before applying any intervention, more appropriate? Maybe immediate corrective action to include formal discipline is required. On the other hand, perhaps introducing an observed deficiency at a command team meeting and seeking help and input from others will lead to a more excellent decision and outcome. The point is that true leaders know their role in driving performance and look for improvement opportunities.

When true leaders observe inappropriate behavior, discover a performance gap, or recognize poor service provided by the agency, they act. They do something about it. As discussed earlier in this chapter, it may involve creating a system or process for follow-up to ensure the right things are getting done. It may include an assessment of organizational policies, priorities, and factors that led to the performance, as the agency's leadership and procedures might be the cause of poor performance by individual contributors. Finally, it may involve coaching from the leader, constantly inquiring and reminding subordinates of the organization's mission and priorities, and keeping performance expectations at the center of their personnel's minds, just as they do.

Furthermore, a leader's actions may involve initiating formal discipline. If that is the case, the leader that executes does not run or hide from this responsibility. In Chapter 2, I described how there were times when I did not take appropriate action in disciplining or correcting the poor performance of members of my work group. This neglect of responsibility did the agency no good, placed an additional burden on the good officers performing admirably, and negatively impacted my reputation as a leader. If formal discipline is warranted, apply the appropriate discipline, and move on. Don't take it personally, don't hold a grudge, and don't put the disciplined subordinate in a box that they can't get out of, where everything they do from that point forward is scrutinized and looked down upon with skeptical and suspicious eyes.

Heeding the words of the author of Proverbs may serve you well as you consider how you discipline personnel. It states, "A gentle answer turns away wrath, but a harsh word stirs up anger. The tongue of the wise makes knowledge acceptable, but the mouth of fools spouts folly" (Proverbs 15:1-2) and "The heart of the righteous ponders how to answer, but the mouth of the wicked pours out evil things" (Proverbs 15:28). Take a moment to ponder about the most appropriate course of action remembering the goal is to improve performance and motivate, not break the spirit and belittle.

THE DREADED EVALUATION

The annual evaluation, if done correctly, plays a role in maintaining high-performance levels by recognizing both positive and negative performance in subordinates. The evaluation is another way to reinforce positive performance and not ignore poor performance. The organization that executes is an organization that evaluates personnel seriously by providing honest feedback on their performance, both their strengths and weaknesses. If we want people to change for the better, we must recognize that "feedback lies at the heart of change."[10]

Personnel need to know where they stand and what they can do to better themselves and the organization. Unfortunately, most of the annual evaluations I have seen, and many I've personally prepared in my early years as a supervisor, were not done correctly and probably did little to improve performance. Some common weaknesses of the annual evaluation process within law enforcement organizations are:

1. Rating performance generally without specific examples of behavior to justify and support the ratings.
2. Focusing on weaknesses and deficiencies but ignoring a person's strengths and positive attributes.
3. Overrating an individual and ignoring deficiencies to avoid conflict.
4. Waiting until the annual evaluation review to discuss poor performance rather than address performance issues throughout the year as they arise.

1. Rating performance generally without specific examples of behavior to justify and support the ratings. When a supervisor makes negative, vague, and general statements as to a person's performance without the ability to support their claims, they open the door to arguments, excuses, and allegations of favoritism and unfair treatment (e.g., "Sgt. Smith never liked me anyway, he's always given me a hard time, I'm not one of the good old boys," etc.). Once a rated subordinate perceives they are being unfairly assessed, whether that perception is accurate or not, the evaluation has lost

[10] Excerpt(s) from *Working with Emotional Intelligence* by L. Daniel Goleman, copyright © 1998 by Daniel Goleman, p. 269. Used by permission of Bantam Books, an imprint of Random House, a division of Penquin Random House LLC. All rights reserved.

its credibility and ability to motivate the employee positively. The process becomes arbitrary, and anything presented beyond this will be seen with suspicious and critical eyes. And you can be assured that the disgruntled employee will share his negative opinion of the process with others who may approach their annual evaluation skeptically.

On the other hand, an employee receiving a stellar review without specific detail on the high level of performance they allegedly provided may be grateful for the positive rating but perceive the entire process as an exercise in futility. The supervisor put minimal effort and energy into preparing the evaluation, which was then quickly reviewed with the subordinate, thus possibly leaving the subordinate to wonder, "Does my supervisor really appreciate my efforts? Does he genuinely believe my performance to be exceptional, or is he taking the easy way out to get the burdensome task of the evaluation process over with?"

How different it may be if the supervisor highlights various examples and specific strengths that the employee brings to the organization. Imagine an employee's feelings and the potential for improving morale when the supervisor documents positive performance from eleven months earlier. The employee may have already forgotten about the incident or believed it to be minor and not noteworthy. Yet the leader remembered and made sure to point it out and memorialize it on the evaluation, which will be forwarded through the chain of command, placed into the subordinate's permanent file, and possibly seen by the agency head. That tells personnel they are important and appreciated for their efforts and their positive work.

Consider the below two examples, with details depicting specific observed behaviors included.

In a category of Work Habits or Field Performance, the supervisor might write,

Officer Smith has been observed numerous times taking notes in roll call as he prepares for patrol. He asks questions in roll call and is genuinely concerned about recent crime trends and calls for service which occurred during his days off. In November 2021, a supervisor noted that Officer Smith read previous reports concerning thefts occurring in his area of assignment on his time off. Officer Smith adjusted his patrol plan accordingly, concentrating on areas of prior victimization. In addition, he was observed conducting surveillance of businesses in his area of assignment when appropriate. Officer Smith observed a deficiency among newer officers in the area of tactics. He completed an impromptu training in roll call for shift members on 12/28 and 12/29.

In the category of Report Writing or Written Communications, the supervisor might write,

Officer Smith has completed 52 incident reports this rating period. Of those reports, 12 required additional corrections prior to submission. Officer Smith handled two incidents in which he decided not to write a report when a report was necessary

(Paramedic Assist 21-12150 and Assist to another agency 21-13254). In both instances, Officer Smith thought it appropriate to rely on other agencies to document his work. Officer Smith's supervisor spoke with him in May about his report writing deficiencies. It appears Officer Smith has made a conscious effort to improve his written reports. Supervisors have noticed increased detail in recent reports completed in the second half of the rating period.

Fortunately, I find this weakness the easiest to overcome because it isn't based upon emotions and the human inclination to avoid conflict and negative feelings like the other described weaknesses. Personnel's performance "is what it is," as the saying goes. The performance, attitude, and behaviors are there, good or bad. The leader just needs to take the time to note them. Indeed, supervisors' own biases and attitudes towards the work and people can affect their perceptions and how they view subordinates' performance, good or bad. Therefore, a supervisor needs to be cognizant of their own subjective opinions to ensure they do not fall into the trap of some leadership voids previously discussed. But if they are true leaders committed to driving performance, they need to just stop and look around, as the performance of personnel is all around them.

Monitoring the performance of subordinates is a primary task of supervisors. Do they take it seriously? Every day, a leader can take note of the performance of their personnel, finding them performing admirably in most cases. It might not be realistic to think a supervisor can put all other responsibilities on hold for making performance observations daily. This may be true, but the performance is still there to be observed, and a committed leader will take advantage of that. At least weekly, I set time aside to think about employees who needed to be recognized. Did I miss any good work that needed to be noted? Are there any negative issues of performance I have failed to address that need my attention? And I document, document, document.

I kept informal files in my office on all direct subordinates I was responsible for evaluating. At the end of the evaluation year, these files would be full of notes that assisted in more accurately understanding personnel's performance, strengths, and weaknesses. These notes also made completing the evaluation instrument much easier as specific facts, cases, and details were available to articulate and justify the performance ratings given to the employee.

Using a standard spreadsheet program, I created a spreadsheet that tracked employees' report writing proficiencies. I started this practice as a sergeant to have a more accurate picture of an employee's report-writing skills for the annual evaluation process. However, the positive results I obtained from this endeavor led me to require it of my sergeants once I was promoted to commander. When I reviewed a report, I would log specific information into the spreadsheet. If the report was not acceptable, the reason was provided with a note. Likewise, if the report was acceptable by department standards, but there was something exceptional, this too would get noted. It took me about one minute per report to log the necessary information, which was not a significant investment of time. After a year of collecting this information, I found a plethora of information available to help me more accurately assess and develop personnel.

The spreadsheet provided both quantitative and qualitative data to assess an officer's performance more accurately. Not only could I say specifically that 74% of Officer Smith's reports were acceptable the first time submitted (which demonstrated room for improvement), but I observed patterns of behaviors repeated over and over, highlighting areas that were strengths or could be capitalized on for improvement. The review of a single report alone may not catch my attention as to an individual's strengths or weaknesses, but a pattern observed among multiple reports over time would. I started to see who understood search and seizure laws and who didn't. Who did the basics to get through the report, and who went above and beyond? Who understood the policy regarding juvenile matters or evidence collection, and who didn't? Were they taking extra steps in their investigations, like conducting neighborhood canvasses and obtaining available video from the business down the block or leaving that for detectives? This simple spreadsheet made my staff evaluations more accurate and provided talking/training points for coaching and development.

Below is an example of one such spreadsheet.

Date	Type of Report	Case	Acceptable	Missed Info/follow up	errors
8/25/2021	Well being check	21-33288			1
8/25/2021	assist to medics	21-33570	1		
8/30/2021	juvenile trouble	21-33922	1		
8/30/2021	ID theft	21-33938	1		
8/30/2021	BTMV	21-34072	1		
9/2/2021	Retail theft	21-30033			1
9/28/2021	battery	21-37809		1	
9/30/2021	DWI	21-37900			1
10/12/2021	consumption by minor	21-39886	1		
10/31/2021	sex abuse inv	21-41468	1		
11/10/2021	armed robbery	21-44531	1		
11/10/2021	poss of cocaine	21-43851	1		

Date	Type of Report	Case	Acceptab	...up	errors
8/25/2021	Well being check	21-33288			1
8/25/2021	assist to medics	21-33570			
8/30/2021	juvenile trouble	21-33922			
8/30/2021	ID theft	21-33938			
8/30/2021	BTMV	21-34072			
9/2/2021	Retail theft	21-30033			1
9/28/2021	battery	21-37809			
9/30/2021	DWI	21-37900			1
10/12/2021	consumption by minor	21-39886	1		
10/31/2021	sex abuse inv	21-41468	1		
11/10/2021	armed robbery	21[illegible]	1		
11/10/2021	poss of cocaine	21[illegible]			

numerous writing errors, wrong name in narrative, missing words and run...

very detailed report. solid understanding of juvenile procedures, promptly notifying parents and supervisor.

failed to check for video of incident from service station.

good understanding and articulation of search and seizure law to justify search.

Similarly, a routine, random review of In-car or body-worn camera videos with documentation in a similar spreadsheet may better educate you on personnel's job knowledge, officer safety, communication, or decision-making skills. Evidence of performance can be found in abundance all around the leader. Do they take advantage of it? A conscientious leader that executes does.

When an employee's evaluation is appropriately based on accurate information and observations that are recorded and can be traced back to specific incidents, actions, and demonstrated behaviors instead of vague claims and overly broad descriptions of performance, it becomes a more credible tool for development and improved performance. For example, it is harder for a subordinate to refute a claim when clear examples of their noted deficiencies are tangible and staring them in the face. Furthermore, it becomes a motivator when positive performance is indicated with specificity, such as when personnel know their good work is recognized and valued and how they benefit the organization.

2. Focusing on weaknesses and deficiencies but ignoring a person's strengths and positive attributes. A common error often made by supervisors is focusing on weaknesses more than strengths. This is somewhat human nature. Looking around the world today, it seems easier to find people complaining and criticizing others, much more than complimenting or recognizing the good work a person has done. The mainstream media and social media companies would be out of business if people had nothing to complain about. I think this is entertainment and a favorite pastime for many people in our society. Unfortunately, the focus seems to lean more heavily toward that which is negative.

Now consider the law enforcement leader. Before his promotion to a supervisory position, he spent several years patrolling the streets in the community, responding to calls for service. And what is the law enforcement professional diligently looking for, people on their best behavior? No, they are patrolling with a focus on the negative, catching bad guys doing bad things. Or the seasoned detective who spends years responding to crime scenes where they see the awful things one human being can do to another. It isn't a far stretch to start thinking the worst of people. These crime fighters, who have dedicated themselves to years of searching out and intervening in situations where people are behaving poorly, are now supervisors. It has been ingrained in them to look for the negative, but now they are expected just to put that aside. It is understandable why this can be a challenge for some leaders, but a true leader can and will overcome it. The true leader recognizes that the drive for performance begins with them. They must set the example and make the changes necessary to obtain the desired level of performance.

When a supervisor spends an inordinate amount of time focusing on the weaknesses of a subordinate, neglecting the person's positive attributes, it becomes a de-motivator, and a "nothing I do is right" attitude develops, which manifests itself into an "If I don't do anything I won't get in trouble" performance level. A police agency or work group does not execute if this is the prevailing attitude. People want to be valued and know they add value to the organization. As depicted previously in this book, you want to improve morale and motivation and drive performance, identify personnel's strengths, reinforce them, and put those strengths to use. This includes recognizing a subordinate's strengths and positive contributions in the annual evaluation. Even the bottom "ten-percenters," your poorest performers, typically have strengths that add value to the organization. Fight the temptation to only focus on their negative performance. Reinforce the positive, and you are apt to get more of it.

3. Overrating an individual and ignoring deficiencies to avoid conflict. Another common error in completing the annual evaluation is exaggerating a subordinate's positive attributes while ignoring or at least minimizing any negative qualities. There are two reasons I can think of as to why this occurs. First, a supervisor may be suffering from the leadership void discussed in Chapter 2, "It's Lonely at the Top". Because of the need to avoid conflict or the desire to be liked by subordinates, the supervisor chooses the path of least resistance. Rather than having to suffer through any discomfort of bringing up and discussing a subordinate's deficiencies, the supervisor highlights the positive behaviors of the subordinate and moves on. The leader abdicates his responsibility for accurately evaluating and instilling the expected performance behaviors of their personnel.

As I have observed, the second reason this occurs is nobler than the first, but still problematic to the law enforcement organization. It involves the psychological complexities often involved in police work as they relate to the police culture and how individual officers relate to each other. Due to the problematic nature of policing, the stress involved in law enforcement, and the life-or-death situations officers find themselves in, officers constantly need to support and rely on each other for their survival. Regardless of what rank an officer may hold, when the going gets tough, and lives are on the line, an officer, supervisor or not, is expected to step up to protect, support, and help another officer. It then becomes a challenge when a supervisor, who once relied on a subordinate officer to protect their very life from harm, turns around, points out, and documents an officer's weaknesses or deficiencies. It is incredibly tempting to avoid such a displeasing task when the evaluation is connected to pay and determines the amount of a raise a subordinate may or may not get.

Some well-intentioned supervisors may do well to coach their personnel or hold verbal counseling sessions where negative performance behaviors are addressed. They consider those discussions adequate to justify leaving negative behaviors off the actual evaluation instrument, not to embarrass the officer or deprive them of a pay raise. In the supervisor's subconscious mind, this reinforces the relationship and psychological connection between the two, who may again have to fight side by side when the next crisis arises.

The problem is that poor behaviors not addressed seldom go away and often become more significant problems. Informally addressing problems may occasionally work, and there is merit to handling some issues this way and with compassion, as the discussion on discipline earlier in this chapter points out. However, reoccurring demonstrations of poor behaviors and lack of performance should be documented to clarify expectations. Appropriate documentation also creates a resource for the agency, such as an employee's track record and valuable information that highlights the strengths, weaknesses, interests, abilities, attitudes, and teamwork of personnel in the agency. Who is promotable, who should the organization's future leaders be, and who can handle specialized assignments as they become available?

On numerous occasions, I have witnessed personnel, when turned down for a promotion or specialty assignment, question why they were not chosen for the position. Their performance deficiencies are subsequently pointed out as to why they did not meet the qualifications for the assignment. The disgruntled employee then presents the last several years of annual evaluations that make them look like a superstar and well qualified because the rating supervisor chose to ignore the subordinate's deficiencies year after year during the evaluation process. The unhappy employee points out this inconsistency to anyone who will listen, along with the allegation that the promotional process is corrupt and the agency leaders are promoting only those that belong to the "good ol' boy" club.

Another version I have observed is the supervisor, at their wits end, who finally comes to management with a statement such as, "We have to do something with Officer Smith. I've had enough of his poor attitude and negative influence on the rest of the shift. We need to get rid of him." However, a review of Officer Smith's yearly evaluations reflects that he is a valuable and hardworking shift member. Yet, the supervisor, who ignored his responsibilities for evaluating personnel and failed to document Officer Smith's poor attitude and performance, now expects management to step up and take the action he should have taken long ago. If you do not believe me, identify your worst employees and review their last few annual evaluations. On paper, will you find documentation of a problem employee or an average or above-average employee?

In my experience, personnel are willing to accept constructive criticism and conversation about negative performance attributes during the evaluation meeting when they feel equal attention and recognition have been given to their positive behaviors. Most people will add benefits somewhere to the agency. If the leader takes time throughout the year to identify and note the positive contributions and bring those to light, people are more willing to accept the negative. After all, each of us has weaknesses too.

4. Waiting until the annual evaluation review to discuss poor performance rather than address performance issues throughout the year as they arise. Evaluating personnel should be an ongoing process rather than something just reserved for the annual evaluation review. But unfortunately, performance evaluations are often reserved solely for the yearly evaluation meeting and are often viewed as a dreaded requirement more than a developmental opportunity. As a result, a supervisor procrastinates until the last possible moment before hurrying through the task of writing up the evaluation, containing no more than a few sentences paraphrasing the category to be rated, sufficient enough to pass until the following year's evaluation.

Several years ago, I decided I wanted to do better for my personnel. They deserved a proper and accurate evaluation that left them with specifics on their strengths (what behavior they excelled at and were expected to continue), those areas where there was room for growth, and how they might achieve said growth. They deserved to know this information. This commitment to improving my evaluations of subordinates led me to pay better attention to their performance and take note of it routinely. It made me a better supervisor, leading to increased daily interaction with personnel. This interaction produced more observations of performance, which in turn helped me better understand their strengths and weaknesses. Routine performance observations create talking points and opportunities for coaching, not just during the annual evaluation review but throughout the year.

There should be no secrets when the annual evaluation review is conducted; personnel should precisely know what they can expect to see on the evaluation instrument. The annual evaluation becomes nothing more than a quick recap of the year and a planning and goal-setting opportunity for the upcoming year when performance is observed, evaluated, and discussed throughout the year.

This process further takes the sting out of any negative notations that might be found within the evaluation instrument. For example, imagine sitting down for your annual evaluation review to find your supervisor with a list of performance deficiencies and errors committed months before that were neither brought to your attention nor discussed nor your feedback or point of view sought. However, now these items are officially recorded in the evaluation instrument. Will this motivate you? Will this inspire commitment to the agency's mission? How do you see this affecting your subordinate-supervisor relationship? Will it flourish or falter?

If I have done my job right throughout the year in observing, candidly discussing, and documenting said performance, then almost always a subordinate's perception of their performance strengths and weaknesses is precisely what they find in the evaluation instrument. When a subordinate sees that you have recognized and formally recorded in the evaluation instrument their strengths and positive contributions from throughout the year, and they have already acknowledged or had the opportunity to discuss their weaknesses and struggles found within the evaluation instrument, the evaluation is perceived to be fair and valid. It thus becomes a more powerful tool for development in the upcoming year. It also improves morale when personnel know you, as a leader, care enough to invest your time throughout the year to see them as valuable and recognize their contributions to the organization. A subordinate who feels they are respected and treated fairly will be more likely to commit to the ideals and mission of the agency, a prerequisite for an organization that executes.

In summary, if you want an organization that executes, you must create a culture of accountability. Accountability will be reached when the agency's leaders do the following:

- Make relentless follow-ups on the commitments and decisions made by the organization part of their daily routine. This follow-up ensures tasks are being completed as expected.
- Create a learning environment where the strengths of individuals and the organization are constantly increased, adding depth and capability to the agency.
- Don't ignore poor performance; identify and address deficiencies in operations and personnel, including disciplining subordinates, when needed.

- Take the evaluation process seriously. Employees want and deserve to know where they stand with the organization. The evaluation process is an essential aspect of accountability and relates directly to the leader's follow-up, promotion of a learning environment, and deficiency attacking responsibilities.

Then repeat!

Section Three

YOU WILL NEVER BE GREAT UNTIL YOU REALIZE YOU AREN'T GREAT!

If this book were to be summarized, I would sum it up as a call to all law enforcement leaders to take the initiative and be proactive in their desire to make a difference in their organizations. The last section was called "Driving Performance." A good leader will continuously look to drive and push performance farther, to improve constantly, even if just in small increments. On the other hand, mediocre or poor leaders will settle into their comfort zone, doing just what is necessary to get by, all along thinking they are someone special and deserving because of their formal title and position. However, the fact is that you will never be great until you realize you aren't great!

When one thinks themselves to be great, at the top of their game, or better than others, they quit, slow down, stop listening to others, and stop trying new things. Why should they? They are already great and have all the answers. So, they think. But, when leaders recognize they aren't great and can't do it alone, they keep listening, learning, and driving performance forward. And the process reinforces itself, continues, and maybe they end up as one of Jim Collins' Level 5 Leaders.

This book has been about making us better law enforcement leaders, improving our leadership abilities, eliminating leadership voids, and increasing the organization's performance. At the beginning of the book, we identified the uniqueness of leading those attracted and recruited into law enforcement positions. Most people in our society can't or won't do the type of work that someone in law enforcement is not only capable of doing but also willing to do.

This book's final section and chapter continue to emphasize the need to be proactive and accountable but from a different perspective. Here, we examine some of the realities of police work. Those who choose this career path and commit to serving the community are true heroes. But they are human, face serious challenges, and have weaknesses. There is an ugly side of police work that our heroes must face that is rarely discussed and primarily unknown by those outside of law enforcement.

For too long, the ugly side of the law enforcement profession has been ignored to the detriment of many officers and their families. As a leader, we must recognize the consequences of ignoring these heroes' personal challenges. We must first acknowledge our own unique challenges and then be proactive in educating and helping our personnel navigate through the difficulties they face in being a law enforcement professional.

If we are to pursue excellence in our police organizations, we must be concerned with the health of ourselves, our families, and, indeed, our personnel. After all, they will determine the strength and success of the agency. Do you want to be great? Then start by realizing you aren't. You are human; you can't do it alone, and neither can they.

Chapter 12

YOU ARE ONLY HUMAN, SO GIVE YOURSELF A BREAK!

You may be a hero, but Superman or Wonder Woman, you are not! Even Superman had a weakness, that being Kryptonite. But Superman wasn't human, and we are. Unfortunately, many weaknesses can cause significant harm to our personnel and us if not kept in check. Referring to them as "weaknesses" is probably an inaccurate and inappropriate term to use. Our officers and deputies are anything but weak. Instead, most people are never exposed to everyday aspects of human nature that can cost the law enforcement professional if not recognized, understood, and prepared for.

I attended a training class a while ago. The instructor began the class by asking, "How much would you sell your family for?" There was a long pause as all the students looked around the room strangely, probably thinking as I did, "That's a stupid question." Then, the instructor asked, "Would you sell your family for a million dollars?" Again, the same result, although some mumbling could be heard among the students, "No, of course not!" I thought, "There is no dollar amount I would sell my family for. Their value to me could never be estimated in any dollar amount." But then the instructor hit home, accurately making his point. How often do we allow the job to take priority and control over our lives, to the point that our personal life, including our families, suffer because of it? The answer is, "Too often!" It happens every day, and for some, possibly all the time. I'll be the first to raise my hand and say, "Guilty."

Consider these rates and how officers and their families suffer because of them. Divorce rates are higher among those in law enforcement than that among the general public. Will that affect the family? Suicide rates are higher than the general public. That will have a profound effect on the family. And then there is alcoholism, prescription drug abuse, and severe health conditions, such as heart disease and digestive problems, all high among the police compared to the average public. Is this just an accident, a fluke, or a coincidence? Or is there something about this job that can lead to such adverse outcomes?

This book has been all about proactive leadership. But there is no other area where proactive leadership is needed more than leading and navigating the challenges found in law enforcement for yourself and those you work with. Your quality of life, your personnel's quality of life, and your agency's performance level all depend on it.

So, what happens? How do many of our young, eager, excited law enforcement recruits, who start the job with a positive attitude and desire to serve and help their community, end up so far from where they began? Many develop a poor attitude, are angry at the world, are married and divorced – possibly multiple times, are often alone, are overindulging in destructive behavior, and hold the job in contempt at the end of their career.

REALITY CHECK – YOU CAN'T SAVE THE WORLD

It doesn't take long on the job until reality sets in. The new officer usually starts their career with high ideals. They have signed up to "serve and protect," and they are anxious about getting started and making a positive difference in the lives of others. And then, they are exposed to the real world. The world that many in society don't think of, refuse to think of, and instead stick their head in the sand wanting to believe such a world could not exist, at least not in the small sphere that makes up their life. Hence, the "it can't happen to me, people like me, or people I know and love" members of society. But it does happen, and it happens every day.

There is real evil in the world. There is genuine hatred, complete 100% selfishness and greed, and violent predators out there; those that will rape, kill, and harm innocent people, including children and the elderly, without remorse.

Then there is a category of people I would not classify as wholly evil or selfish, yet they have lost their way and are making choices that harm themselves and others. For example, the drug addict who steals to support their habit and has found themselves alone with no help or support because their criminal behavior, and seemingly selfish actions, have separated them from any family support. They can't maintain employment because of their addiction, and so the criminal behavior continues, not only to support the drug habit but to survive. Another person within this category could be the juvenile runaway, who flees an abusive home seeking safety and companionship but finds themselves among others living on the streets. Unfortunately, their attempts to survive the street lead them into behaviors that only reinforce a poor outlook for their future. The influences of those they encounter on the street, who take advantage of them, and their need to survive often lead to dysfunctional behaviors, such as drug addiction, drug trafficking, theft, and prostitution.

Then consider the catastrophic events and accidents that occur in the world; they are not criminal in nature but still bring about real pain, death, and destruction. Sometimes these events are more challenging for those in law enforcement because they are random and no respecter of persons. Compared to criminal acts, which result from a conscious decision made by an individual or individuals. Even victims sometimes make poor decisions that lead to their victimization. Random occurrences of injury and death brought on by traffic crashes and workplace accidents, as well as by Mother Nature herself through floods, hurricanes, and tornadoes, on the other hand, prey on innocent, unsuspecting persons that leave officers and deputies asking "why" such things must occur. They often realize there is little to nothing they can do about it.

Law enforcement professionals get exposed to aspects of this pain, death, and or destruction daily, year after year. After taking that "Oath of Office" and hitting the streets, their world begins to look a lot different than ever before. And ever so slowly, they begin to change, to transform into someone different, with a different perspective and outlook. They have entered into the police culture.

I believe law enforcement officers see reality better than most people in society. Because they don't just see the warm and fuzzy "life is good" version, which is how many people want others to see and think the world is. Oh no, they get to see the ugly, people at their worst, and the harm caused to others because of it. This changes their outlook, and a behavior change often follows.

As a father of five, when they wouldn't get their way, some of my children used to tell me how much they hated my job because of the suspicious perspective on the world I held. We tended to stay on top of our children's whereabouts more than most. "You want to hang out with a friend? I'll need to talk with their parents," was one of my typical responses. We wanted to know where they would be, who they were with, what adult supervision was present, and whether the adult was a responsible parent. And then there would be the occasional surprise checkup to ensure they were where they were supposed to be. I knew the evil that could happen and wanted to protect my family from it. But it wasn't always easy from a family or parenting standpoint, as dad was often the bad guy. The job changed me.

Let's make no mistake; some change is required for the officer who will excel at the job. Returning to this book's introduction, we recruit, hire, and train those I affectionally call "action junkies and control freaks." That's what we need when things are going wrong, people are dying, or lives are at risk, and evil is knocking at the front door – people who will take action and control. These officers are of great necessity in our society. They are indeed heroes.

We further train and reinforce our heroes to be suspicious. Because we know evil does exist and may be lurking around the next corner, officers are always expected to be hypervigilant. After all, they are a community's watchmen and caretakers. They must be prepared to confront crime and chaos at a moment's notice before harm is brought to those they have sworn to protect.

My family knows what seat I require at a restaurant. And I think most law enforcement families know this too; the seat with the back to the wall facing the entrance is the seat a cop wants so they can see who is coming and going. We are constantly watching, even when we're not on the clock. When the last few rows of pews at my church were removed, I recall how out of my comfort zone it caused me to be. I was used to sitting in that last row, where I would get the first look when someone entered the church building, enabling me to be the first line of defense. So, it took me a while to get used to not having my watchtower disguised as a pew.

This hypervigilance and untrusting perspective most law enforcement officers possess is responsible for many evil people and criminals being removed from the streets and crime prevented. It works. But it can come with a cost if not understood and balanced appropriately.

When I started my career thirty-two years ago, I found a lot of fun and humor in the job. I would come home, and my wife, Wendy, often asked me how my day went. I would go into a long explanation of any significant incident, emphasizing, and maybe even exaggerating from time to time, anything that might get a good laugh. I saw stupid people making stupid decisions; some results were downright hilarious. I would see things occur working in the prison that people would never believe because it was so bizarre and inconceivable. Even when I tried to tell them, they would sometimes not believe me.

Today, I could have seen a fatal wreck, responded to a shooting, worked a murder/suicide scene, been involved in a severe child abuse case, or participated in breaking up a bar fight. But upon arriving home, even when asking me about my day, Wendy would probably still not receive much more than, "It was okay." After filling my head with so much over the years, I don't want to think about it or talk about it any more than I must. So, it becomes just another day, another bad incident. When I go home, I just want to sit in peace, not relive the ugliness or frustrations I've experienced.

I used to think dealing with intoxicated people on the street was fun. They acted so silly and would do and say the dumbest things. It would make me laugh. Arresting a drunk person was like entertainment. I was getting paid to be entertained. Today, I have lost all patience for dealing with drunks and intoxicated people. I've seen the damage they cause – the lack of self-control over their lives, the poor decisions they make, the families ruined, and the harm caused to themselves, their families, and society. Innocent lives are lost due to drivers driving drunk, and immense pain is caused to families whose loved ones are both the perpetrators and the victims. Additionally, the pain and helplessness experienced by a family whose child is addicted to drugs can be overbearing. Because of the victimization our communities suffer by the impaired in our society, I simply no longer see the humor.

I have been blessed to have a wonderful wife that has stood by my side, despite the changes this career has caused in me. My wife, Wendy, must be a saint, as she has tolerated my mess; there certainly have been times when I haven't been there for her because of the job or haven't been as responsive to her needs as I should have been. Our marriage has sustained a decades-long law enforcement career, probably more because of her love for God than her love for me. She takes her commitment to love very seriously, even when I don't deserve it or don't reciprocate as I should. The point is, I'm not the same person I was when we met. The job has changed me. She likely never would have married me if I was the person then that I am today. She would have probably said "No thanks" and walked away. And many wives, who do not possess the extraordinary commitment that Wendy does, do just that.

I used to be fun, spontaneous, open, and certainly more sensitive to her needs. Today, I am a little more serious, withdrawn, closed off, and judgmental. I keep to myself and certainly lack patience for anyone practicing stupidity. It's not necessarily a recipe for a good marriage, but I am not alone. I am just one of the thousands who share similar experiences.

Don't get me wrong; I'm not disgruntled with my career choice or desiring to convince anyone not to seek such a career. No, I love the opportunities I've had. I can't imagine having done anything differently. I'm not sure what else, if anything, I might have enjoyed or been good at. However, I believe we need to better educate those choosing employment in law enforcement about what a healthy perspective may look like.

Help people? Absolutely! Everyday! Save the world? Let's not get ahead of ourselves.

ALL THAT, AND FOR WHAT?

One of the first questions asked of an applicant desiring to become a law enforcement officer typically is, "Why do you want to be a police officer?" And a typical response is usually something like, "I want to help people," "I want to serve and protect," or "I want to make a difference in the community," etc. Having participated in many interviews involving police recruitment, I have heard this rendition many times and in different ways, but they ultimately are saying the same thing – they want to make a positive difference in the world. And I believe it. My response was similar when I was asked that very question many years ago.

The purpose and calling of the law enforcement officer are intrinsic. Something special inside them leads them to sacrifice themselves for others. Like our armed forces heroes, they want to make a difference. Let's face it; you don't sign up for a career in law enforcement or the military to get rich. That just isn't likely to happen. The primary motivation is to make that positive difference. And they do. They take their oath to serve and to put others above themselves. And all but the very few who possess the wrong motivation, and disgrace the badge, make that difference.

They are willing to risk their lives every day, trying to protect others from pain and suffering. They face the violence and horror of the real world, taking that on themselves so others can live safely and peacefully, and don't have to deal with the mess. And this commitment to serving others is not taken alone. The law enforcement officer's family shares in that service, as they must often sacrifice themselves, their desires, and their comfort.

Anyone in law enforcement is familiar with missed birthdays, holidays, special events, and even ruined dinner plans and vacations. I missed Wendy's birthday about five years in a row because I was out of town helping coordinate an annual training conference in which I was heavily invested. Years ago, a law enforcement friend made the statement, "What is this Christmas thing you speak of?" His point? He wasn't used to celebrating Christmas with his family because for years, as a police officer, he worked Christmas Day so that others could celebrate their Christmas safely, in peace, and without the fear of someone breaking in their front door and doing them harm.

My family didn't always get the support they needed or deserved because I was preoccupied with work. It was not uncommon for me to get that phone call about a significant crime that had just occurred about the time the food hit our table at the restaurant. So, I'd say, "Pack it up; I have to go," and out the door I'd go. So much for a pleasant evening with the family.

When Wendy was eight months pregnant, she was stuck in a flooding sump pump well because our pump went out during a storm and threatened to flood our basement and belongings. I was at the beginning of a sixteen-hour shift. I was the only on-duty supervisor covering two shifts and could not come home. So, as the muddy stormwater was rushing in, Wendy, with a Home Depot employee on the phone talking her through how to change a sump pump, got the job done because I wasn't there to help.

Then there have been the night shifts and the unexpected extra hours an officer must put in when bad things happen and additional personnel are needed. The community has expectations that someone will come when they call 911. Leaving the street unmanned is usually not an option. When another officer calls in sick, or there is an emergency and additional manpower required, you don't always get to go home as you planned.

Like me, my father-in-law was an avid baseball fan. At the time, he lived in Phoenix, Arizona, and my family and I were still in Chicago. Although we had never attended a major league baseball game together, we had talked a lot about baseball. During his later years, he visited us in Chicago, so I took the liberty to buy us tickets to a Chicago White Sox game. I was excited about the opportunity to spend this time with him at the ballpark. However, criminals don't care about your plans, and the day I was to enjoy special time with my father-in-law was a prime example. I was a detective at the time, and that morning there was a theft of $70,000 from an armored car, and I was assigned the case.

As I worked the case with the assistance of other detectives, we identified a suspect. And I had to decide whether to put the investigation on hold for the weekend, follow up with our suspect the following Monday, and thus preserve my night at the ballpark with my father-in-law or immediately move forward to locate and apprehend the suspect. A lot could happen over a weekend; the suspect might flee the area, and evidence may go missing, including stolen money, either spent or hidden. On the other hand, by waiting several days, the suspect may believe we didn't have much of a case, thus providing him the confidence not to cooperate. So, we decided we needed "to strike while the iron was hot," which meant I would not be attending the baseball game with my father-in-law. We continued the investigation into the night; the suspect was located and arrested. He confessed to the theft, and we recovered the stolen money. Sadly, my father-in-law passed away before we could reschedule that missed game.

Three months after I uprooted my family and relocated them to North Carolina, a kidnapping and murder of a well-known and respected community member occurred. Now, away from their friends and our extended family, I had to miss my son's 10th birthday because of work. This kidnapping and murder occurred on his birthday, which kept me away from home for that day and most of the upcoming week. Not only was it his birthday, but my father had arrived for his first visit to our new home in North Carolina. I never really got to visit with my dad that entire week. I came home late after a long day, went to bed, got up early, and returned to the office to continue working on this homicide. On several occasions, my dad met me for lunch as I broke away for a few minutes before returning to work. When the week ended, I almost cried as I said goodbye to my father, who was returning to his home in Chicago, as I prepared to head back to the office. I didn't get to visit him the entire week and didn't know when I would see him again.

These are just a few stories that come to mind over a career of events. Everyone in law enforcement has their own stories, including those involved in deadly force encounters, where they fought for their lives or maybe had to take the life of another. They committed to serving and protecting, which often resulted in sacrificing. It comes with the job. But when the support of those you sacrifice for, the community, is not there, it can leave you frustrated and asking the questions, "Why?", "What's the point?", "Is it worth it?" and "Am I making any real difference at all?"

It often seems like people rarely notice the positive work done by officers but are quick to line up and point out the faults and mistakes. As someone who has held various leadership positions within law enforcement agencies, I certainly have responded to many more complaints than compliments. And then there is the media.

In his book *American Soldier*, General Tommy Franks recalls his reporting of an operation in Afghanistan. General Franks reported the operation as "an unqualified and absolute success." Although, unfortunately, eight military members had died, and many others had been wounded, hundreds of the enemy were killed, and the objective was met. But media members were critical of the operation because eight soldiers had died. How could that ever be considered a success?[1]

What signal does that criticism send to the soldiers putting their lives on the line? How is that for troop morale? What would these reporters say about World War II? Imagine where our nation would be today had we lost World War II. No doubt a success for our country, yet how many were killed? Hundreds of thousands!

The media continues to portray law enforcement personnel and operations similarly. Any adverse outcome or harm gets attributed to a failure in law enforcement. They seem to forget that the criminal also has a choice, and their choice sets the stage and puts in motion most events that often lead to bad outcomes. The drugged-out or violent criminal doesn't have rules to play by, yet law enforcement does and is quickly criticized when they step outside those bounds, even under the most life-threatening and stressful incidents. The criminals can do as they please: fail to comply with laws, prey on members of the community, resist the efforts of the police, physically fight and attack police, and then when there is a bad outcome, and officers aren't perfect in their assessment and response, all of the blame is laid at their feet. The media completely overlooks that the criminal had a choice and made decisions that led to the law enforcement encounter. What message does this send to law enforcement personnel? How is that for officer morale? I expect this type of response from the public, frequently promoted by the media, is

[1] Franks, Tommy General (2004). *American Soldier.* Harper Collins, New York, NY, pp. 380-381.

mainly responsible for the staffing crisis and mass exodus of law enforcement officers retiring or leaving the profession entirely. A crisis that ultimately has left our communities less safe.

Our officers are expected to be experts in communication, psychology, the law, and the medical field and excel as race car drivers, MMA fighters, and military strategists. And when they don't make the perfect decision within the few seconds provided, they are labeled incompetent losers and deadbeats. The public expects a lot from law enforcement, including personal services and benefits, and it demands this service until the service negatively impacts them. For example:

- If someone tries to break into a person's home, the police can't get there fast enough. But, if an officer activates his emergency lights to go through a red light at an intersection, he is impatient and abuses his authority.
- The police don't do enough to stop crime, they say, until it is their kid who gets arrested for committing a crime.
- Someone calls the police because their teenager is out of control, only to complain about the deputy because they could not fix in twenty minutes what the parents spent seventeen years screwing up.
- They demand traffic enforcement to stop the speeding cars in their neighborhood but expect a warning when they are caught speeding.
- They are perfectly fine allowing officers to perform various minor services, such as providing taxi services to their children, changing a flat tire on their wife's car, replacing the smoke detector batteries in their elderly parents' home, or removing the raccoon from their backyard because they are too fearful of doing it. But let them see the same officers sitting at a local restaurant or stopping for a cup of coffee, then those same officers are lazy and not doing their job.

This list could go on and on. After many years of what feels like no support to those officers who have committed themselves to helping and serving, it is understandable that many become frustrated and lose the motivation they once had. The trust in the community they swore to care for wanes. They begin isolating themselves from anyone outside the law enforcement circle because those people don't understand and can't be trusted. Their outlook can change from the passionate drive to make a positive difference in the world to something that isn't at all positive. Unhealthy habits and adverse outcomes for the officer and their family may result. But it isn't just the reality of a dangerous and sometimes evil world law enforcement professionals live in, or the perceived lack of support from those whom officers swore to serve and protect, that causes all the problems. As law enforcement leaders, we must also look inward, within the law enforcement agency, for leadership voids that might be harmful and move our personnel in an unhealthy direction.

THE BAD GUYS AREN'T ALWAYS THE PROBLEM

Stop and think about what you hear members of your law enforcement organization complaining about most often. Is it external to the department, such as how the public treats them? The difficulties of responding to serious and often violent calls for service? Or is it internal, such as the policies, procedures, formal and informal processes, and people's attitudes inside the agency?

If you are a police chief or sheriff, you may be shielded from the reality of the situation today as your personnel may want to please you and want you to think the best of them. Or they may fear the consequences to their careers if you knew what they honestly thought. So, you might not be hearing the truth. Just this week, I turned the corner to find three officers going from an active conversation on some topic to dead silence when they saw me breach that corner. What could they have been discussing or complaining about?

If you find yourself at the top of the organization's hierarchy, stop and think about previous positions you held, maybe as a sergeant or lieutenant. Or better yet, think back to what you used to spend your time and energy complaining about as an individual contributor long ago. When you met side by side in your patrol vehicle with another officer, what were you frequently discussing? Was it the increase in violent crime? Was it the gruesome crime scene you witnessed? How about the drunk you had to wrestle to the ground? Or how your fellow officer missed the deranged drugged-out man trying to attack and sprayed you in the face with pepper spray instead of him? Probably not! You signed up for that and know that it comes with the territory. More often than not, your people are most frustrated with and complaining about the agency's internal workings. Not what we want to hear but know to be true.

I was a member of the Northern Illinois Critical Incident Stress Management Team. They are a great group of professional people who committed themselves to helping those that helped others, police, fire, EMS, and emergency room personnel. It was always amazing to me when I would respond and provide services to officers involved in a critical incident, such as an officer-involved shooting or exposure to a traumatic event where multiple persons, including children, were killed, it wasn't the incident itself that was causing problems for these officers. Instead, it was often how their agency had responded to it that frustrated, angered, or caused them the most distress.

An officer was in the fight of his life, almost died, and had to use deadly force, taking the life of another, but that wasn't what kept him up at night.

Instead, it was the lack of support from his administration, such as being forced to write a report the day of the incident before being allowed to go home. For others, it was how some officers involved in the deadly force event were treated differently than others.

Employee complaints cover a spectrum of issues. Some involve the arrogant leader, who thinks they are more important than anyone else in the department (this leader suffers from the "It's not about you" leadership void). Others involve the chaos caused by the incompetent leader (described in Chapter 4). And the leader who takes no time to understand the "small things" that are vital to their subordinates (discussed in Chapter 5). To the arbitrary and authoritative leader who gives nobody a voice or any control over the decisions that affect them (discussed in Chapter 6). These employees want a voice against the unfair promotional process, the poor equipment, or the lack of equipment. Or their complaints could center around the lack of accountability for the poor performance of the bottom "ten-percenters" or the unfair discipline, where some employees are treated differently and more harshly than others. Do these complaints sound familiar?

The fact is the internal grumblings and dissatisfaction within the law enforcement agency are as responsible, if not more so, for the long-term distress and lack of satisfaction with the job than the lack of public support and the high stress calls for service to which they are routinely exposed. But when exposed to all three of these dynamics found in a career in law enforcement over time, it is understandable that many of our law enforcement heroes suffer significant negative consequences in their lives and those of their loved ones. It's no wonder law enforcement officers are getting divorced at high rates, are addicted to various substances, and have other dysfunctional behaviors.

So, what can we do? Can we make it better?

My suggestion is to start by remembering the number one rule of leadership...

It's Not About You!

The message is not a negative one. It's not about complaining or whining about how lousy police officers have it. Instead, keeping with the proactive nature of this book, the message is positive. It is another opportunity for proactive leadership. If we are to pursue excellence, we need to recognize these challenges in law enforcement for what they are and take the opportunity as leaders to make the necessary improvements.

First, recognize reality for yourself. Have you experienced these challenges and frustrations? Have they led to negative consequences in your life? If so, start by giving yourself a break. You are not alone. Don't beat yourself up over something natural if not kept in check. Thousands of law enforcement professionals are experiencing similar challenges. Commit first to care for yourself, but remember it is not just about you.

Next, it's time to give your personnel a break, as they, too, are only human. If you only improve your personal circumstances, then obtaining excellence is limited. Identify realities that affect you and provide opportunities for positive change. Work towards those changes, and then you will be better positioned to improve the quality of life for those working for you or around you. The people in the organization need to be healthy if the organization is to be healthy and successful. Remembering "It's not about you" puts you and the organization in a better position to win and excel.

Indeed, we are starting to see a greater emphasis on officer well-being in the law enforcement environment. This is a good thing. We must educate officers on the importance of eating right, staying physically fit, maintaining appropriate sleep habits, and having a proper work-personal life balance. Providing resources, such as Employee Assistance Programs (EAPs), peer counseling, critical incident stress management services, and various counseling services, are all good, but I suggest insufficient.

Recognizing the number one rule of leadership, "It's not about you," and avoiding this void in leadership is the starting point of pursuing excellence. It is the crucial point where a leader's influence begins. Daily influence can significantly impact a person or organization's effectiveness more than just offering the availability of resources, such as the EAP, and then walking away.

What can the leader do to mitigate the frequent negativity and frustration in the law enforcement profession?

REMIND THEM WHY?

Personnel need to know they make a difference. After all, that's why they took the job to begin with. In addition, if a person sees value and meaning in their work, they will likely be more satisfied with it and continue to act in a manner that reinforces that personal satisfaction.

Keep the organization's mission at the forefront. Make sure subordinates know the role they play in achieving the mission. This book has provided numerous examples of how a leader may carry that out, be it notes of appreciation, public acknowledgment, a formal award, or some form of recognition. Ensure your personnel know how important they are to the agency, as success or failure truly lies in their hands.

I keep several items in my office on the corner of my bulletin board to remind me why I do the job and the difference I know I've made. In that corner lies a book marker with a young child's picture. That child, at one-year's old, died after slipping under the water and drowning in the bathtub. Officers gave CPR to that child, trying desperately to save her life, and the call took an emotional toll on the responding officers. The mother gave that bookmark to each officer that was there that day and me.

What gave me a different perspective and warranted this bookmark landing on the corner shrine of my bulletin board was that each officer was already familiar with the mother. She was someone who had been in trouble with law enforcement multiple times. Each of us had probably arrested her at least once. She was someone we usually would not associate with or give much time to. But on this occasion, after losing her beautiful child and seeing the effort and the emotions the police put into trying to save her child, her perspective and attitude toward law enforcement changed. The mother wanted to make sure the police knew she was thankful to them for the service they provided. And the lesson I'm reminded of when I see that bookmark is that, as long as a person is alive, tomorrow is a new day and an opportunity to change. People do change. Some not-so-good people can end up being great people. And sometimes, law enforcement can be the catalyst for such a change.

A picture of a forty-year-old man in a business suit is in the same corner of my bulletin board. I never met the man, but he also is a reminder to me. I was presenting to a community group, and I made a comment related to the discussion and topic at hand. The comment was an accurate statement and was appropriately understood by most participants. However, as soon as I made the statement, which referenced deaths from drug overdoses, I felt the mood of the audience shift. I knew I was in big trouble. However, the audience's mood settled down as I continued the presentation. After the presentation, I noticed an older woman in tears approaching me. The realization that I was about to be confronted was apparent. She graciously thanked me for my time and the presentation but did tell me she thought my one comment was insensitive. She explained how her forty-year-old son had recently died from a heroin overdose and how my comment devalued his life. The entire audience, other than me, had been aware of his death. As she cried, I apologized the best I could. I hugged her and held back my own tears.

This encounter ate at me, as did my insensitivity, so I later tracked down who this woman was, obtained her address, and wrote her a letter. In the letter, I again apologized and asked for her forgiveness. Later, I received a lengthy letter in which she granted me the desired forgiveness for my insensitive statement and the hurt I caused her. Along with that letter was that picture of her son. Not only did she and I become friends, but she became a big supporter of mine. I learned that, as law enforcement professionals, no matter what we may think of those we encounter, they remain someone's child, parent, spouse, sibling, or friend. They may have made bad choices that brought about terrible consequences, but they are still human and, most likely, still loved by someone. A little compassion and mercy can go a long way.

And then there is the card from young seven-year-old Henry thanking me for helping him with his problem. Henry was attending his brother's Little League game at a local ball field. Henry and his friend played catch behind the field as the game continued. Unfortunately, their ball ended up in the backyard of a house adjacent to the park. Henry, doing the right thing, notified his mother that he had lost his ball in the backyard. His mother took him to the house, where a marked police vehicle sat in the driveway. They knocked on the front door to ask permission to go into the yard to retrieve the ball. After no one answered the door, Henry's mother told Henry he could walk down the narrow sidewalk into the yard and retrieve the baseball. The next thing his mother heard was screaming. She ran into the yard to find an off-duty police officer yelling at her seven-year-old son. He threatened to have Henry sent to a juvenile detention center and his mom arrested for trespassing. Both Henry and his mother were terrified by the officer's behavior.

Later that evening, Henry hid under his covers, crying and asking his mother how long she would have to go to jail. In hopes of remedying the damage caused by this so-called police officer, Henry's parents decided to bring him to the police station to talk to an officer. I was that officer. I spent time with Henry and the family, reassuring young Henry that the police were good and genuinely there to help. Unfortunately, this police officer worked for another jurisdiction, so I was limited in what I could do about him. However, I did work with Henry's parents on how to best file a complaint with the officer's department, which they did follow up on.

A week or two later, I revisited Henry and his mother. This time I came with a gift. Through work contacts, I obtained a baseball signed by Ozzie Guillen, the 2005 World Series Champion Chicago White Sox manager. I am a lifelong White Sox fan. I didn't have a signed baseball by Ozzie Guillen and would have liked to have had one. But a seven-year-old boy was more important, and when I saw the responses from both Henry and his mother, I never had any regrets. There was never any doubt whether I was making a difference to them.

These are just a few personal reminders that give me perspective, have kept me grounded, and remain committed to serving the community. Leaders need to help subordinates see the difference they make every day. What they do is essential, and our society and freedoms could not continue without them.

I attended a community event at a local park a couple years ago. I was in uniform and walking among the crowd talking with community members. A young girl, cute as can be, with her mother standing behind her in support, approached me, handed me a bag of potato chips, and said, "Thanks for your service." I quickly knelt and thanked her. They then walked off into the crowd before I realized the valuable gem I was holding in my hand. Stapled to the bag of chips was a business card. On that business card was the "Thin blue line" and the following words: "When this job (and humanity) has you questioning why you were even doing this, think back to why you started doing it. The reason is the same. You cannot save the world, but what you can do is help one person at a time. That is all you must do. Do that, and yours is a life lived well."

That encounter and the card given by that young girl were additional reminders that I needed to keep a healthy perspective and keep me driving on. That card was the next installation to the bulletin board in my office.

About a year later, I would be fortunate to meet this young encourager again. Once again, I found my friend, Kennedy, handing out encouraging business cards to first responders at another community event (see Figure 10).

Figure 10. My young friend and encourager. I first met Kennedy at a community event in 2021 where she and her mother were handing out cards of encouragement to first responders.

I often reminded officers about all the people they didn't know in the community. Indeed, there are people and houses in the community that law enforcement is all too familiar with and has the stories accompanying them. "The guy who lives in this house is the one who attacked Officer Smith." "The teenager in that apartment has overdosed four times already." "That house is full of gang members." Or "We did a search warrant on that house last summer." But that isn't the case for most homes in our communities. As law enforcement patrols their neighborhood, they pass by house after house that they have never been inside and don't know who lives there. These, I remind officers, are the people we work for. The good, hard-working, tax-paying, trying to raise their children right, people. We often don't meet this group because they live right and make good decisions. It is helping this group that should keep our law enforcement professionals engaged and moving forward.

But it's easy to get dragged down by negativity, frustration, and lack of support from those who should be supporting us. That's why true leadership is needed to ensure this doesn't happen. Ensure your people know their value and encourage them to continue to make a difference, one day and one person at a time.

FIND A SAFE PLACE – BE A SAFE PLACE

Law enforcement needs a safe place to vent, share, and discuss the challenges, frustrations, and stressors they are routinely exposed to. Holding and internalizing anxiety and emotions daily and year after year is unhealthy. Adrenaline and stress must go somewhere. It cannot be held in forever. Any attempt to hold in or hide the internal buildup of pressure and frustrations will manifest itself in unhealthy ways, i.e., anger, resentment, isolation, lack of patience, poor coping mechanisms, etc. Fortunately, the days of encouraging officers to keep everything hidden inside themselves, discouraging the sharing of feelings or showing of emotions because it signaled weakness are not as prevalent as it once was.

Traditionally, groups of officers gathered at the local liquor establishment after shift, specifically if they had experienced a significant incident earlier in the day. There was a benefit from being around other officers and sharing their experiences with each other, discussing what they had seen and done and their thoughts and feelings about it. But the excessive intake of alcoholic beverages, which often accompanied these tavern counseling sessions, likely reduced the benefit of coming together with other officers under those circumstances. Sharing experiences could quickly turn to griping and complaining about the incident, the unappreciative populace, or the unsupportive law enforcement organization. This, in turn, could increase anxiety levels instead of decreasing them and encourage self-pity.

Moreover, the benefits received from camaraderie with fellow officers might be offset by the angry spouse waiting on them, tired of them coming home late, intoxicated, or otherwise unengaged with the family. And then, of course, the mysterious woman at the end of the bar seemed to be the only person in the world who could possibly understand what the officer might be going through. With this mysterious woman, an officer finds consolation and, as could be predicted, infidelity and another ruined marriage.

Law enforcement professionals must have a support network, which should be a positive one. They need safe places to be themselves without fearing judgment or being perceived as weak. The benefits of discussing and processing the various challenges they face and struggle with within a positive environment can keep officers grounded and in balance.

I had two such resources I routinely relied on. First was Wendy. I could go home and vent to her as needed. She would sit and listen, respond with ideas or suggestions if appropriate, or remain silent, just listening and encouraging if that was best.

Second was my friend Don Pasquarella, better known as Pac-Man. I considered him a mentor. When I first became a police officer, he took me under his wing after I had finished my formal training. I'm not sure why we connected as well as we did, as he was many years my elder, older than my father. But he would show up on my calls, keep me safe and out of trouble, and provide guidance as needed. Of course, I didn't always take his advice, sometimes having to figure things out myself or learn the hard way. But his advice was always good; I would never go wrong listening to it.

This mentorship turned into a friendship. When frustrated or unsure of myself, angry with the organization's decision, or feeling mistreated by a supervisor, I could always find a listening ear with Pac-Man. He didn't always give advice. Often, he just listened and encouraged me as I talked through and processed what I was going through. Pac-Man has been retired for many years but is still a great friend, a person I love talking and venting to. He is a safe place. He has never betrayed my confidential discussions, so I could always count on him as that safe place (see Figure 11).

I've tried to be that person for others. Often, I would get visits from officers, many of whom didn't work directly for me. I suppose they perceived my presence as a safe place. They would visit and share some of their concerns or problems, whether they were marital problems, issues with their children, or addiction circumstances. There was often nothing I could do to help with the problem at hand other than just listen and validate their concerns. Hearing themselves put their thoughts into words and processing them was often all they needed to find the solutions.

Figure 11. My mentor Pac-Man (Don Pasquarella) and I. He kept me smiling and safe. The jokes weren't always great, but his advice was.

As a leader in our organizations, there will be times when we must wear the supervisor hat. The organization must come first, and inappropriate conduct or an officer not fit for duty must be reported and addressed as it's in the agency's best interest. There are other times, however, when providing that safe place for your personnel to talk and process their challenges and frustrations is in the organization's best interests. It relates to the officer's health, directly affecting their attitude and performance. It doesn't mean you must agree or take sides on an issue. Just being available and demonstrating concern for your organization's people tells them they are valued and worth investing in.

GIVE CONTROL

Law Enforcement officers are typically control-oriented people. It is these personalities who tend to navigate towards police work. They want to make decisions, and when responding to a crisis or a significant event that allows them the opportunity for control and decision making, they are probably at their best, or at least feel their best or fulfilled. Watch and listen to them interact after a significant event requiring quick and decisive action. They feed on it.

But the paramilitary or autocratic structure and leadership style of many law enforcement organizations tends to limit or remove opportunities for individual control and decision making. Most agencies will have mounds of policies, rules, and standards that detail what officers should and should not do, leaving little room for individualized decision making. This "lack of control" can frustrate employees whose personalities cry out for control.

Officers often feel a lack of control after a major event, such as a disaster, where a significant loss of life causes distress and adverse effects on their personal life. Now consider a career of events where the lack of control is felt by a group of people whose primary drive is to help people and make a difference.

In his book *Emotional Survival for Law Enforcement*, Dr. Kevin Gilmartin addresses law enforcement's need for control. Dr. Gilmartin recognizes this lack of control as a reason for some negativity among officers. However, acknowledging that officers don't always have a "say so" or ability to control many aspects of the work environment, he emphasizes the importance of making decisions in their personal life. Dr. Gilmartin's book is one of my "must-reads" for all law enforcement officers and a good starting place for making a positive change in the life of the law enforcement professionals around you.[2]

Due to the high risk involved in law enforcement activities, it is understandable that many tasks within the work environment require strict guidelines without room for deviation. However, much of the officer's or deputy's role allows for customization and individualized decision-making opportunities. A proactive leader will look for or create such opportunities. The many benefits of encouraging decision-making by subordinates were emphasized in Chapter 6, "An Outdated Leadership Model." Giving personnel a voice not only benefits the organization but can enhance the quality of life and well-being of employees personally.

Two decision-making models I would frequently share with subordinates and encourage them to use and try to master are the "worst case scenario" and the "if a supervisor asks" model.

When the need to make a decision is present, and it is either a decision that should not require a supervisor's input or intervention or there is no time to seek out and obtain a supervisor's input, the officer can weigh various alternatives by considering what the worst case might be for each choice. For example, you should ask yourself, "If I choose option A, what is the worst thing that can happen?" How about options B, C, D, etc.? Often when

---

[2] Gilmartin, Kevin M. P.D. (2002). *Emotional Survival for Law Enforcement.* E-S Press, Tucson, AZ.

considering what the worst case might be, it will become evident as to which option or options are best. For instance, you may decide that option A, making an entry into the room of a mentally unstable person, may escalate the incident and provoke a use-of-force encounter. In contrast, option B may utilize time and cover to the officer's benefit and allow the opportunity for de-scalation, which reduces the chance of a use-of-force incident. Very quickly, one can determine, if there is no immediate threat of harm to anyone, that option B may be a wiser choice than option A.

In the "If a supervisor asks" model, the decision maker questions and challenges their motivation for making a decision. Whether it is an officer's direct supervisor or the agency head, if they were to ask you why you chose option A instead of option B, C, or D, can you articulate it and answer it, demonstrating that it was a reasonable and professional response under the circumstances?

As leaders, we cannot expect everyone in our agencies to think just like we would. That is not realistic or desirable. So, should we be looking for the perfect solution? The best solution among all possible alternatives? Or what we would do if we were making the decision?

I believe leaders should expect their personnel to make reasonable decisions based on the circumstances and information known at the time, with an eye toward the organization's mission. If a decision maker, working within the "if a supervisor asks" model, starts to recognize their motives and intentions aren't consistent with the agency's mission, and they wouldn't want to explain their reason for the decision to the supervisor, then they are probably considering a wrong alternative and should reconsider. For instance, if, in deciding whether to write an incident report after a call for service, an officer recognizes his motivation is to go home on time and not have to hold over beyond their standard quitting time to finish the report, they are probably about to make the wrong decision.

With practice, these two decision-making models can be learned and become second nature, and decisions can be made quickly, even under stress. But, more importantly, it allows personnel to make decisions, giving them a voice and some control over their work. Most law enforcement officers crave control, so give them some. You may be surprised at the results you get.

CONCLUSION

Law enforcement is all about serving others. We aim to continuously add value to our communities, improving the safety and quality of life for those who live, work, travel, and play in our respective neighborhoods. From a leadership standpoint, we must realize that the officers and deputies on the front line possess the power and ability to make the most significant difference. When law enforcement leaders recognize how much their front-line personnel matter and treat them respectfully, they will likewise treat the people they serve as though they matter.

If the law enforcement organization treats officers like professionals, it is expected they will, in turn, respond professionally to members of the public. How do we get there? How do we obtain this excellence we are pursuing? We start with the self; we look inward. Recognize our weaknesses and natural human inclinations that may hinder us, which could ultimately stunt organizational progress. In other words, realize you aren't great, and maybe someday you will be.

APPENDICES

Appendix A

REQUEST FOR FEEDBACK SURVEY

CID Supervisors:

You are receiving this because we are interested in your feedback referencing the selection of the upcoming Street Crimes Sergeant. It is vital to the success of the Street Crimes Unit that we identify the most qualified candidate for this position. As depicted below, this person will be required to balance multiple interests, being responsive and cooperative with all other units within CID. This is the person that you, as CID supervisors, will be directly working and communicating with, and who will be supporting your units. I ask you to please take some time to consider these job expectations and provide your feedback directly to me. Having worked with these officers, and perhaps also having a personal relationship with some or all, you have had opportunities to view and assess their strengths and weaknesses, and how those identified strengths and weaknesses may apply to the expectations of the street crimes sergeant position.

DEADLINE FOR PROVIDING FEEDBACK IS WEDNESDAY JANUARY 24th AT 1500 HOURS

The five candidates are:

Kelly Adams
Patty Henderson
Tim Johnson
Brian Jacobson
Jack Williams

The Street Crimes Unit will be expected to focus on areas related to the strategic plan.

- Warrants will require prioritization, focusing on the most serious offenders identified by the strategic plan, i.e., Breaking & Entering offenders, targeted violent offenders, etc.

- The Street Crimes Unit will be expected to proactively patrol and conduct enforcement in High Crime Areas (HCA), including areas of recent crime activity, regardless of whether that falls into an identified HCA.
- The Street Crimes Unit will be expected to be familiar with known Breaking & Entering offenders and to cooperate with the Property Crime Unit in locating and taking enforcement action against them as needed.
- The Street Crimes Unit will be expected to be responsive, when practical, to all other units within CID, lending assistance that will enhance that CID unit's investigations and service to the community.
- The Street Crimes Unit is a proactive unit, spending most of its time in the field. The unit is expected to demonstrate results in arrests, warrants served, informants developed, etc.

Therefore, the qualified candidate is someone that must:

- Be able to multi-task and successfully balance the many competing interests of CID.
- Be able to communicate openly, candidly, and respectfully with all other supervisors.
- Be able to prioritize, schedule, and direct their personnel to ensure all required expectations are met. Often personnel may want to complete the tasks they enjoy or deem important, and the qualified supervisor must ensure all areas are accounted for. Likewise, the qualified supervisor must have the strength and integrity to ensure street crime activities remain balanced and neutral, and that one CID unit doesn't obtain excess support from street crimes at the cost of other units.
- The qualified supervisor should be a self-starter, well-versed in search and seizure laws and field operations.
- The qualified supervisor should have the desire and ability to develop their personnel to conform to and excel at the requirements of the Street Crime Unit.
- The qualified supervisor should be able to "think outside the box," deriving innovative ideas to tackle the issues at hand.
- The qualified supervisor will be expected to maintain and furnish reports on street crime activity on a routine basis.

I would prefer your feedback in writing but understand some may be more comfortable discussing it in person. I will be happy to accept the feedback in the manner you prefer. The information I collect will be kept confidential and combined together as a whole. I will not identify specific information with the provider but rather share all the information once gathered and combined.

Therefore, no one other than I will know who provided what information.

Please rank the five candidates from 1 to 5, with 1 being the most qualified and 5 being the least qualified. Again, your input will remain confidential. I will average all the numbers together and just share the final list with my chain of command.

1. ____________________
2. ____________________
3. ____________________
4. ____________________
5. ____________________

The ranking of candidates as part of the feedback requested should be supported by additional information/feedback provided to support your opinion. The ranking is meant to give an overall picture of the opinions of present supervisors on the various candidates once averaged together. The final average might show two or more candidates are very closely perceived as qualified candidates.

The feedback requested is informational only and not binding on the final decision. Having worked closely with the candidates, you may possess important considerations unknown to the command team that may provide valuable insight and should be considered. Ultimately, however, the Police Chief maintains complete authority and discretion in the matter of promotions and the recent request for feedback about the candidates does not alter that.

Thank you for your time and assistance in this process.

Captain Smith

Appendix B

LEADERSHIP SURVEY

This survey represents your opinions and perceptions as they relate to the performance of **Captain Smith.** How is Captain Smith doing with the below behaviors within the Operations Division? Please circle the most accurate response. There is room for comments after each statement. After the survey, there is additional room for any comments unrelated to the ten behavioral statements. Once completed please submit as explained on the cover sheet.

1. Recognizes the value of diverse views and opinions.

Strongly Agree	Agree	Neutral / Undecided	Disagree	Strongly Disagree

   <u>Comments:</u>

2. Creates an environment where people focus on the "big picture" versus focusing on personal interests.

Strongly Agree	Agree	Neutral / Undecided	Disagree	Strongly Disagree

   <u>Comments:</u>

3. Creates and communicates a clear vision for the division

Strongly Agree	Agree	Neutral / Undecided	Disagree	Strongly Disagree

   <u>Comments:</u>

4. Effectively involves people in decision making

Strongly Agree	Agree	Neutral / Undecided	Disagree	Strongly Disagree

   <u>Comments:</u>

5. Ensures people receive the training they need to succeed

Strongly Agree	Agree	Neutral / Undecided	Disagree	Strongly Disagree

Comments:

6. Provides recognition for others' achievement

Strongly Agree	Agree	Neutral / Undecided	Disagree	Strongly Disagree

Comments:

7. Gives people the freedom they need to excel

Strongly Agree	Agree	Neutral / Undecided	Disagree	Strongly Disagree

Comments:

8. Understands his own strengths and weaknesses

Strongly Agree	Agree	Neutral / Undecided	Disagree	Strongly Disagree

Comments:

9. Strives to understand the perspective of others

Strongly Agree	Agree	Neutral / Undecided	Disagree	Strongly Disagree

Comments:

10. Encourages creativity and innovation in others

Strongly Agree	Agree	Neutral / Undecided	Disagree	Strongly Disagree

Comments:

Additional Comments:

Appendix C

STRATEGIC PLAN

Goals, Objectives, And Strategies

Goal 1: **We will use our financial and human resources fairly, efficiently, and effectively**

Objective 1.1: Expansion and maintenance of Agency-wide Leadership Continuum

Strategy: 1.1a – Implementation of Sheriff's Leadership Academy for all first-line supervisors	**Division/Person(s) Responsible:** Chief Deputy /Professional Standards Captain
Description: Our first-line supervisors are the heart of our chain of command. They are the communication link between the employees and administration, and they have great responsibility concerning employee productivity, morale, and development. We want to better equip our supervisors by implementing a leadership course based on the challenges they face. We will add squad-level leadership opportunities after the successful completion of training.	**Status:** *In process* **Completion Date:** January 19, 20XX Sgts. complete February 16, 20XX Cpls. complete (Creation and first round of implementation)

Strategy: 1.1b – Ensure continuing executive-level training for Lieutenants & above	**Division/Person(s) Responsible:** Professional Standards Captain/ Command Team
Description: Focus Group has been completed. Executive Training through FBI National Academy, SPI (Major & Above), AOMP, and Northwestern University (Lts. & Captains). Through the promotional process identify those candidates most likely to promote further within the agency to attend Executive Training (Command Team).	**Status:** *Complete* **Projected Completion Date:** Completed & Ongoing

Strategy: 1.1c –ICS Leadership Training for Supervisors	**Division/Person(s) Responsible:** Professional Standards Captain, Patrol Captain, Major
Description: Incident Command System (ICS) training with full field training exercises in conjunction with partners will be offered annually to supervisors.	**Status:** *Complete* **Projected Completion Date:** Completed & Ongoing
Strategy: 1.1d – Annual Tactical training for Sworn Personnel	**Division/Person(s) Responsible:** Professional Standards Captain
Description: Tactical training for sworn personnel was completed in the fall of 20XX. Like training will be planned and rolled out in the fall of each year.	**Status:** *Complete* **Projected Completion Date:** Completed & Ongoing

Objective 1.2: Comprehensive SOG Manual

Strategy: 1.2 – Standard Operating Guidelines	**Division/Person(s) Responsible:** Staff Attorney/Command Team
Description: Develop and deploy Standard Operating Guidelines (SOG) for all divisions.	**Status:** *In Process* **Projected Completion Date:** Operations Bureau, Support, Communications, VIP complete. Detention *In Process* February 28, 20XX

Objective 1.3: Physical Fitness Incentive Program

Strategy: 1.3 – Physical Fitness Incentive Program	**Division/Person(s) Responsible:** Operations Major/Professional Standards Captain
Description: Creation and review for implementation of Physical Fitness Incentive Program begins by December 31st, 20XX. Program to be completed annually voluntarily by staff. Fully implemented by December 31st, 20XX.	**Status:** *Completed* **Projected Completion Date:** Creation and Review-December 31, 20XX Completed & Ongoing

Objective 1.4: Creation of Community Support Team

Strategy: 1.4 – Creation of Community Support Team	**Division/Person(s) Responsible:** Staff Attorney/Patrol Lieutenant/ Volunteer Coordinator
Description: Creation of Community Support Team with inclusion of all volunteer services by December 31st, 20XX with full implementation by December 31st, 20XX.	**Status:** *In process* **Projected Completion Date:** Creation- December 31, 20XX Implementation- December 31, 20XX

Strategy: 1.4a – Community Emergency Response Team (CERT)	**Division/Person(s) Responsible:** Patrol Captain/
Description: Creation of a Community Emergency Response Team (CERT) within the Community Support Team model. CERT will allow citizens to provide basic disaster response to the community. Sheriff's Office will continue to partner with local emergency services, hospitals, and medical providers to better coordinate response and plan for future needs.	**Status:** *In process* **Projected Completion Date:** Creation- December 31, 20XX Implementation- December 31, 20XX

Goal 2: We will reduce agency targeted crime in the County

Objective 2.1: Reduce Domestic Violence recidivism rates within the county by 15% by December 31, 20XX

Strategy: 2.1a – Community Approach to Offender-Focused Deterrence	Division/Person(s) Responsible: CID Captain/Patrol Captain
Description: We will utilize a community approach that brings all stakeholders to the table working within the model known as Offender Focused Deterrence. Partnering with the Domestic Violence Advocates, Social Services, regional law enforcement agencies, and the District Attorney will hold offenders accountable while offering better care and easier access to victims.	**Status:** *In process* **Projected Completion Date:** Ongoing

Strategy: 2.1b – Training of Patrol in DV response	Division/Person(s) Responsible: Professional Standards Captain
Description: All our patrol employees will receive (initial and ongoing) training in domestic violence response and the cycle of violence.	**Status:** *Complete* **Projected Completion Date:** Completed & Ongoing

Objective 2.2: Reduce Part 1 crimes in high crime areas in the County by 10% by December 31, 20XX

Strategy: 2.2a – Identify the four highest crime areas (HCA's) in the County	Division/Person(s) Responsible: Crime Analyst/CID Captain/ Patrol Captain
Description: Identify the four highest crime areas (HCA's) in the County based on Part 1 crime occurrences and disseminate by March 1, 20XX. Will be recalculated every March for the life of the plan (Crime Analyst). The Captains of Patrol and CID will ensure all personnel participates in directed patrols as a routine and hold accountable those who do not. Sergeants shall monitor their personnel logged direct patrols and submit them to their Division Captains monthly. Division Captains will make these monthly reports available at the next available command team meeting.	**Status:** *Complete* **Projected Completion Date:** Completed & Ongoing

Strategy: 2.2b – Continue weekly Crime Analysis Meetings	**Division/Person(s) Responsible:** Chief Deputy
Description: To maximize the results of our crime analysis, we will continue weekly Crime Analysis meetings with the intent to focus efforts in all strategic plan areas and ensure accountability.	**Status:** *Complete* **Projected Completion Date:** Completed & Ongoing

Strategy: 2.2c – Focus enforcement activity on crime during regular patrol	**Division/Person(s) Responsible:** Patrol Captain
Description: The shifts in our crime data analysis will allow our patrol enforcement activities to be both reactive and proactive to the crimes being committed. We will continue to utilize this data to assign surveillance and enforcement in high burglary areas to continue on our successful trajectory in combatting Breaking & Entering offenses.	**Status:** *Complete* **Projected Completion Date:** Completed & Ongoing

Strategy: 2.2d – Utilize a targeted approach to focus on B&E crime offenders	**Division/Person(s) Responsible:** CID Captain/Street Crimes/ Property Crimes/Warrants
Description: We will develop and disseminate intelligence, as appropriate, about repeat offenders committing targeted crimes. Partnering with other local law enforcement agencies and the District Attorney will hold criminals accountable while offering better care and easier access to victims.	**Status:** *Complete* **Projected Completion Date:** Completed & Ongoing

Objective 2.3: Develop and implement solvability factors in incident reporting to increase clearance rates for Part 1 crimes by 10% by December 31, 20XX

Strategy: 2.3a – Solvability factors training	**Division/Person(s) Responsible:** CID Captain/Patrol Captain / Professional Standards Captain
Description: Conduct training for detectives and patrol deputies on the benefits of tracking solvability factors and how they increase clearance rates. Report writing class for sworn personnel and detention officers completed in May 20XX. Fingerprint training provided to patrol squads by CID.	**Status:** *In process* **Projected Completion Date:** Ongoing

Strategy: 2.3b – Solvability factors equipment	**Division/Person(s) Responsible:** CID Captain/Patrol Captain/ Professional Standards Captain
Description: Fingerprint kits distributed by CID to all patrol squads. Cameras distributed to patrol squads for improved documentation and collection of photographic evidence. Training with Crime Scene Technician for patrol complete by May 31, 20XX.	**Status:** *Complete* **Projected Completion Date:** Completed & Ongoing

Objective 2.4: Reduce Controlled Substance Overdose Death Cases by 15% by December 31, 20XX

Strategy: 2.4a – Expand efforts to educate, prevent and fight abuse of prescription medication	**Division/Person(s) Responsible:** Support Captain
Description: We will partner with community advocates and medical and mental health professionals to expand our efforts to educate, prevent and fight the abuse of prescription medication throughout the County. Partners will include...	**Status:** *Complete* **Projected Completion Date:** Completed & Ongoing

Strategy: 2.4b – Focus Narcotics Unit toward prescription drug diversion cases	**Division/Person(s) Responsible:** CID Captain
Description: The agency has staffed a Dedicated Drug Diversion Agent and will continue to identify and support initiatives to reduce prescription drug diversion. The agency will assist in educating medical professionals who dispense prescription narcotics about risk factors for drug diversion.	**Status:** *Complete* **Projected Completion Date:** Completed & Ongoing
Strategy: 2.4c – Connect with pharmacies and health care providers for education and intelligence gathering	**Division/Person(s) Responsible:** CID Captain
Description: Local pharmacies and health care providers need to be involved in preventing the diversion of controlled substances and educated on how to rapidly identify and respond when diversion is detected. The Narcotics Unit will educate these shareholders, gather intelligence, and establish a system for prevention and reporting.	**Status:** *Complete* **Projected Completion Date:** Completed & Ongoing

Strategy: 2.4d – Create and disseminate resource materials to inmates	**Division/Person(s) Responsible:** Detention Captain
Description: Create & disseminate resource materials regarding rehabilitation for those incarcerated in the County Jail and continue to partner with community resources, Jail chaplains & the Prison and Jail Ministry to assist those incarcerated.	**Status:** *Complete* **Projected Completion Date:** Completed & Ongoing

Strategy: 2.4e – Narcan dissemination and training for all agency personnel	**Division/Person(s) Responsible:** Professional Standards Captain
Description: Professional Standards has partnered with Community College to educate and train officers with Narcan - a medication that will help prevent and fight overdoses and overdose deaths in the County. Narcan training will continue as part of the In-Service Training Program.	**Status:** *Complete* **Projected Completion Date:** Completed & Ongoing

Strategy: 2.4f –Family Risk Assessment for Health Care Professionals (FRA)	**Division/Person(s) Responsible:** CID Captain
Description: Formulation and training for Family Risk Assessment for Health Care Professionals (FRA) to administer to patients.	**Status:** *Complete* **Projected Completion Date:** Completed December 31, 20XX

Strategy: 2.4g – Conduct various pill drop campaigns	**Division/Person(s) Responsible:** Evidence Custodian/Professional Standards Corporal
Description: Conduct various pill drop campaigns in the community beyond the pill collection box (minimum one per quarter).	**Status:** *Complete* **Projected Completion Date:** Completed & Ongoing

Objective 2.5: Maintain the B&E&L reduction of minimum of 15% from 20XX levels through December 31, 20XX

Strategy: 2.5a – Continue weekly Crime Analysis Meetings	**Division/Person(s) Responsible:** Chief Deputy
Description: To maximize the results of our crime analysis, we will continue weekly Crime Analysis meetings with the intent to focus efforts in all strategic plan areas and ensure accountability.	**Status:** *Complete* **Projected Completion Date:** Completed & Ongoing

Strategy: 2.5b – Focus enforcement activity on crime during regular patrol	**Division/Person(s) Responsible:** Patrol Captain
Description: The shifts in our crime data analysis will allow our patrol enforcement activities to be both reactive and proactive to the crimes being committed. We will continue to utilize this data to assign surveillance and enforcement in high burglary areas to continue on our successful trajectory in combatting Breaking & Entering offenses.	**Status:** *Complete* **Projected Completion Date:** Completed & Ongoing

Strategy: 2.5c – Targeted deterrence to B&E&L crime offenders	**Division/Person(s) Responsible:** CID Captain/Street Crimes/ Property Crimes/Warrants
Description: We will develop and disseminate intelligence, as appropriate, about repeat offenders committing targeted crimes. Partnering with other local law enforcement agencies and the District Attorney will hold criminals accountable while offering better care and easier access to victims.	**Status:** *Complete* **Projected Completion Date:** Completed & Ongoing

Objective 2.6: Reduce inmate on inmate physical assaults by 10% by December 31, 20XX

Strategy: 2.6a – Identify potential risk inmates through state-mandated classification system	**Division/Person(s) Responsible:** Detention Captain
Description: Classification will complete an assessment of all inmates that enter the Detention Center and assign housing as necessary.	**Status:** *Complete* **Projected Completion Date:** Completed & Ongoing

Strategy: 2.6b – Review inmate keep-away orders on a weekly basis to segregate potential high-risk inmates	**Division/Person(s) Responsible:** Detention Captain
Description: Classification will review keep-away placements in the jail and make adjustments as necessary.	**Status:** *Complete* **Projected Completion Date:** Completed & Ongoing

Strategy: 2.6c – Staff will manage inmate movement to reduce the potential for fighting	**Division/Person(s) Responsible:** Detention Captain
Description: Detention center staff, supervisors, and classification staff will work together to manage the placement and movement of inmates within the facility.	**Status:** *Complete* **Projected Completion Date:** Completed & Ongoing

Strategy: 2.6d – Work with medical and mental health staff to identify and counsel potential high risk inmates	**Division/Person(s) Responsible:** Detention Captain
Description: Once potential high-risk inmates are identified mental health staff will counsel and evaluate those inmates to make recommendations for housing with the Detention facility.	**Status:** *Complete* **Projected Completion Date:** Completed & Ongoing

Strategy: 2.6e – Train staff quarterly on early identification of high-risk inmates	**Division/Person(s) Responsible:** Detention Captain
Description: Detention Supervisors will train their staff quarterly on the identification of high-risk inmates.	**Status:** *In process* **Projected Completion Date:** Ongoing

Goal 3: We will provide high quality service to the citizens of the County

Objective 3.1: Continue on-going Quality of Service Survey through December 31, 20XX

Strategy: 3.1 – Continue on-going Quality of Service Survey	Division/Person(s) Responsible: Operations and Support Major/ Communications Director
Description: Will be managed and reviewed by the Major on a monthly basis, with Command Team report each week. The database will ensure survey results remain ongoing, accurate, and functional. Focus areas will be designated on a quarterly basis to be reviewed by division Captains who then submit changes as applicable for the upcoming quarter. Beginning January 1, 20XX data will be pulled utilizing the following criteria; • Every 5th victim from a Breaking & Entering report taken (Crime Analyst to assemble) • Every 5th Domestic Violence Victim (Crime Analyst to assemble) • Every 15th Concealed Carry Weapons Permitee (Support Services Captain will assemble) • Every 15th Handgun Purchase Permitee (Support Services Captain will assemble) • Every 75th Caller to the Business line in Communications (Director of Communications will assemble) • All survey follow-up calls will be one month after the incident. All follow-up survey questions will use uniform standardized questions.	**Status:** *Complete* **Projected Completion Date:** Completed & Ongoing

Objective 3.2: Answer 92% of 911 calls within 10 seconds of receipt (NC 911 Board standard) by December 31, 20XX

Strategy: 3.2a – Utilize administrative call takers	**Division/Person(s) Responsible:** Communications Director
Description: Utilize administrative call takers to answer administrative phone lines, allowing telecommunicators to focus on answering 911 calls more efficiently.	**Status:** *Complete* **Projected Completion Date:** Completed & Ongoing

Strategy: 3.2b – Answer all 911 calls within two rings	**Division/Person(s) Responsible:** Communications Director
Description: Utilize staff of telecommunicators and call takers to answer all 911 calls within two rings.	**Status:** *Ongoing* **Projected Completion Date:** Completed & Ongoing

Objective 3.3: Dispatch 80% of emergency fire calls (NFPA standard) within 60 seconds of receipt by December 31, 20XX

Strategy: 3.3a – Utilize administrative call takers	**Division/Person(s) Responsible:** Communications Director
Description: Utilize administrative call takers to answer administrative phone lines, allowing telecommunicators to focus on dispatching 911 calls more efficiently.	**Status:** *Complete* **Projected Completion Date:** Completed & Ongoing

Strategy: 3.3b – Dispatch all emergency fire calls as soon as the call type is determined before further questioning	**Division/Person(s) Responsible:** Communications Director
Description: Dispatch all emergency fire calls as soon as the call type is determined before further questioning.	**Status:** *Complete* **Projected Completion Date:** Completed & Ongoing

Strategy: 3.3bc – When possible, one Telecommunicator will dispatch the call while another is completing caller interview	**Division/Person(s) Responsible:** Communications Director
Description: When possible, one Telecommunicator will dispatch the call while another is completing a caller interview.	**Status:** *Complete* **Projected Completion Date:** Completed & Ongoing

Objective 3.4: Increase random deputy patrols to our schools

Strategy: 3.4 - Deputy Patrols of Schools	**Division/Person(s) Responsible:** Patrol Captain
Description: In addition to the law enforcement presence created by our School Resource Deputies, we pledge to increase random deputy patrols to our schools.	**Status:** *Complete* **Projected Completion Date:** Completed & Ongoing

Objective 3.5: Provide Community Education (Sheriff's Community OutReach and Education S.C.O.R.E.)

Strategy: 3.5a – Offer Sheriff's Community OutReach and Education (S.C.O.R.E.) programs that educate the community	**Division/Person(s) Responsible:** Crime Prevention Coordinator
Description: Programming will include programs such as: • Children's outreach, giveaways, Sheriff's Office tours, and presentations • B&E/Theft prevention education program • Sheriff's Overwatch Program – Creation by December 21, 20XX • Town Hall Meetings occurring on a monthly basis throughout varying areas of the county. Meetings will promote accessibility, transparency and give citizens a direct connection to the Sheriff's Office and staff • Refuse to Be a Victim • Church/Organization Safety Training • Gun Safety Education and gun lock giveaway	**Status:** *In process* **Projected Completion Date:** Ongoing

Strategy: 3.5b – 911 Community Education	**Division/Person(s) Responsible:** Communications Director
Description: Provide Community Education by establishing a 911 Education Coordinator to work with elementary schools to educate children on the proper use of 911 and provide information about 911 resources such as Smart911 and Nixle. The Education Coordinator will contact one school per month to schedule an educational session. Will meet with and provide educational materials to all 4th-grade public school classes and will schedule 911 Center tours for school classes upon request.	**Status:** *In process* **Projected Completion Date:** December 31, 20XX

Objective 3.6: Support the Sheriff's Citizens Academy

Strategy: 3.6 – Sheriff's Citizens Academy	**Division/Person(s) Responsible:** Crime Prevention Coordinator
Description: The Sheriff's Citizen's Academy is an in-depth program providing education and crime prevention skills to the public. The program consists of 13 diverse classes. The Sheriff's Office will continue to support and provide instructors for this program.	**Status:** *Ongoing* **Projected Completion Date:** Ongoing

NORTH CAROLINA ASSOCIATION OF CHIEFS OF POLICE

GOALS FOR THE NCACP'S STRATEGIC PLAN, WHAT MUST BE ACHIEVED?

1. Provide for the Sustainability of NCACP
2. Develop 21st Century Police Leadership

OBJECTIVES, WHO DOES THE WORK?

The members decided on a five-year strategic plan with action items set at 1 year, 3 years, and 5 years to achieve their goals. Since the NCACP has standing committees the work will be assigned to committees or the President can appoint special committees. Financial planning or marketing can be contracted out to professional services with the approval of the Board of Directors.

Objectives by Year 1	Who Does the Work?
Increase membership in NCACP to 300 Chiefs	Regional Directors
Create a social media group, to promote information exchange	Staff
Increase participation of metro chiefs on the board or committees	Board of Officers
Engage chiefs by recruiting/appointing those who have not served on a committee to serve	President
Develop curriculum for newly appointed chief's course	Training Committee
Appoint a Sustainability Committee	President

Objectives by Year 3	Who Does the Work?
Teach pilot of new chiefs' course and evaluate	Training Committee
Offer the new chiefs' course three times across the state	Training Committee
Introduce a statutory requirement for all new chiefs' to attend the course	Legislative Counsel
Hold summit with the Sheriff's Association on matters of mutual interest	Emerging Issues Committee
Produce a financial plan for the Association	Budget Committee

Objectives by Year 5	Who Does the Work?
Have statutory requirement for new chiefs' course adopted and funded by the state	Legislative Counsel
Create capital fund	Sustainability Committee
Identify a location for the permanent office of NCACP	Sustainability Committee
Acquire physical location for NCACP	Board of Officers
Review staffing needs and plan for additional staffing as needed	Board of Officers

GOAL 1: PROVIDE FOR THE SUSTAINABILITY OF NCACP

Objective	Description - Activities (Date to be completed)
1.1	Increase the membership of NCACP to 300 Chiefs - Challenge Regional Directors to each recruit 6 new members by NCACP Chief's meeting at NC Police Executives conference (Jul 20XX) - Assign to Membership Committee if that goal is not met (Jul 20XX)
1.2	Create social media group for the exchange of information - Assign to a staff member (Jun 20XX) - Survey membership to see if there is an existing platform they find useful, what would they use? - Select some format and test with existing members (Jan 20XX) - Approve and launch by Spring Board of Directors meeting
1.3	Recruit and appoint chiefs who have not previously served on a committee to serve on a committee - Acquire a list of member Chiefs from staff for review (Jun 20XX) - ID committees with vacancies or ones to add positions - Have existing Board and Committee members recommend chiefs by the NC Police Executive Conference (Jul 20XX) - Make contact with chiefs by phone or at the conference
1.4	Appoint a Sustainability Committee - Discuss at the conference and get input from the members on who should lead and be nominated for this committee (Jul 20XX) - Recruit members and meet with the group for direction (Nov 20XX)

1.5	Hold a summit with the NC Sheriff's Association - Pitch the idea to the leadership of the NC Sheriff's Association, members from both associations could meet for a day and discuss what items of mutual interests could we collaborate on? - If there is any interest assign a combined group to organize the summit - Select a date and location for the summit - Hold the first summit in the Spring of 20XX or sooner
1.6	Produce a financial plan for the Association - Assign to the Budget Committee (Jul 20XX) - Budget Committee meets and discusses options on how to create a financial plan (Oct 20XX) - By the winter training conference have a recommendation for the Board of Directors on how to develop a financial plan - Begin developing a plan and meet quarterly, give updates on progress to the President following each quarterly meeting - Outline steps to be taken by the Spring 20XX NCACP Board meeting - Approve plan at NCPEOA meeting (Jul 20XX)
1.7	Create a capital improvement fund to acquire NCACP office - Assign to Sustainability Committee (Jan 20XX) - Meet with Budget Committee developing the financial plan, consider having a member on each committee for coordination - Assess the initial costs of permanent office space and identify potential ways to raise that capital (Jul 20XX) - Create a capital improvement account, with minimum amount (Jan 20XX) - Outline capital improvement campaign project, and recommend to Board of Directors (Spring 20XX) - Conduct capital improvement campaign during 20XX and 20XX - Raise minimum necessary to provide office space for the first five years (Dec 20XX)
1.8	Review staffing needs and add additional staff where needed - Meet with the Board of Officers to discuss future staffing needs, succession planning for existing staff, additional staff needed for a permanent office (Jul 20XX) - Assign one or two members to do a staffing report - Meet individually with the current Executive Director, Legislative Counsel and Clerical Support for their input (Oct 20XX) - Discuss the report findings and recommendations by the Winter Conference (Jan 20XX) - Make assignments based on the recommendations (Jan 20XX)

1.9	Identify location for permanent office of NCACP - Assign to Sustainability Committee (Jul 20XX) - Meet to consider options for a Raleigh location, space needs, location, price per square foot, budget, etc. (Sept 20XX) - Conduct a search for available space, report options to the Board of Officers (Mar 20XX) - Prioritize locations identified, review lease options, and make a recommendation to the Board of Officers (Dec 20XX)
1.10	Acquire office for NCACP - Board of Officers takes the proposal to sign for a location to the Board of Directors for approval (May 20XX)

GOAL 2: DEVELOP 21st CENTURY POLICE LEADERSHIP

Objective	Description - Activities (Date to be completed)
2.1	Develop a curriculum for a new chiefs' course - Assigned to the Training Committee (Jun 20XX) - Training Committee members meet to assign tasks and discuss (Jul 20XX) - Collect curriculum from other states (Georgia and Virginia were mentioned) as samples (Sept 20XX) - Review the topics/modules collected and create an outline for the course. It was suggested to keep the course under a week and possibly break it into a couple sessions to make it easier for some to attend. (Oct 20XX) - Full Training Committee meets to agree on a purposed outline, assign lesson plans to writer or rewrite. (Dec 20XX) - Review draft lesson plans (Mar 20XX) - Approve new chiefs' course and outline (Jun 20XX)
2.2	Teach a pilot of the new chiefs' course and evaluate the curriculum - Select date for the first delivery of the new course (Jul 20XX) - Select a location for the instruction and recruit a panel of instructors. (Aug 20XX) - Deliver the first course to a class of NCACP member chiefs, so they can evaluate the material and instructors. Including some new chiefs as students is an option as well. (Jan 20XX) - Training Committee meets to finalize the lesson plans based on the course evaluations (Mar 20XX) - Final lesson plans approved and ready (Jun 20XX)

2.3	Offer new chiefs' course three times across the state - Select dates and locations to teach the course three times in NC. Fall 20XX, Winter 20XX, Spring 20XX (Jul 20XX) - Confirm instructors and advertise for class. Class size between 10 and 20 for newly appointed chiefs, less than one year experience as chief. - Conduct training and evaluate the course. - Training Committee meets and reviews all the evaluations for the course, makes any recommended changes (Jun 20XX)
2.4	Introduce a statutory requirement for all new chiefs to attend the course - Assign to legislative counsel for research (Jun 20XX) - Draft a legislative or regulatory change necessary to require all new chiefs to attend the course (Dec 20XX) - Identify a sponsor for the legislation (Mar 20XX) - Present to members of the legislature committee for consideration (Jun 20XX)
2.5	Have the statutory requirement for the new chiefs' course adopted and funded by the state - Report progress to NCACP Board at director's meeting - Work through committees and legislators until adopted (Jun 20XX)

Appendix D

MEMORANDUM: PATROL DIVISION MONTHLY REPORT

TO:	Deputy Chief Jones
FROM:	Commander Smith
SUBJECT:	February 20XX Patrol Division Report
DATE:	March 8, 20XX

During the month of February, the following directed patrols/activities were completed as a means of responding to community issues and the prevention of crime.

Overnight Theft related crimes (burglaries, BTMV, vehicle thefts, etc.) for Feb. 20XX occurred as follows:

Echo 1 – (15) to include tire thefts from Enterprise & (4) separate occurrences of tools stolen from work trucks
Echo 3 – (6) to include garage burglary w/ offender apprehended
Echo 2 – (3)
Echo 4 – (5)

Last (4) months of theft related activity

Echo 1 – (47) 54%
Echo 3 – (19) 22%-**76% of thefts occurring on the north side of town**
Echo 2 – (8) 10%
Echo 4 – (12) 14%

Extra patrol units were assigned to the north side of town, with specific emphasis on the Industrial Park to include hotels and car sales lots.

Fourteen extra patrols in the area of TransRun Trucking (176 N Main) were conducted over the weekends due to the recent and frequent target for tire thefts after hours. Several cut holes in fencing surrounding the business were located but determined to be old and previously reported.

Several incidents of graffiti have been reported late in the month and the beginning of March, primarily in the Echo 3 area. Most reported dates of occurrence incorporated the weekend, which is the most likely time of occurrence. Officers have been instructed to monitor the residential areas, looking for pedestrians, juveniles, etc., and challenging same. Officer Hanson took the initiative to conduct foot patrols and surveillance of the affected areas.

Officers disrupted a college party involving underage drinking at 541 W. Lorraine (XX-6762). Five people were charged with the Consumption of Alcohol by Minor. The case was forwarded for Chronic Nuisance.

Officers continue to monitor the activities around the One Stop bar. There were no new reports of damage in the area of the bar or city parking deck. There were several arrests made related to bar activity in or near the One Stop. These arrests included:

- (1) arrest for trespass (refusing to leave the One Stop) and resisting arrest
- (1) DWI arrest of patrons leaving the One Stop
- (2) disorderly conducts for public urination

Officers continue to monitor the closing of the One Stop on weekends. Only one complaint was made in February (Feb 23rd) about loud noise at closing. There has been ongoing contact with the complainant, a resident of Crescent Court Condominiums seeking feedback reference officer's efforts to control unruly and inappropriate behavior at closing time. Officers have been provided the sections of various ordinance violations that may apply to the ongoing issues at One Stop. Sgt. Chance also forwarded a letter to the local cab companies requesting additional cabs at closing time. The lack of cabs is the primary reason patrons congregate outside after closing. Extra patrols and assigned units at closing time will continue.

There were (92) bar checks conducted.

There were (73) hazard notifications completed for garage doors found open overnight and valuables, such as GPS units being left in vehicles in plain view.

Patrol addressed the following citizen complaints:

- Subsequent to citizen requests, traffic details were carried out at the following:
  - o Avoiding traffic control device-North & Main behind X Sport (8 citations & 3 warnings issued)
  - o Speeding on the 100 block of Farmers Dr. (3 citations & 2 warnings issued for non-speeding violations)
  - o Speeding on the 100 block of Elm St.
  - o Stop sign @ 3rd & Main.
- Additional patrol at 972 S. Carter after evidence of drug usage was found behind the business. No new signs of illegal activity or suspicious persons were located.

Patrol participated in two bike safety presentations.

Patrol officers participated in a tour of the college to familiarize themselves with the locations of various buildings and procedures to use in an emergency response to that location. Discussions referencing emergency response and what resources were available at the college were discussed with security personnel.

After responding to a "check on well-being" call involving a young autistic boy who refused to talk with officers and physically resisted their efforts to help, an article referencing law enforcement's response to autistic individuals was presented to all patrol officers. Additional training on the topic is planned for a future date. A recommendation for department-wide training in this area is suggested.

Officer Jacobson was assigned to the detective division for two weeks of cross-training.

This month all members of patrol were trained on the Pursuit Policy (Policy 314).

Incidents of significance or interest occurring during the month include:

- Burglary arrest (XX-5660). Officers responded to a burglary in progress at 210 Elm. After a perimeter and short foot chase the offender was apprehended. A Unit Citation was requested for the officers involved. A card of thanks and appreciation from the victim was subsequently received by the shift.

- Officer Goodman responded to a full arrest of a 68-year-old woman (XX-5761). He utilized the AED and then performed CPR reviving the victim. A Life Saving Award was requested.
- A violation of an order of protection investigation was initiated where officers suspected the offender was frequenting the prohibited area. Officers monitored the area over multiple days locating and arresting said offender for a violation of OOP (XX-41789).
- Officers responded to an armed robbery and battery of a taxi driver. Within minutes, two of the three offenders were located and taken into custody. With the assistance of the detective division, the third offender was also located and arrested. All three offenders were charged with the robbery and transported to County Jail. A Unit Citation Request was submitted in reference to this incident (XX-5824).
- Officer McFarland was assigned a theft report at the hospital with a suspect. Officer McFarland obtained a confession over the telephone and then convinced the suspect to come to the station to meet with him. At the station Officer McFarland continued with the interrogation of the suspect and obtained a confession on two additional, unknown, and unreported thefts. The suspect was charged for all three separate thefts (XX-5857).

Respectfully Submitted,

Commander Smith

Appendix E

MEMORANDUM: PROPERTY ROOM AUDIT

TO:	Deputy Chief Jones
FROM:	Cmdr. Smith
SUBJECT:	property room audit
DATE:	March 24, 20XX

On 3/21/XX at 1415 hours, I conducted an audit of the property room. Twenty-three items from different cases were randomly selected through the Evidence Records Management System (RMS). I, along with Property and Evidence Technician Roberts inspected said items to ensure they were located in their designated and appropriate area and entered/packaged properly. One item, being item #10 from case #XX-21595, was listed as being stored on the shelf in section 1000E. This item was located one shelf away in section 1000F. The item was then placed in the correct designated location.

All other items were located appropriately. Items of evidence were packaged correctly and the general appearance and organization of the property room were satisfactory.

I've included the items randomly selected for inspection to this memo.

Sincerely,

Commander Smith

REFERENCES

Abrashoff, D. M. (2002). *It's Your Ship: Management Techniques from the Best Damn Ship in the Navy.* New York, NY: Warner Books.

Axelrod, A. (2006). *Eisenhower on Leadership.* San Francisco, CA: Jossey-Bass Publishing.

Bossidy, L., & Charan, R. (2002). *Execution: The Discipline of Getting Things Done.* New York, NY: Crown Business.

Bratton, W. (1998). *Turnaround: How America's Top Cop Reversed the Crime Epidemic.* New York, NY: Random House Inc.

Bratton, W., & Tumin, Z. (2012). *Collaborate or Perish.* New York, NY: Crown Business.

Charan, R, Drotter, S, & Noel, J. (2001). *The Leadership Pipeline; How to Build the Leadership Powered Company.* San Francisco, CA: Jossey-Bass Publishing.

Coleman, J. L. (2010). *Police Assessment Testing.* Springfield, IL: Charles C Thomas, Publisher, Ltd.

Collins, J. (2001). *Good to Great.* New York, NY: Harper Collins Publishers, Inc.

Covey, S. R. (1989). *The Seven Habits of Highly Effective People; Powerful Lessons in Personal Change.* New York, NY: Free Press.

Enter, J. E. (2006). *Challenging the Law Enforcement Organization: Proactive Leadership Strategies.* Dacula, GA: Narrow Road Press.

Franks, T. (2004). *American Soldier.* New York, NY: Harper Collins.

Fuller, J. F. C. (1957). *Grant & Lee.* New York, NY: MJF Books.

Gallup. (1999/2016). *First, Break All the Rules; What the World's Greatest Managers Do Differently.* New York, NY: Gallup Press.

Gilmartin, K. M. (2002). *Emotional Survival for Law Enforcement.* Tucson, AZ: E-S Press.

Goldsmith, M. (2007). *What Got You Here Won't Get You There.* New York, NY: MJF Books.

Goleman, D. (1998). *Working with Emotional Intelligence.* New York, NY: Bantam.

Giuliani, R. W. (2002). *Leadership.* New York, NY: Hyperion.

Guilfoyle, S. (2013). *Intelligent Policing: How Systems Thinking Methods Eclipse Conventional Management Practice.* Charmouth, UK: Triarchy Press.

Harari, O. (2002). *The Leadership Secrets of Colin Powell.* New York, NY: McGraw-Hill.

Human Capital Institute. (2013). *Leadership and Emotional Intelligence: The Keys to Driving ROI and Organizational Performance.*

Heintze, H. (2013). *The Schaumburg Police Department: An Agency in Transition, An independent assessment and strategic roadmap.* Chicago, IL.

International Association of Chiefs of Police. (1999). *Police Leadership in the 21st Century: Achieving & Sustaining Executive Success.* Recommendations from the IACP President's First Leadership Conference.

International Association of Chiefs of Police. (2008). *Police Chiefs Desk Reference: A guide for newly appointed police leaders* (2nd ed.). New York, NY: McGraw Hill Learning Solutions.

LeBoeuf, M. (1985). *The Greatest Management Principle in the World.* New York, NY: Putnam Publishing Group.

Marquet, L. D. (2012). *Turn the Ship Around; A True Story of Turning Followers into Leaders.* New York, NY: Penguin Group.

Maxwell, J. C. (2001). *The 17 Indisputable Laws of Teamwork.* Nashville, TN: Thomas Nelson Publishing.

McDevitt, D. S., & Field, M. W. (2010). *Police Chief; How to Attain and Succeed in this Critical Position.* Springfield, IL: Charles C Thomas, Publisher, Ltd.

Office of Community Oriented Policing Services. (2006). *Law Enforcement Tech Guide for Creating Performance Measures that Work: A Guide for Executives and Managers.* Washington, D.C.: U.S. Department of Justice.

Peters, T. (1987). *Thriving on Chaos.* New York, NY: Alfred A. Knopf Inc.

Phillips, D. T. (1992). *Lincoln on Leadership.* New York, NY: Warner Books Inc.

Police Executive Research Forum. (2007). *Good to Great Policing: Application of Business Management Principles in the Public Sector.* Washington, D.C.: Police Executive Research Forum.

Police Executive Research Forum. (2009). *Leadership Matters: Police Chiefs Talk About Their Careers.* Washington, D.C.: Police Executive Research Forum.

Police Executive Research Forum. (2014). *Future Trends in Policing.* Washington, D.C.: Office of Community Oriented Policing Services.

Roberto, Michael A. (2013). *Why Great Leaders don't take Yes for an Answer.* Upper Saddle River, NJ: Pearson Education.

Sabin, N., & Curtis, B. (2005). *How Good Do You Want to Be?* New York, NY: Ballantine Books.

Sanborn, M. (2004). *Fred Factor.* New York, NY: Waterbrook Press.

Terry, D. D. (2015). Community Policing: What Style of Leadership Works? *Law Enforcement Executive Forum, 15*(3), 39-44.

Welch, J. (2005). *Winning.* New York, NY: Harper Collins Books.

Willink, J. (2020). *Leadership Strategy and Tactics Field Manual.* New York, NY: St. Martin's Publishing Group.

INDEX